STILL LIFE IN REAL TIME

Post-Contemporary

Interventions

A series edited by

Stanley Fish and

Fredric Jameson

STILL LIFE IN

THEORY AFTER

DUKE UNIVERSITY PRESS   *Durham & London 1994*

REAL TIME

T E L E V I S I O N

Richard Dienst

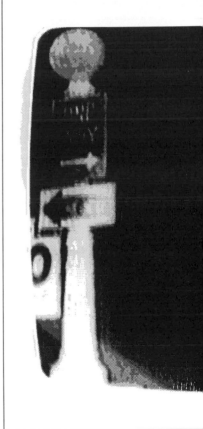

© 1994 Duke University Press
All rights reserved
Printed in the United States of America on
acid-free paper ∞
Typeset in Berkeley Medium by Keystone Typesetting, Inc.
Library of Congress Cataloging-in-Publication Data appear
on the last printed page of this book.

I, from the orient to the drooping west
(Making the wind my post-horse), still unfold
the acts commenced on this ball of earth.
—Shakespeare, *2 Henry IV*

This is an expressive nation that produced CNN and MTV.
We were all born for the information age.
This is a jazzy nation, thank goodness, for my sake,
that created be-bop and hip-hop and all those other things.
We are wired for real time.
—President Bill Clinton, *New York Times*,
February 28, 1993

CONTENTS

PREFACE

When Jacques Lacan, the famous psychoanalyst, appeared on television in 1974, he opened his discourse with these words: "I always speak the truth: not all of it, because there's no way to say it all. Saying it all is materially impossible: the words are lacking. It's even through this impossibility that the truth holds on to the real."[1]

Lacan begins by saying that he cannot finish what he is starting to say, at least not on television. And in that peculiar, inexorable way in which everything that appears on television somehow becomes essentially televisual, Lacan speaks for the apparatus that carries his picture and his words. (Whether he still speaks for himself under such circumstances is another question.) Like Lacan, television cannot say everything, although it always looks as if it is trying, as if it is about to get everything out. Lacan's gesture, which summons the whole by admitting the impossibility of articulating it, provides the point of departure for the essays that follow: once a start is made, there will be no way to finish, no way to say it all.

Perhaps it would be better to say that there will be no way to *see* it all, since this study begins by assuming that seeing and saying are fundamentally intertwined and unavoidably textual processes. Each chapter will approach television by finding and making its own "images" within various theoretical frameworks (including historical, economic, existential, and discursive dimensions). Following the example of the thinkers examined here, I treat theory as a highly mobile kind of cultural practice, provided that it is understood not as the pursuit of a "true picture of things" but as the invention of concepts, or more precisely, the invention of *theoretical images* that link up with images produced through the machine itself.[2] I leave it to the reader to decide how these theoretical images contribute to our thinking about television and the world. Although television may sustain those older values invoked by Lacan— "truth" and "the real" in their mutually limiting configuration—it also allows us to imagine new values for the visible image and the visual realm without resorting to the ultimate privilege, or the ultimate evasion, of the invisible. As all too many people know, invisibility can be disastrous.

In addition to this utopian challenge to thinking, television offers a strategic site for cultural and economic negotiation over new technologies, even as it shows signs of an irreversible expansion into other spaces. It should not be assumed that new technologies will simply do away with older forms and materials: precisely because there are strenuous efforts to adapt and revalorize old investments, the prospect of "life after television" (title of a high-tech pep talk by Reaganite guru George Gilder) can only be envisioned as the apocalyptic victory of one transnational corporate bloc over another.[3] "Theory after television," on the other hand, is the project of using television to spur new speculations about the forces and powers that drive our already "postcontemporary" world.

The first chapter details the ways television was recognized by its earliest theorists as a (new kind of) figure for a (new kind of) global whole. Whether optimistic or pessimistic, these descriptions of television assume it to be an empty technology, a mechanism of transparency and simultaneity. But as soon as some kind of content is thrown into this chain of glass boxes, the fabled immediacy of television turns out to be an imaginary mirage, a staging of time and space through images. The problem then becomes more concrete: how does this particular technological ensemble construct its spaces and temporalities of viewing? The answer lies not in terms of the single subject or the aesthetics of reception, although television produces all kinds of subjectivizing functions, many of them clustered around the archaic organizations of "experience" and "representation." We cannot read an itinerary of experience from a circuit of images; on the contrary, there is every reason to suspend localizing interpretations until the generalizing movement of the circuit has been traced. Through a critique of the notion of "flow," we may reveal the systemic scale of the televisual apparatus and thus define an urgent problem for current cultural theory.

The second chapter proposes that economics is the basic level at which to diagram television's system. The geotelevisual system does not merely facilitate consumption of commodities but produces a substance of value all its own: socialized culture time. Just as factory machines helped to aggregate and abstract human labor (as labor power) in the steam age and thereby defined the metaphysical foundations of capitalist wages and money, so now television, as a late capitalist machine, makes possible another exchange system in which time is again aggregated and valorized en masse. We work at television, participating in the creation of value that appears to us in the form of images. This work can be characterized as a general circulation: value is generated to the extent that we serve as efficient conductors of signifying charges and as calculable markers of ever more differentiated cultural tastes (upon which the ratings, advertising systems, and especially the new projects for "interactive" television depend). To perform this job for capitalism, television does not need to offer meaning or pleasure, just a structure of time and a mechanism for profit.

Between the first set of theoretical explorations (which deal largely with issues of history and political economy) and the second set (which propose a series of philosophical and theoretical speculations), I have placed three detailed readings, which connect the theoretical discussions to particular slices of North American television. Like the surrounding chapters, these readings do not pretend to be universalizing accounts; on the contrary, they demonstrate that the point of critique is to allow contingencies, aberrations, and exceptions to contest the terms of analysis rather than merely to confirm them. I can think of no better figure for this kind of theoretical traverse than changing channels, lingering here and there when something catches the eye. Zapping channels, like reading or writing or working, is always "interested," and here I am frankly interested in using these programs to reinforce and anticipate issues raised elsewhere in the book—I can hardly claim to have crossed the entire network. The analytic thread running through these three readings is the category of televisual time, which will allow us to integrate a range of questions about history, subjectivity, value, and the construction of images.

Temporality, then, provides a starting point for further theorizing about television and its world. Turning to the grand philosophical account of time and technology in Heidegger—in which television plays a remarkably pivotal role—I argue in Chapter 6 that, instead of thinking television in terms of our perceptions (which would draw us back to phenomenology), we must think of this object in terms of whatever is supposed to ground it: the world, the real, or Being. But once television confronts Being it is no longer easy to say when the ground ends and the deviation, distortion, or diffusion begins. Rather than proving faithless to the course of human existence so far, television confirms all its axiomatic anxieties and leaves us roughly where we started, at the brink of the latest modernity, waiting for the metaphysics of representation to give up the ghost.

The penultimate chapter switches from Heidegger to Derrida to argue that television, like other great programs of the West, works through a certain errance. In spite of its economic and existential immensity, the televisual system is structured on tenuous textual networks held together by an unfounded guarantee that messages always reach their destinations. Perhaps, Derrida suggests, a little uncertainty in the right places is all it takes to disturb this network. Or, just as likely, a little uncertainty in the right places keeps the whole thing together. A deconstruction of television maps both sides of the ideal communicative equation: disturbances and bonds, gaps and attachments, displacements and localizations, constant breakdowns and unlimited relays.

Using Deleuzian categories the final chapter analyzes the historical place and the temporal vectors of televisual processes. Caught between older technologies of the still image and newer technologies of pure electronic flux, television oscillates between modes of appearing and disappearing, between composition and decomposition. Deleuze, of course, does not seek to resolve these two poles into a single synthetic operation: the explanatory value of his terms consists in their capacity to move along with their putative objects. This last set of theoretical images, then, deals with time scales (the instantaneous and the automatic) projected before and beyond the operations of memory, representation, or narrative. Only by withholding full acceptance of these classical schemes—which indebt us as spectators to the autonomy of the image—can the radical potential of thinking beyond television be pursued. For his part, Deleuze locates this potential in avant-garde filmmakers like Godard, a recurring character in these reflections, who may still offer valuable lessons to would-be practitioners of a transformed television. In the Nietzschean spirit of Deleuze's work, however, I treat theory itself as the best available technique for remaking televisual images and reclaiming the power to create images of our own.

Although these diverse explorations offer nothing more radical than a call to think about television differently (both more carefully and more boldly), I hope these essays will alert readers to the most radical and dynamic currents in the televisual world, so that we might learn better to see past it.

ACKNOWLEDGMENTS

This project began under the direct guidance of five teachers. I want to thank each of them. Fredric Jameson has provided both the essential stimulus and constant reference point for this entire project. I am grateful for his personal and intellectual example. Barbara Herrnstein Smith has been an exceptionally generous critic, an extremely careful reader, and a genuine model of savoir faire. Jane Gaines was a source of energy and an enthusiastic expert in film and television studies. Janice Radway did not hesitate to give her help, advice, and kind encouragement at every step of the way. Ken Surin was wonderfully attentive and responsive, showing me the best way to be active in thought. Other teachers have provided crucial help and inspiration, whether near or far to the work at hand: V. Y. Mudimbe, Franco Moretti, Jean-Joseph Goux, Terry Eagleton, and, ultimately, Masao Miyoshi. Over the years I spent at Duke's Graduate Program in Literature, Sandy Mills continually surpassed herself in kindness and good spirits. I am deeply indebted to my friends in Durham—especially Henry Schwarz, Michael Speaks, Loris Mirella, Saree Makdisi, and Cesare Casarino—for all the conversations, stories, meals, and all-purpose support. In the final stages of writing, Vince Leitch provided steady encouragement and perceptive advice. Somewhere out there are two excellent anonymous readers who helped me rethink the final shape of the work.

At Duke University Press, I want to thank Jean Brady for guiding the manuscript to print and Reynolds Smith for being the coolest editor around.

I also want to thank my parents, Carl and Peggy Dienst, for everything they've done since day one.

And thanks to Karin . . . who knows the reason why.

An earlier version of Chapter 2 was published in Jane Gaines, ed., *Classical Hollywood Narrative: The Paradigm Wars* (Durham: Duke University Press, 1992). An earlier version of Chapter 4 was published in Peter Brunette and David Wills, eds., *Deconstruction and the Visual Arts: Art, Media, Architecture* (New York: Cambridge University Press, 1994). A different version of the "Crime Story" chapter appeared in *Polygraph* 2/3 (1989). I am grateful to the editors and publishers for permission to reprint.

PART I *Televisual Flows*

ONE *The Outbreak of Television*

Television is for pleasure, for bringing the family together, and for killing time. Those are the three functions of commercial TV.—Silvio Berlusconi, Italian media magnate

Television, like modernity and capitalism, has not always existed. It is a dynamic thing, a concrete machine, a collection of working parts: it had to be invented, produced, reproduced, and placed here and there upon the earth in numbers we can still count. To be sure, modernity and capitalism are dynamic things, too: whatever they are and whenever they emerged, they also work upon the earth without being visible or comprehensible all at once. Although the term "television" seems specific in a way "capitalism" and "modernity" (not to mention "postmodernity") do not, it definitely belongs to the same plane of abstraction, the same scope of materiality, and hence the same theoretical hesitation. Each of these terms names an elusive and unresolved object—perhaps not an object at all, but a "problematic"—something whose processes, functions, and domains cannot be fixed in a stable discursive field. Directed at such global abstractions, our thinking is forced to follow the very motions of dispersion and unification that would define the thing itself in its full contours. In light of all the interlacing questions about saying, doing, showing, and knowing that have been raised in contemporary theory, it is no longer possible to define television in a single set of terms, to treat it as merely derivative of the current mode of production, or to let its place in the history of writing systems go unexamined. If theoretical questions can dislodge television from its cosy nest of familiarity (lined with empirical certainties and ideological disclaimers), perhaps this thing can look strange again.

To approach and apprehend "television" in general, we must engage in creative speculation, combining and recombining all kinds of images, some supplied by television, some not. For if there are fleeting images visible on television, there must also be persistent images of television, visible somewhere else, which may be harder to discern.[1] What abstract images—what rules of composition, figural devices, representational structures, or conceptual frameworks—can be built into and out of the concrete images on television? How do we know what television can show us? To explore these questions I will begin by working through three distinct historical images of television, to see how television looks before people begin to watch it. Later, I will outline two related sets of images—the technical and the theoretical—along with the narratives of invention they bear, in order to mark out the questions that occupy the rest of this study.

Imaginary Totalities

In debates about globalization, cultural imperialism, dialectics of enlightenment, and so on, "television" assumes a power beyond that attributed to its programming, as if its mere existence ensured certain effects, both ideological and physical. All of a sudden, at some point that should be within living memory, television seemed to flood the social sphere with a new kind of power. But the question is not: when does television begin? but: when does television begin to function to the second power? When does television replace the "communication" of discrete messages with the profuse "diffusion" of images? When does television cease functioning merely as a movement between distant points and begin shaping its own "world," gathering distances into itself in order to redistribute them according to its own program? And the answer is: from the start.

The dreams of television at its birth were already global. On the basis of the most rudimentary experiments in image transmission, televisuality was immediately imagined as an all-encompassing putting-into-view of the world. In its future ideal state, television would override the irreducible gap between speaking and listening (telephone, radio) with a field of total instantaneous visibility, where relays of cameras and monitors would speed up and finally erase the distinction between seeing and being seen (that old residue of the self-conscious subject, with its inevitable emphasis on "perspective" and "framing"). The earliest partisans of television saw no reason why anyone would refuse this offer of transvisibility, since it included the promise of mutual recognition, equal exchange, and an immediate symmetry between transmission and reception, ultimately a kind of immanent Absolute Knowledge.[2] An admirably succinct statement of these hopes comes from Rudolph Arnheim, writing in London in 1936, where public TV broadcasts were just beginning.

> Wireless, with television, is the last phase of a development that was begun by the first seafarers and nomads. Man leaves his birthplace, crosses lands, mountains and seas, and exchanges produce, inventions, works of art, customs, religions and knowledge. European doctors, missionaries, educational officials in Asia and Africa; Chinese, Japanese, Indians and negroes at European universities; the African fetish in the metropolitan drawing-room and the stiff collar round the neck of the black chief: and to-day a voice singing, teaching, preaching, conquering, going everywhere, coming from everywhere and making the whole world participators in everything . . . [Wireless] and television enable any number of people to hear and see simultaneously what is happening everywhere in the world.[3]

Arnheim celebrates broadcasting not only because it perfects the lopsided cultural exchange in which Western religion, education, and medicine are swapped for the decorative exotic "fetish" (he got that right!). More important, he listens to the radio with an eye on the prospect of television and hears a new Gestalt: a single voice that sweeps up all the others into a placeless ubiquity, a circulatory transcendence from "anywhere" into "everywhere." Although Arnheim did not clearly recognize it, television would be the best finale for his story, returning us at last to a settled state of existence unknown since the primordial nomadic disruption. Stilled by the sight of television, we are supposed to say: let images and voices travel in our place and the world will be one.

Television's first imaginary horizon is the utopia of uninterrupted free trade, already transnational, a realization of specifically metropolitan, imperialist geopolitical ambitions. The "worlding" image of television, with its ideals of total flow and tendential completion of the network,

bears the unmistakable stamp of post–World War I Anglo-American corporate optimism and liberal universalism. Like an archaic legacy, this ur-
image persists through subsequent developments. Indeed, each turn in
the history of television's invention generates new images of its world.
There is no way to separate a technical advance from the ultimate uses
and deployments imagined for it. Even the assumption that television
was invented to transmit images includes a certain understanding of
what an "image" is, what "transmission" does, and "who" might be involved. The creation of television's world requires a textual protocol that
emphasizes reproducible verisimilitude over representational veracity,
requiring an acceptance of transmission as the possibility of instantaneous exchange and co-presence between here and an elsewhere, or
rather, since sites of sending and receiving can be multiplied outward,
countless heres and elsewheres. It is a long step, but taken immediately,
from recognizing the light on the screen as a transmitted image to accept-
ing that the world can be assembled under a single rule and process.

Television's apparent capacity to project and bind an abstract totality
was not lost on those opposed to global capitalism. Eleven years before
Arnheim, the visionary Soviet director Dziga Vertov predicted that television ("radio-eye") could itself be overturned to prepare for the completion of an alternate world economy, communism.

> Technology is moving swiftly ahead. A method for broadcasting
> images by radio has already been invented. In addition, a method for
> recording auditory phenomena on film tape has been discovered.
>
> In the near future man will be able to broadcast to the entire world
> the visual and auditory phenomena recorded by the radio-movie
> camera.
>
> We must now prepare to turn these inventions of the capitalist
> world to its own destruction.
>
> We will not prepare for the broadcast of operas and dramas. We
> will prepare wholeheartedly to give the workers of every land the
> opportunity to see and hear the world in an organized form; to see,
> hear, and understand one another.[4]

Vertov understands television as the combination of two distinct operations—recording and broadcasting—that together can organize a world.
The "visual facts" collected by the camera pursue their truths on two
levels. First, since the radio-eye presents every image as a fact drawn from
the real world of production, each would represent a single product in an

endlessly unfolding economic cycle. Second, the relation between any two images must testify to a necessary bond, a mutual material link, which would consist neither in the "content" of the images nor in the syntax of the presentation, but in the system itself, in the indivisible unity of a world acting as an integrated economy. This link between images must be "produced" each time by tracing a kind of ideological algorithm, which, insofar as it demonstrated the laws binding together all work and life, would itself presage the concrete realization of international communism. Relationships between images would not only figure but enact reciprocal relationships between workers. Television would be, in good Leninist fashion, "cinema plus electrification,"[5] a dialectical procedure in which an expansion in the quantity of images would generate new qualities of representational power.

Both Arnheim and Vertov visualize television as an unlimited economic utopia. (Seen from this perspective, McLuhan did no more than repeat pretelevisual ideas long after their historical moment had passed.) But as soon as television systems began to be set up on the ground, it became clear that governments and private enterprises would not necessarily hurry to saturate the social field with television. In fact, the means of saturating the social field would vary from nation to nation, depending on the level of public and private capital available for investment in the machinery and programming. In starting a broadcast system, the first strategic decision is how best to generate and occupy a particular social space through the distribution of transmitters and receivers. Access to television can be regulated at both ends. The actual placement of receiving and transmitting devices, as well as the crucial ratio between them, will be the product of intense competition between interests, sometimes of outright class struggle. For it is by no means obvious whose interests would be served by putting receiving sets (let alone transmitters) in every home. Nor is it obvious that television becomes "total" only when it is visible everywhere. The second strategic decision, then, concerns the way in which all these machines, working together, can project a specular totalization of the social field through the textual power of images.

The most familiar techniques for such a grand task were borrowed from the existing discourses of state and cultural authority that immediately informed the creation of broadcasting institutions. In Europe, television (like radio) began as an instrument of government, so that official messages could be voiced in the distinctive timbre of a ruling culture. In each case, there was a tension between state functions and cultural production, since providing "public service" required maximum diffusion, and unifying "public demand" required a consistent aura of "distinction" and even exclusivity. Public monopolies like the BBC and ARD/ZDF, regulated and sometimes financed by the government, were charged with the dual task of promulgating information in the national interest and expanding the demand for cultural training (generally in a universalizing bourgeois mode). For as long as it holds, such a compromise prevents the formation of either an official state culture or a fully privatized, commodified one. (In the case of Italy, for example, there was an especially strong swing from one to the other.) After World War II, all of western Europe followed the route of public service and state stewardship, with its characteristically limited broadcast hours and allowances for regional and private company productions. The Soviet Union and the United States, on the other hand, bypassed prolonged periods of compromise and pursued the expansion of television according to their respective centralized and commercial network models. As other countries joined the television club, and as older members renegotiated their start-up agreements, the distinctions between the models have blurred. To generalize quickly: in places where television is not simply ruled by government, broadcasting authority is becoming highly hybridized, with state and public corporations running alongside local entrepreneurs and transnational conglomerates. (For the purposes of this discussion, the word "broadcasting" includes all telecommunication of programming.) In the face of such mixtures, and with the promise of further heterogeneity, the imaginary work of television cannot be assumed to be linear, cumulative, and transparent; on the contrary, as its machinery becomes more available, its powers of visibility threaten to become more uneven, competitive and preemptive.

But the European models were not easily exportable: the successive waves of decolonization offered opportunities to rethink the status of broadcasting authority. In 1961–62, as he was preparing the second volume of the *Critique of Dialectical Reason*, Jean-Paul Sartre devoted some sketchy but suggestive notes to the question of how television brings about a transformative collusion among state power, elite culture, and new forms of capitalism. In examining the limited expansion of television in Gaullist France and revolutionary Cuba, he distinguishes between two lines of potential totalization, which we can call the ideological and the technological. These two totalizations do not proceed along parallel tracks toward an assured completion but rather interfere with each other every step of the way. For Sartre, the story of television must be told dialectically, through the disjunctures of scale between the concrete apparatus and the discourses it sets in motion. Initially, insofar as television's discourses continue to obey class interests and established cultural patterns, its way of addressing the populace will be irreducibly contentious, provoking by exclusion as much as by inclusion. A social contradiction therefore occurs as soon as there are a few TV receivers, since ideological unification at the level of the broadcast is immediately undone by the scarcity of access to the technology. In a "bourgeois democratic" society, the first solution will be technological: more machines will fill out the imaginary gaps in the social field.

> If the tiniest number owns a TV, it appears both as positing itself for itself within the totality . . . which for its part, remains deprived of TV, and at the same time—inasmuch as *it precisely is* the totality—as representing the condition to which the totality must accede. If no practical frontier divides the field, the solution is without real violence: the field *organizes itself* to be totally supplied with TV sets . . . In relation to the owner, equality replaces inequality, in the sense that *everyone* will see TV.[6]

But Sartre suggests that this solution brings the original enterprise into a new contradiction: a material totalization outstrips the imaginary one that justified it, and television assumes its own synthetic "voice," spoken by an impossible third party in a dialect that is no longer that of the state, the nation, or even the falsely universal bourgeois culture. "[Television's] unifying policy: ideological propaganda, but *without saying anything; unity is negative, and consequently serial. Saying what pleases everybody. But nothing pleases *everybody*. So you have to say *nothing*. On this basis, there is TV thought, TV behavior, etc., which belong to the practico-inert. It is simultaneously other-direction and senseless discourse" (CDR II, 440–41). The development of the apparatus cuts across individuals and groups, reconstituting them as parts of a larger ensemble. These human parts are no longer linked through older cultural practices or a common project but through the machine itself, which replaces their active mutuality with the whole system's inert, inaccessible absence. Thus television, like other machines and material systems, produces a "serial" unification which simultaneously joins and separates each participant in a grid of Otherness. In this second solution, then, the machine that might have serviced bourgeois culture now betrays its historical mission and henceforth dictates its own terms, generating cultural forces that confront human individuals, groups, and collectivities from the outside, as their destiny.[7]

The analysis of seriality—which is for Sartre the very logic of work, culture, and everyday life in capitalist societies—is carried out in ominous detail throughout the first volume of the *Critique*. Sartre discusses such pertinent examples as the radio broadcast (as a passive "indirect gathering"), the free market (as a "milieu" of alterity), and the Top Ten list (as a composite expression of nobody's tastes).[8] The concept of the "serial" designates a general logic of identity and organization, where individuals and objects alike are constituted only as functions of purely external processes. Seriality erodes the collective dimension of social life, pounding down groups to the rhythm of a deadening dialectical synthesis, realigning and reabsorbing dispersed actions around the empty ordering of thinghood and Otherness.

But here Sartre adds a new step to the story: the possibility of undoing seriality through broadcasting. (He names this possibility "Cuba," but perhaps we should understand this as Sartre's own private Cuba.) If technology and class ideology continually override each other in the capitalist evolution of television, the revolutionary use of television would offer another unfolding, where the demands of "popular culture" would force an ever-greater expansion of the televisual system. In other words, although Sartre suggests that seriality is an unavoidable product of the apparatus, he holds out hope that the serial disarticulation of groups can be undone when television is directed to the "total distribution" of popular culture (CDR II, 440). This potential is based not only on the rearrangement of the conditions of watching television (forming genuine groups around the tv set), but on the capacity of television to draw all individuals and groups, however serialized, into an immense simultaneity that would delimit a space for future cultural unification. To distribute "popular culture," then, is to posit a movement of radical totalization for the whole nation: "So you need a carnival, or the apocalypse, or some upheaval, in order to make a comparison (one million people assembled, etc.)" (CDR II, 438). To unify a collectivity, it is not enough, of course, merely to aggregate serialized groups; television must produce this synthesis without freezing it into a permanent goal or an achieved image of the collective, which would merely resegment the social field around a new inert center. In a revolutionary society television should inhabit culture, not the other way around: even in the process of making a new kind of culture possible, television would have to hold back, remaining partial and discontinuous, preventing itself from imposing its laws of distribution on the practices of popular creation. It should come as no surprise that Sartre leaves this problem for Castro to solve, because it is exactly analogous to the larger dilemma of the *Critique:* how can the revolutionary group maintain the dynamic that fused it without turning to the terrors of institutionalized power? Sartre finds television no more capable of overcoming the antinomies of political organization than humans are; at best it can, under certain historical conditions, dissolve the isolating pull of seriality by becoming ever more present, eradicating the material pressure of scarcity and the ideological expressions of elitism, thereby establishing a formal equality and freedom with respect to the machine. We might read Sartre's hesitation over the revolutionary potential of television as his suspicion that the incessant dialectic of seriality and fused groups cannot be resolved by bumping up its scale of operation to the level of the national culture or even the class struggle. Television appears to offer just one political gambit—the material and ideological unification of a practical field—but no class, party, or state seems capable of ultimately controlling the terms and the structure of that process. In Sartre's account, finally, the machine will survive the designs of its initial producers only to direct the production of the next ensemble, whose energies will be challenged to remake what confronts them. And so it will go, one struggle after another playing out through these linkages until the apparatus is either transformed or destroyed.

Quite apart from the theoretical interest of Sartre's account—some of its economic and existential aspects will reappear in later chapters—it here leads to the final piece of our schematic narrative of television's ongoing birth. Television first offered a transparent *world;* later, it has wavered between the regimes of a governing *state* and a unified *culture* (with their qualifiers "national," "mass," and "popular"), and at last it revolves around the exigencies of a *market*. These four positions or perspectives are not a necessary historical sequence or logical succession of forms; instead, they offer a shorthand map of the systemic relations between televisual mechanisms and discourses. Since all actually existing television systems are in some sense a failed totalization of an ideal visuality, the task of comparing systems requires a hypothetical typology that conjugates historical and imaginary frameworks in order to illuminate contrasts and tensions. Each of these key images—world, state, culture, market—organizes in its own way the three abstract components of any adequate description of television: its quasi-phenomenal domain of representation, its specific system of interests, and its concrete deployment in a practical space.[9] Every attempt to describe television inevitably encompasses its mechanism, its economy, and its representational capacities, although one or another component may appear to hold sway over the others.

Every image of television is, then, first an image of a particular social organization held together (or not) on several levels at once. The resulting balances and repressions show us some striking contrasts between different ideal types and historical actualizations of the machine. At the level of perception and presentation, for example, the image of television as world promises immediacy and immensity, where all possible subjects and objects are co-present to each other. But when television develops its image of the market, visual extension is replaced by visible distinction, and the general address of seeing becomes a tentative offer to choose and consume. By the same token, the image of television as instant global immediacy appears decidedly wispy against the social scientist's image of an international media market with complex, overlapping, and uneven hardware topographies. In some places, the state's hand will be visible onscreen; elsewhere, cultural signals will plot the coordinates of group identity and conflict. Each alternative implies its own scale, organization, and degree of technology; both state- and culture-television can be regarded as restrictive strategies to close the system against other kinds of images. On the other hand, once a television system has become fully plugged into other systems, it confounds the images of world, nation, culture, and market, since the latter often claims all of the others as its proper domain. We should remember, in the pages that follow, that the expansion of television we are witnessing everywhere today means the expansion of television as market—geotelevision—at the expense of any other image of television's future.

Technical Imaginaries

The radical theorization of television took a great leap forward in 1974 with the publication of Raymond Williams's book *Television: Technology and Cultural Form*.[10] In a deceptively modest volume, Williams tries to produce dual images of television: first, as a technology whose historical course is not irreversible, and second, as a cultural construct comprising nothing less than a new structure of visibility. Perhaps sensing that any attempt to glimpse these two images simultaneously would set television adrift in parallax, Williams (as usual) neatly shuffles his terms together, leaving us an unsolved problem jammed into the title's serene formula. What does it mean that something can be both technology and cultural form, without one simply becoming the other? To answer that question, we must retell the emergence of television in somewhat finer grain, beginning with Williams's own telling of the tale.

If television signals a new, inextricable combination of what used to appear as separate practices—the levels of market-based economics, technological deployment, and ideological representation discussed a moment ago—the theoretical question of its limits, balances, and pressures takes on an urgent political direction. Williams's answer is couched in terms of the tectonics of Gramscian time, the upsurges and sinkholes of cultural conjunctures that race ahead or slump back in unreliable syncopation with the political fortunes of the class struggle. Indeed, a ribbon of panic runs through his book: for Williams, although television might once have offered an incredible opportunity for oppositional cultural growth it has now instead choked off those impulses and poisoned the air for the future. Here is the short version of his story: A specific technology captures multiple cultural forms and remakes them as television, which then, as a unifying and singular cultural form, serves both state and commercial interests by dispensing ideological messages in local currency. The critical task becomes two-fold, says Williams: first, to read existing television through the mutual determinations of technology and cultural forms; second, to rescue both the technology and the project of culture from the dead-end embrace of present-day television. Crisscrossing between utopian values and muted pessimism, Williams confronts the spectre of an increasingly powerful televisual system that threatens to become more than simply dominant. The power of this system—its technological capacity to absorb and circulate every kind of cultural energy—must therefore be named and analyzed.

Williams first approaches his subject by cataloguing the variants of technical determination in historical writing. Distinguishing a pure "technological determinism" (in which social change is explained by reference to this or that invention or machinery) from a "symptomatic" account (in which a given technology is grouped with other elements to express an overall social disposition or paradigm), Williams finally opts for a third path, in which an "intention" must be built into the account, that is, technology must be interpreted as the outcome of specific interests and forces, as a social intervention rather than an act of scientific curiosity or genius.[11] Such an emphasis would be compatible with the most radical versions of scientific and technological history (as seen in Latour or Feyerabend), provided that Williams's "intention" is heard in its full dialectical tenor. During the process of a technical "development," the efforts of every historical player are subject to drastic reorientation, in which the "ends" they envision are absorbed into a still-unfolding complex of historical determinations, solidified, and returned to the field as new demands and exigencies. The definition and pursuit of scientific objectives do not lead straight up to the present: rather, each point is a complex of alternatives and contingencies in its own right. (This denial of a *telos* and of teleology, which we have already seen in Sartre, is an appropriate first move in the study of an open tele-system, sent from afar but not entirely destined).[12] Williams resorts to an apparently subjective language ("intention") to bind technology to the ensemble of practices that circulate through a historical situation. Then it becomes possible to recognize that the very notion of technological determinism, or more broadly, the appearance of a world dominated by "technology," is itself a product of certain processes, not only technological, that regulate the visualization and conceptualization of human existence. At the same time, the whole language of social "needs" and "uses"—indeed, the very presupposition of "the social" itself—has to be recast in terms of the administration and contestation of interests (the class struggle, patriarchy, and so on).

Apart from performing the usual materialist caveats, Williams makes historical claims for television that make sense only through the social/economic dimension of "intention." Television appears, then, not because of a utopian desire to see at a distance, but because a range of imperatives directed the course of technological research. The demand for "communication," in particular, should not be taken at face value—there is no such thing as communication in general—always "communication" is framed in specific terms, with requirements of transmittability, quantity, and potential reciprocity. Every technology of communication installs limits of these kinds; at the same time, there is no communication outside an apparatus, though an apparatus is no guarantee of communication. This lesson has been unlearned repeatedly, from McLuhan to Baudrillard: a surplus of different technologies does not mean that absolute communication is at hand.

Williams wants to distinguish radio and television from all previous technologies of communication by indicating that their development moved completely through capitalist processes and decisions, operating at necessarily larger and larger scales, integrating "scattered technologies," and responding to political and economic crises.[13] From this general background, he draws a startling conclusion: "radio and television were *systems primarily devised for transmission and reception as abstract processes, with little or no definition of preceding content*. When the question of content was raised, it was resolved, in the main, parasitically."[14] We may read this statement in a number of ways, not all of them within the range of Williams's argument. The statement expresses Williams's anxieties about television's relation to all of previous culture. In the opposition between "means of communication" and "content," he draws a sharp line between technology and culture: one is the product of a certain highly developed stage of economic activity where individual inventions are absorbed into the agenda of corporate capital, and the other consists of a range of artifacts, forms of expression, and events—comprising a certain reality—that will be snatched up and circulated by this new machinery. Above all, this is a picture of television as the usurper and profiteer of public discourse: it implies an expansion of capitalist logic into a new realm of commodification, where the varied spaces and times of everyday life are packaged and sold in measured lengths of representation and reception.

In the distinction between "means" and "content," however, Williams argues that television's specific forms of content are secondary, accidental, or arbitrary. As he tells it, the capitalist manufacturers (RCA, Westinghouse, and G.E. in the United States, EMI in Britain) invested initially in developing the transmitting apparatus, selling the receiving sets, and only then produced something to broadcast. Williams isolates "content" in order to exempt it from this unhappy and alienated mechanical birth and to hold out the possibility that an intervention at the level of television's programming could reverse the social determinations that produced its technology. Unfortunately, he stubbornly refuses to follow the logic of determination to the point of recognizing that the construction of a broadcasting system creates its own market space, filled with its own kind of goods. Television could be launched precisely because its very mode of transmission implies its own distinctive production of content. Although Williams misreads the "intention" of the early corporations, it is still worth asking if the developers of television indeed acted as if their system were an immaculate, abstract mechanism of communication. If so, this belief would be a useful starting point for a critique of broadcasting protocols, whose assumptions about the technical efficiency of televisual transmissions orient everything from programming schedules to shot framing and editing. At the level of an operating ideology, the idea that "means" take precedence over "content" can be attributed directly to a rationalizing economic logic.[15]

Although Williams recognizes that technology imposes constraints on what is transmitted or received, he overlooks the possibility that the very notions of transmission and reception—the forms in which these practices are socially figured—belong to the apparatus itself. In Williams's parasitic hierarchy, television leeches its lifeblood from objective cultural products—events, news, artistic productions, and cinema. To ears schooled in post-structuralism, however, a "parasitic" relation works in both directions at once, inverting the norms it presupposes. In other words, the question of "content" was the crucial one all along, so that television's apparently innocent appropriation and reproduction of its material must be considered the primary characteristic of its mode of transmission. The place-marker called "content," then, which had formerly been defined at the level of the preexisting real, instead owes its very existence to the defining instance of distribution and diffusion. We would have to clarify Williams's statement by saying almost the opposite: that television produces "content" only in the abstract process of transmission and that its so-called "parasitism" is not secondary but programmatic. To be sure, the "content" of television was not "defined" in advance, or, rather, it was always defined in the plural (at formal and generic levels). But in what communication system is there initial or final determination of "content" by "means" or vice versa? Any attempt to oppose these terms, especially by speaking of the "abstraction" of one bringing the "parasitism" of the other, obscures the questions of what television's technical and social characteristics have been all along and of whether the transmission functions of the technology could ever be separated from the signifying functions of its material. Note that a system of alphabetic script (to mention another kind of communication technology), because it allows "content" to be produced at any moment, never really sorts out the difference between either its processes (writing and reading) or its contents (signifiers and signifieds).[16] Is television really any different? Aren't "abstraction" and "parasitism" aspects of all communication systems, insofar as they are conceivable as systems?

Before framing answers to these questions, we must briefly reconsider the history of television's design with an eye to the crucial problems and constitutive features. One major account of this process appears in Bryan Winston's *Misunderstanding Media,* in which the invention of television is juxtaposed with other information technologies (computers, comsats, telephones).[17] Winston offers a wealth of information but at the same time arranges each story according to a single invariant sequence: each technical development is likened to a complete linguistic utterance. Thus every invention presupposes scientific "competence," it is galvanized as an idea, it is produced and adjusted to its context, only to suffer an unavoidable fate in which its most "radical potential" is blocked as a condition of its eventual social acceptance. This sequence leaves aside all the force of Williams's insistence on an overall competitive capitalist framework, which can only intervene in Winston's plan alongside a jumble of other assorted "supervening necessities." Those necessities include such miscellaneous determinations as the importance of regulating commodity consumption after World War II and an imputed Western appetite for "realism" in culture.[18] But Winston is certainly on the right track: a range of forces, from the most specific to the most general, play a role in the complex development of any technological "event."

To give a technical description of television, then, necessarily involves more than operating instructions. It would be difficult to produce an answer that did not include components that also belong to other kinds of machinery, since all technological products are in some sense provisional hybrids. A first general definition of television, for example, might be "transmission of a moving picture," though transmission can happen in several ways, by broadcasting, by metal wire, by laser technology. Each mode of transmission depends, however, on the common two-step process that I will call the *de-screening* and *re-screening* of light through a video signal. These awkward and untechnical neologisms will be helpful if we do not want to prejudice the whole matter by saying that television already deals in "images," either given or received. (Of course television also includes sound, often sent by FM radio waves; though not inessential, sound does not enter this story until we try to theorize television reception in the next section.)

What is transmitted, at the simplest level, is simply a stream of pulses that scan a field at a certain speed: light entering the camera hits a plate where it can be registered line by line, translating a two-dimensional spatial arrangement of light into a sequential signal. When this signal reaches the other end, it is translated back into a field by projecting the electrical intensities line by line onto another screen. The transmitter strips light from one place, and the receiver traces it back in another. That is it: a one-way, synchronized movement of electrical devices, beginning and ending with the shape as a luminous rectangle, lasting only as long as the signal goes.

There are a number of important technicalities.

(1) Note that there is no provision in this account for recording signals: in fact, this technology—video recording proper—would come much later, as we will see.

(2) Note that the transmitter is not necessarily a "camera." Although television was developed to transmit optical information, it is easy to imagine (especially in the age of computers) how other kinds of mechanisms could also generate information in a screenable format. Computer animation, for example, does not require the drawing and photographing process of cinematic animation: it can be produced by programming incremental alterations in a given set of data, which are finally generated in the space and time of a video screen.

(3) An application of phosphorescence to glass (pixelation) is necessary on the monitor (receiving) screen if it is to be illuminated from behind. Otherwise (and this is the case with many large-screen systems), the signal can be projected onto a plain white surface. Not incidentally, phosphor technology was later the key to the development of color television.

(4) Television transmission is not constructed on any kind of passive or sensory model, unlike analog audio technology (in which sound is transmitted or recorded through a device that reproduces a physical motion) or film (which receives and records light on a material surface). Television treats light and sound as raw input, to be rebuilt using a complex and easily manipulable electronic code.

(5) The transmission is essentially instantaneous (moving at the speed of electricity): hence the technical basis for "immediate" or "live" visibility. Because there is no necessary storage of the signal, a camera can send continuous information to a monitor as long as there is a power source. (Surveillance cameras typically work this way.) If not infinite, televisual transmission is at least open-ended. The formal scandal of cinematic long shots—their uninterrupted stretches of duration—would be a trivial effect for a video camera and monitor plugged into a steady power source. Clearly, then, the invention of television was not an adaptation of cinematic means, but a way of starting over.

From the start, the key to televisual technology and aesthetics was *scanning,* which mediates at both ends between visible screens and electrical currents: it is above all a way of translating and framing light as information. The transmitter scans a field with an electron beam, traversing it back and forth, top to bottom and back again, cutting it into a number of impulse tracks or lines that are recomposed later. These "lines of resolution" have been standardized; contemporary televisions use either 525 lines (in the United States and Caribbean) or 625 lines (everywhere else), with each frame being scanned twenty-five times a second. High-definition television, now in development, will use 1,025 lines; a French system using 819 lines has already been discontinued.[19] "Resolution" indicates the precision of the scanning as well as the light sensitivity of the screens. In the early prototypes of television, scanning was done mechanically: the field was exposed to the electron source by means of various moving parts (e.g., the Nipkow disc, a perforated spinning wheel that exposed the field as arcs of light). With the breakthrough "image dissector" of Philo Farnsworth (1927), the scanning system was directed entirely by electrical signals: a cathode ray swept the image plate from side to side, each cycle alternating lines, guided by timed magnetic impulses. From that point, the transmitted signal would have to carry, as part of its load, the timing-prompts that direct the scanning device, telling it which lines to draw and when to repeat its cycle. The Farnsworth scanner produces a complexly interlaced, self-sealed message, complete with directions for its own decipherment that only another machine could read.

Scanning sacrifices the auratic or Gestalt spaces of optics to the telematic balance between transmission and reproducibility. For Williams (writing in the early seventies), television's visual "inferiority" to cinema has to be weighed against the benefits of broadcasting's "whole social intake"— as if television compensated for its perceptual poverty with an abundance and variety of generic forms, which begin to approximate the entire range of cultural offerings.[20] But there is no reason to approach this basic relation (which is, again, between technology and cultural forms) according to the norm of cinema; the continuing improvement of television's scanning resolution does not force it to adopt the modalities of cinema.[21] On the contrary, a range of visual textures persist on television, cut loose from any regulating ideal.

What Williams sees as television's weakness, its abandonment of a will-to-photography, should be taken instead as its strategic, epoch-making strength. Experimenters were content from the start to transmit blurry outlines of faces, silhouettes, cartoon cats, and easily recognizable symbols. One of Farnsworth's first transmissions was a dollar sign,[22] and the initial goal of both Baird and Alexanderson was a satisfactory close-up, so that a facial expression could be read. In 1927, AT&T engineers ran an experimental program that included a speech, a vaudeville actor delivering lines in an "Irish brogue" and "negro dialect," followed by another humorous "dialect talk."[23] And starting in 1928, C. F. Jenkins broadcast shadow pantomimes (including a baseball game, Sambo, and the Little Dutch Girl) to a scattered audience of hobbyists.[24] In these early prototypes, a transmission could be considered successful as long as an image took shape against the choppy grey static: "Can you read me?" says the crackling screen. But if these images rush to make a claim on reality, it rests on the fact of transmission—reproduction at a distance—not on the veracity of its representations. Perhaps it would be more accurate to say that the distance becomes part of the representation itself. A capacity of diffusion, its range and efficiency, preceded the development of anything like a televisual syntax or *langue*. Unlike cinema, which from the beginning constructed object-images using nineteenth-century industrial (or even preindustrial) techniques, television began by testing its ability to circulate the most ordinary expressions and stereotypes of a solidly, even proudly, philistine corporate imagination, treated as raw data for the machine.

A televisual image has to be established and sustained onscreen moment by moment. With transmission, images and sets of images pass the time and fill out the current: in this sense television is always "live." On film, on the other hand, the image appears in a here-and-now necessarily separate from the then-and-there of its production. At this technical level, before recording, television promises to revoke the Bazinian ontological distinction between the "natural" profilmic event and the inevitable "fall" into some kind of visual language. Insofar as its instantaneity (or, more broadly, its diffusion) has always risked its legibility, television proves that it is not built to produce images (like cinema), but to open and frame *fields of visuality* where a number of images, or any image whatsoever, can be constituted as *points of visibility*. Rather than reversing this topography, later technical innovations have reinforced and extended its scope.

There are several ways to illustrate this point. At the scale of microseconds and electrons, scanning cannot deliver an image all at once—its composition is always in process, and a "stable" frame can be instantaneously switched midway through. Although pixels can retain luminosity long enough to await the next scanning cycle and thereby approximate the succession of discrete filmic images, the fact that no image is ever constituted entirely in a single instant grants television a range of technical options for framing and editing, including incision and torque of the image's surface. Mixing and decomposition, as Godard has shown in his video work, are essential characteristics of the technology: the plane of the image can be broken without adding layers or dropping into depth. Nam June Paik's 1963 "prepared television" sculptures dramatized how altered magnetic fields could derange the reception of broadcast signals, slashing pictures with jagged lines of static, an act of destruction that leaves no ruins.[25] It is a general rule that there may not be an image onscreen all the time, or, what amounts to the same thing, that everything onscreen has to be seen as an image, in a new and specifically televisual sense.

Another set of clues about the relation between images and fields of visuality inhabits the combined trajectories of sound recording, cinema, and television.[26] Obviously, both phonograph recording and photography are means of recording, and the cathode ray tube is not. Early television experimenters and broadcasters depended on film equipment for two purposes. First, film was included as an intermediate step within specially built broadcasting machinery: a scene was shot on film, the film was run straight through a developing process in less than a minute, and the resulting footage was shot by either a mechanical or electronic scanner for transmission. Such arrangements were employed by BBC's first studio (ca. 1937) as well as the German Fernseh AG operation in Berlin (ca. 1935). Because lighting could be better controlled, these television cameras scanned flat images more easily than three-dimensional scenes.[27] Second, early broadcasters used film to record separately any televised material deemed worth the extra expense, which was a very small portion indeed. For many years, well into the 1950s, television programming consisted mostly of shows sent off "live," with motion pictures (i.e., 35-mm products of the big studios) and television films (16-mm) being added to the mix relatively late (in the late 1940s).[28]

Together, these intersections imply that the creators of television systems were content to poach components of film technology as temporary solutions to the persistent problem of recording. To be sure, television systems did not require the capacity to use or make recorded material: many broadcasting services were launched without waiting for it. What, then, would television do with the power of recording once it arrived? If the first phase of television can be described as the emergence of crude visuality through the persistence of radio formats and institutions, then the next stage—television after the advent of taping technology and widespread broadcast of filmed productions—became a much more complicated industrial effort in direct competition with other media, which were not destroyed so much as redefined as tributaries to televisuality. This period, lasting into the 1970s, also brought the first stage of internationalization, as more and more developing nations began television operations, often reaching only small population segments with a combination of local and Western programming.[29] To enter and service these new markets, American production and distribution companies peddled their secondhand wares globally, even as their erstwhile partners, American electronics manufacturers, saw their dominance slipping.

A third phase of technical elaboration began when recording technology (i.e., the VCR) became available at the receiving end. Videotape changes the basic relation between the transmission and the production of images. As a technology, the VCR depends on two developments: the improvement of plastic-magnetic tape manufacture (beginning in the late 1940s) and the invention of increasingly miniaturized and efficient magnetic heads in the machine itself. The magnetic tape recorder was developed in Germany and then the United States for use in the music industry, reaching the standard of radio broadcasts—which it was designed to augment—by the late 1940s. (Bing Crosby, like Edgar Allan Poe and Mark Twain in their respective eras, invested heavily in the technology of his trade.)[30] As improvements were made in the recording heads (which transfer the signal onto the tape surface), changes had to be made in the quality of the tape itself so that it could receive more information. After the grain of metal powder that coats the plastic base was refined and the tape width expanded, magnetic tape could retain the denser, more detailed impulses of video scanning. The first reel-to-reel video system by Ampex (1956) used two-inch tape; a series of European and Japanese competitive maneuvers led to Sony and JVC's late 1970s Betamax and VHS cassette systems, which then fought it out between themselves before VHS became the de facto standard for the 1980s.[31] Although Sony lost the format battle, it led the field in the innovation of helical-scan recording heads, which attained an unsurpassed capacity to distribute a video signal onto increasingly small segments of tape, squeezing and wrapping bands of electronic intensities tightly. Videotape storage fixes the signal without re-screening it: the recondite black tape holds images in their broken-down form, invisible as electrons, awaiting playback.

If scanning and transmission create one potential space for images, videotape clears another space, obeying new rules of reproduction and temporality. As long as the means of recording belonged to broadcasters, the television system expanded only through repetition and multiplication of programming on an ever larger and intensified scale. At the level of the apparatus we are tracing here, a recording and replaying device transforms the way programming is screened: now everything onscreen can be intercepted, its electronic immediacy stripped, its line-by-line information archived with little loss. Though subject to decay and fatigue, the tape offers viewers a chance to rearrange, slow, duplicate, and even manipulate signals that once crossed through as irretrievable events. Nevertheless, taping broadcasts for later viewing ("time-shifting") does not necessarily diminish the power of the program.[32] Rather, the vcr permits a virtual synchrony of the program, assuring its continuous availability. Far from delivering viewers outside the system (as implied in statements like "video recorders are agents of popular power"),[33] the vcr allows the semantics of televisual signification to persist outside the restricting temporalities of syntax.

Once the possibility of recording is put in place, programming can pursue new kinds of serial fragmentation and diversification. Meanwhile, video release of motion pictures, like showings on pay-cable systems, now offers the film industry a way to redistribute its risks and rationalize production along marketing lines cleared by television. Remarkably, statistics indicate that in countries with multiple and diverse broadcasting institutions (like Japan and the United States) the dominant vcr use remains time-shifting, while countries with a narrow range of programming are the largest users of films on video, often imported. In addition, complex subsidiary patterns have emerged in regions like Southeast Asia, where large numbers of bootlegged films and television serials circulate.[34] But the general tendency seems clear: until the overall social basis of broadcasting is overturned, each new technological "advance" is an extension of industrial-institutional interests and power, even when that order cannot completely control the tremendous profit potentials it has unleashed.

The ramifications of the vcr are still being charted. Curiously, Williams slights cassette recording in his 1974 book, giving it only a nod or two—noting both its multicorporate international scope and its potential to open new alternative markets for independent producers.[35] (With hindsight, it is clear which of these two tendencies would prevail.) In a separate essay, however, Williams attempts a theoretical typology of devices that would account for the distinction between television broadcasting and video recording. Again he begins with an "abstract" definition of television technology as pure means of transmission via a multidirectional ("two-way") channel. Furthermore, he bases his notion of communication as an essential good (the more of it, the better) on the claim that "[in] all modern and all foreseeable societies, physical speech and physical non-verbal communication ('body language') remain as the central and decisive communicative means."[36] He then outlines three kinds of technology in which these fundamental "communicative means" can be transformed: "amplificatory" (which distributes messages), "durative" (which stores messages) and "alternative" (which alters the form of messages). Because speech remains the assumed norm, these transformations take shape as, respectively, radio, recordings, and writing. The difficulties of this classical position become clear when Williams tries to decide where the various current technologies fit: radio and television, since they have travelled so far from direct interchange between autonomous individuals, must be grouped together with the other alternative means (video and film), which all share with writing the faint but unmistakable stigma of requiring an elite literacy.[37] Williams's critique of media then becomes an exercise in measuring how far from "physical" communication each medium has gone and in finding ways to reorient those practices toward the direct speech model, so that they may become the "vast network of pipes" envisioned by Brecht as the ideal mass medium.[38] Significantly, Williams skips one implication of his earlier argument, namely, that such technologies as radio and television have to be recognized as fully produced by capitalist priorities and pressures, and that the dominant structure of "centralized transmission and privatized reception" is not at all an accidental overlay but part of the technology's built-in socioeconomic "intention."[39] Instead, Williams maintains that television bears within it at least the technical essence of free communication, waiting to be realized in a new social context where radio, television, and video would simply circulate direct speech everywhere.

One need not be versed in deconstruction to recognize the logocentric axioms at work in Williams's argument or to be skeptical of any political critique and radical blueprint based on an ideal of "direct speech." Nor does one have to know much about the current state of the television/video industry to realize that the new flexibility and multiplicity of video techniques have not brought crisis to the institutions of power. On the contrary, despite a booming pirate and black market, video has arrived just in time to offer new modes of valorization for the television and film industries worldwide, largely by reinstating the centralized/privatized distribution structure that Williams identifies. Each of the major uses of video equipment reinforces a dependency on one or another product: blank cassettes, programming, and equipment. And all of these depend on the established presence of television. Williams usefully reminds us that the politics of television are still being fought on the level of capitalist control of technology. As we have seen, he also wants to emphasize that the televisual apparatus remains potentially contestatory, even though he risks essentializing the very object he wants to situate as a product of concrete historical forces. If, as he argues, television as technology can be adapted to a radically new social agenda or "intention," it would be absolutely crucial to identify which of its powerful effects or applications can be saved and which can be avoided and scrapped. In surveying the whole televisual scenario, where does Williams see danger, and where does he look for hope? Or is it possible that everything visible today would have to be rejected?

The tension which runs through and structures Williams's book can be summed up as the crude opposition between the thing—television as such—and its many and varied uses. In much leftist discourse, this opposition takes on economic coloring, where the thing is first of all a product of labor, caught in exchange relations, and the moment of its use stands apart as the goal, end, or fulfillment of its exchange value. Sartre refuses to let "use" float free from the object: insofar as something is produced by labor (especially in commodity productions), its "use" is inscribed in its very material, ready to engage in a kind of struggle with living praxis. Either objects bear a "use value" as the material basis for all value (as Marx and Sartre would say) or objects are necessarily open to all kinds of uses that can be reconstructed only after the fact (an unspoken assumption behind many current theorizations of television). We will delve more fully into economic descriptions of television in the next chapter; for the moment, we note the privilege Williams invests in the "use" of television, since this weak spot will become, in some of his commentators and critics, a blind spot.

Itinerary of a Concept-Image: the Vicissitudes of "Flow"

Midway between the forces of technical determination and the freedom of cultural usage, and at the center of Williams's argument, is the notion of the program and the concept-image he substitutes for it, "flow." This nodal point mediates the basic terms. "In all developed broadcasting systems the characteristic organization, and therefore the characteristic experience, is one of sequence or flow. This phenomenon, of planned flow, is then perhaps the defining characteristic of broadcasting, simultaneously as a technology and as a cultural form."[40] As technology meshes with cultural form, so does the broadcaster's planned sequence mesh with the viewer's experience. Williams does not leave it at that, but goes on to refine each side of the equation. "Planned flow," the schedule of shows, becomes a "real flow" with the addition of commercials, announcements, and previews of upcoming shows. Let us consider what this theoretical merging of transmission and reception has brought about in Williams and his critics.

The "experience" that Williams confesses in the face of this real flow is one of bewilderment and entanglement, "a single irresponsible flow of images and feelings."[41] Messages are no longer discrete. Narratives are cut up. Constant interruption has been transformed into something like its opposite, continuity. Overall, the "flow effect" defines how programming seizes its viewers, promoting the values of "speed, variety, and miscellaneity," which then become part of the structure of expectations.[42] One person's doped inertia is another's rapt fascination or bored indifference, but all of these responses would have to be described as an "experience" of flow. To be sure, "experience" is as misleading a term as "intention." Throughout his oeuvre, Williams places such subjective terms in large conceptual determinations; recall his famously paradoxical phrase, "structure of feeling." We have to wait a while for a similar move in the television book. But at the end of his catalogue of flow-effects (which he outlines at several Metzian scales, from montage to generic sequence to schedule), Williams offers this startling, totalizing summary: "In all these ways, and in their essential combination, this is the flow of meanings and values of a specific culture."[43]

After this general outline, Williams abandons flow, closing his book instead with a discussion of social theory and socialist alternatives to commercial broadcasting. In that context flow appears to be nothing more than a byproduct of the commercial system. Williams advocates "universal accessibility" and "open skies," but without asking the formal question, that is, without wondering whether that new kind of television would end up looking like the same crowded, "irresponsible" flow. In a later work, he proposes an expanded pay-per-view system, which would both finance a separate tier of independent producers and make television viewing more like choosing to go to a cinema.[44] Such a system would certainly break flow into chunks but would not necessarily break the market hegemony of the larger production companies, with their familiar generic and ideological repertoire. A similar problem exists today for alternative channels and programming (like the Paper Tiger/Deep Dish TV project), which plunge into commercial flow, wearing their low-tech production approach as a badge of resistance.[45] But if the flows of a broadcasting system are arranged through a logic of distinctions—and charting these distinctions is the tantalizing field of inquiry opened by Williams's chapter on flow—then alternative production efforts must constantly resist an overcoding by the network, which will attempt to shape radical "content" into just another slot within a complex *combinatoire* of viewing options.

Before there can be talk of escape from this semiotic cage, the implications of Williams's analysis of the current system must be probed more fully. What kinds of televisual operations would have to be included in any definition of flow?

A certain existential odor clings to the very notion of flow, an uncanny sense that its essence has always already flowed out of reach. Certainly the term points to different, though interdependent, levels of textual construction. That those internal relations—among images, minutes, series, weeks, seasons, and the illimitable horizon of the future—are both provisionally legible and fundamentally undecidable has to be granted at the start. As the examples drawn from early television indicate, a mixture of generic forms appears even on the briefest transmissions. If flow designates a movement of multiplicity within a single channel, it has always been with us.

But flow also defines potential movement between separate channels.[46] Now some qualifications are in order, since we cannot assume that television always brings plenitude on the scale of American cable systems (approximately 30 channels on average), let alone the Italian system (with 17 national and 850 local channels). Today, when television transmission facilities are practically universal, only a few countries receive just one channel of broadcast programming.[47] In most places, then, several programs usually overlap, even when broadcasting hours are limited to a few hours a day. Moreover, many non-Western national systems are relatively dependent on imported programming, which is likely to break up each day's broadcast into an uneven mixture of materials.[48] (Significantly, this uneven circulation of programming—largely north to south, with Brazil as the primary exception—is also called "flow.") With a satellite dish, of course, there is hardly a spot on earth that cannot gather a crowd of signals. Hence, the intensification of the geotelevision network will bring the possibility of cross-channel flow closer, often as a result of relaxation of government controls under pressure from external interests. In the densely channeled Western systems, a grid of flows already determines the programming strategies of each broadcaster, whose response will vary according to prevailing market logics and tendencies. For example, music video television, home shopping networks, nonstop televangelists, and specialty movie channels are just some of the recent American offerings, ready for export. The future promises much more in the way of repackaging than of programming innovation.

The actual coexistence of all these channels poses yet another dimension of flow. In place of an inaccessible total output, a new object of study has been substituted: the practice known as zapping.[49] With electronic remote-control units, zapping between channels can occur at split-second intervals, allowing the viewer to cut across programs indiscriminately. (Slowing down to discriminate, then, returns to the problematic of a single-channel flow's mechanisms of continuity.) Zapping may have a kind of infantile, tactile fascination about it that existed before the remote control: a child learns to change channels easily, discovering just how much pressure is required to turn the knob, to overcome the lump of mechanical resistance between one slot and the next, how to roll the knob to make everything spin past, until stopping short at one channel, just as the finger can stop a globe from turning by suddenly pressing down somewhere. Zapping reveals how television channels are always just that: grooves dredged out of airspace by the antenna and the knob, somehow more solid than the smooth glide of the old radios (which have now largely acceded to electronic tuners as well). With zapping comes the union of two kinds of digitality—of the fingers and of the signal. The remote-control button makes changing channels into a kind of cut, but unlike editing, the loss is both temporary and absolute. A channel, once abandoned, is completely beyond recovery until turned to again. Even television sets capable of making a composite image from two channels at once cannot make the leap from the single visible to the many virtual images. Both the structure of predictability and the flowing verticality of the program grid itself now appear as the broadcaster's attempt to overcome this absolute absence, to offer relief from the emptiness on all sides. At best, zapping reintroduces a moment of circumscribed chance, making a transverse cut through the grid from one programmed zone to another until sense appears.

For the past twenty years, flow has been a central notion in Anglo-American television theory. I will confine my discussion of that theory to places where the concept-image of flow is explicitly developed. In John Ellis's *Visible Fictions*, flow is dismissed almost immediately in favor of an analysis based on television's "segmental commodity."[50] Ellis charges that Williams overlooks the fact that television produces "unrelated" but discrete segments, on the model of the advertising spot and the news report, which are also the building blocks of larger forms (such as the serial and the series). Ellis's notion of the segment depends on two features: its "internal coherence" and its amenability to repetition and combination into larger sequences.[51] The segmentation he describes explains neither the succession of images nor the appearance of standard forms like the soap opera: at best, he could claim that all of television is more or less segmented according to some standard of coherence, but he does not then ask how the "intelligibility" of any segment is produced (except by reference to a grab bag of large- and small-scale terms borrowed from film theory, which is Ellis's basic point of comparison). He has it both ways—television can be seen as both fragmented and full of miniaturized, fully functioning text-segments.

In an exemplary account of the ideological value of television's technical immediacy, Jane Feuer again links "flow" with "segmentation," but she adds the crucial point that the relation between the two is "without closure."[52] She continues, "Flow, as a seamless scanning of the world, is valorized at the expense of an equally great fragmentation."[53] Through its quality of "liveness," flow packages an ideological message for the spectator, bypassing its contradictions via the clicking rhythm of a manufactured urgency. Feuer stops short, however, of theorizing how that transmission of a message *happens*. Flow remains in an undecidable relation to the individual text's "means of address" and "ideological problematic." If we recognize these latter two formulations as unsuccessful attempts to rename the opposition between "form" and "content," then Feuer's reasons for withholding a final verdict become clearer, for that is the very opposition challenged by thinking about "flow."

Rick Altman's essay "Television/Sound" amplifies a point about flow made by Ellis: that the soundtrack not only designates its images, but holds the distracted attention of the television viewer/auditor more flexibly than the sequence of images could.[54] He proposes that the flow of sound mediates and "harmonizes" between the visual sequence and a "household flow," which is his phrase for any environment of reception. Sound, then, is a kind of long leash that allows the eye to wander because the ear is always attached. Altman's argument depends on a basic assumption about the mental organization of sensory perception—that although sound is secondary and supplemental with respect to the image, it is a more effective carrier of information and a more absorbing, perhaps even more physical, kind of continuity. His argument further depends on a series of assumptions about the viewing habits of people in a variety of cultures. Although Altman confines most of his analysis to commercial networks, he nevertheless posits a universal law that higher fluxiveness— the intensity of perceptual attachment produced by textual devices—will appear as soon as a system is commercialized. Since he claims that televisual flow arises from competition for audiences, it can be cranked up wherever the household flow is more busy, turbulent, and distracted (his assumed norm in capitalist countries). In a more empirical form, this argument has also been made by Tania Modleski, relating women's housework to daytime television.[55] It is not clear in Altman's account, however, why increased sequential choppiness will always invade the household more fully (unless increased flow is equated to sheer sensory stimulation), or why anyone would ever change channels. Although Altman does not say it, MTV would be the perfect realization of his characterization of American TV, for it uses most of the aural tactics he describes. The question would then become: Why isn't all television like MTV? Like Feuer and Ellis, Altman identifies flow as the capture of viewers by formal means, as the engagement of attention through mesmerizing spectacle and tantalizing verbal lures. (Williams furnishes some precedent for this view: in an odd passage about television's "visual mobility," he suggests that we need to turn off the sound to recognize what is new about television's "primary processes of the technology."[56] If Altman still allows for a degree of variability in the way programs can flow and flow can program, he does so not to critique the circularity of the model, but to locate its functioning as both more versatile and unyielding. And rather than questioning the founding axiom of the ratings system (which also claims that subjective attachment to the screen synchronizes with its textual devices), Altman assures us that ratings, however inflated, still speak the sad truth about flow—that we have already been caught, one way or another, whether by sight or sound.

One danger of these readings of "flow" consists in just this premature interpretive summary, where flow totalizes rather than blocks the functioning of a communication regime. In these latter accounts, where film theory provides the basic terms of analysis, televisual flow is constituted as the endless message that calls for dissection and interpretation. Depending on the choice of model, different visual/textual units will be carved out and presented for analysis. That flow works on the scale of the message, the enunciation, or the subjective interpellation is taken for granted. But this emphasis on segmentation domesticates and normalizes the concept of flow, reconstituting a stratum of sense exactly at the point where its appearance is most radically uncertain and contingent.

A cautionary note about an alternate trajectory in cultural studies: It should be clear that flow in Williams's usage implies a rather bleak version of television's ideological work, which we have seen partially elaborated by his critics. One leading critic, John Fiske, has broken away from this critical stream to offer a sunnier picture. His 1977 text, *Reading Television* (coauthored by John Hartley)[57] does not address Williams's book (it is, however, cited in the bibliography), but his 1987 discipline-forging textbook *Television Culture* does,[58] and his use of Williams displays symptomatic problems. He sees in flow the "textual openness" of television, first as the "associative" sequencing of images and texts, second as the holding of viewers in the loose grip of the program. Since Fiske, a semiotic libertine, is above all concerned with describing a televisual scenario where viewers are free to make "meanings" and "pleasures" (the two keywords), flow's "openness" lets everybody get what they want, uncoerced and carefree. Television reveals itself as a curiosity shop that viewers enter and leave at will, rummaging through the textual shards for delight and perhaps edification. Their task is eased by the cooperation of the texts, which offer themselves—through the weak links of flow—as rich morsels of indeterminate meaning, waiting to be brought home and blended into each viewer's polysemic, kaleidoscopic experience. (Although I may be parodying, I am condensing and clarifying as well.) Fiske, in sum, whistles a happy tune of resistance whenever the dark clouds of ideology gather. His brief and simplified reading of Williams's chapter on flow signals an unwillingness to challenge the most prevalent assumptions about cultural history and textuality.

For a more nuanced reading of Williams, we turn to Stephen Heath and Gillian Skirrow's "Television: a world in action" (1977),[59] which analyzes a single show to indicate how it belongs to "television itself," that is, to argue from particular significations to a definition of general practices.

To define television's general practices, Heath and Skirrow refract each point of their specific analysis through a framework of semiological distinctions among television, cinema, and the novel. They insist that the "movement" of flow can be measured only through the "stasis" of its regularities.[60] At the end of the analysis, however, all of those regularities operate at the level of ideological message (using "dramatic" figures), and flow opens something else, a channel of "communicationality,"[61] television's special contribution to the institutional construction of socialized individual subjects. What had seemed peculiar to television—its "immediacy" supported by the "experience of flow"—is then revealed as its inescapable ideological snare, flow as the passage of a heterogenous time bound together by abrupt shifts between levels of signification, its approximation of a world always neutralizing its own definition, always unavailable to any single viewer.

The impulse of Heath and Skirrow to seek constant formal constraints through a specific case seems valid, even if it leads them to tag a theoretical no-escape clause onto an empirical content analysis. Though they reject parts of Williams's analysis, they nevertheless retain his terms, choosing finally to emphasize the "abstraction" of the televisual transmission over the detail of its material. But as long as television's "abstraction" is described as the suspension of the viewing subject's rules of order, the novelistic norm is maintained, coupled with a conception of ideology as the coddling of classically formed bourgeois individuals. "Experience" becomes the empty category in which all the findings of textual analysis—contradictory and diffuse, full of specular identifications—are deposited. All talk of television's "effects" posits the viewing subject as the only point of consistency, the floating tensor of intelligibility tugged and tempted by every image.[62]

An opportunity to elaborate and revise this argument came in 1984, when Heath and Skirrow interviewed Williams[63] and raised two relevant points of debate. Heath sketched an extreme version of his own argument, where television preys on popular cultural forms and restages them as spectacle. Williams responded with a strong statement of his own, repudiating any attempt to make "radical" versions of "other kinds of cultural forms" and in effect claiming that a challenge to television can come only on the level of form.[64] But when Williams is asked to define that very level, "flow" is once again the chosen term. Heath offers a clarification: as form, flow refers to the "sheer quantity" of televisual output; but as "experience," flow designates a "qualitative" response. Williams answers by speaking again of flow as the "normal television experi-ence" of a program's miscellaneous continuity.[65] The exchange is telling because both parties are willing to abandon the analysis of television in terms of particular segments, and both are anxious to specify the "content of the form" of existing broadcasting. Whereas Heath suggests that tele-visual flow sends out a meta-ideology of inclusion, Williams reads flow as the (passive) intake of a decomposed message whose only unity has to be posited (actively and critically) beyond the reach of viewing. In either case, television survives through flow, whose transmission washes away the particularity of its messages along with the differences between them, and whose reception drains perception of its resistant holding powers of distance and memory. Thus flow absorbs the entirety of the televisual textual process.

It does seem, then, that every definition of flow tries to touch ground somewhere in raw materiality. Stephen Heath himself, in a 1986 essay that stands as the brilliant and extravagant end point of a long theoretical road, equates flow with history itself.[66] What is so dazzling about his argument is its own flow: he does not let any of the old ideas go, does not disqualify any concept, but precisely lets them run together—Heath is a film theorist so overwhelmed by all these images that he can no longer choose one to examine. Still, "reality" and "experience" bob to the surface once again as the inescapable reference points for flow. Once those words are uttered, there seems to be no way of effacing them, just as the word "flow" itself seems to trap us irrevocably in the dichotomies of form and content, medium and message. If flow beckons to an irresistible way of thinking about the historically original televisual blending of a real world and points of subjective experience, it is nevertheless unable to leave the hermeneutic circuit between them. Flow remains the blurry image of unresolved metaphysical impulses in the theorization of television. It retains all the charm of an aesthetic fetish.

All of this theorizing of television—its discourses, its apparatus, its interests—settles sooner or later on the place of the viewer, the recipient, the site in front of the screen. Time and again, each theoretical snapshot tries to take into account what Sartre would call the "facticity" of tele-vision, the impression that it stands over against us, soliciting and re-pulsing our efforts to engage it constructively. Our best tactic may be stubbornness: staring down the images onscreen, looking at television as if it were not already there, and thereby producing our own fields of visibility.

Another Beginning

In 1977, three years after Mozambique won its independence, the government contracted with Jean-Luc Godard's television production company (Sonimage) to investigate the possibility of instituting a television system for the country. Godard and his team made several visits to Mozambique, held classes, journeyed around the country, and planned several television films of their own for French television that were never finished.

Godard's account of this encounter is a remarkable text: a montage of snapshots (in black and white) and prose-poems entitled "The Last Dream of a Producer: North Against South or The Birth (of the Image) of a Nation."[67] Here is how Godard described his mission:

> To study the image, the desire of images (the wish to remember, the wish to show this memory, of making a mark, of departure or arrival, a conduit line, a moral political guide with a view to one end: independence).
>
> To study the production of these desires of image(s) and their distribution via airwaves (oh! Sirens) or cables. To study production just once before diffusion muddles it up. To study programmes before making a grid, behind which there will be spectators who will no longer know that they are behind—trailing behind—the postal system, and not in front of it as they believe. (73–74)

An unmistakable fatality pervades Godard's peculiar text. He considers himself the unwilling agent of an unhappy baptism. In a photograph of Godard with several Mozambicans in a field, he sets up a camera while they watch. His caption, "an image never to be seen again," communicates a sense of fear and apprehension that in the space of the next moment something will be irrevocably lost. This foreboding is matched by an optimism of radical rethinking. Godard fills a page with the command: "learn, learn, learn." His lesson consists in showing how a single image implies several human supports: "always two for one image" he writes beside a picture of two men discussing a camera. The truthfulness of the image is not at stake, but the active construction of relationships that every image implies, although so many disguise. Godard did not try to show the Mozambicans how to produce an image; they showed him how they will produce their country by making images together. Within the boundaries of the experiment, Godard presents the moment of creative production as the only moment of radical action, the time when the images are not yet fixed anywhere, when the apparatus has not yet taken control. Before the image is sent off, it still belongs to an open process of learning and decision; as soon as it moves somewhere else, it becomes text. "First production or first diffusion. An image of me for others, or an image of others for me" (105). The moment of production must be prolonged. Failing that, it must always be reconstructed from out of the passivity of reception. Can there be production without subjecting anybody to the transmission? Godard waits to see how long his experiment can last. On one side, Godard counsels a generalized apprenticeship in an ethics of making images, and on the other, an exposure to techniques of reciprocity as the ethics of spectatorship. If everyone cannot ultimately become an image-maker, then the best a new nation can hope for is that everyone becomes cognizant of the necessity of collaboration. Those who produce images will produce for this unborn audience; those watching the images will abruptly add their own, exercising their right to speak, their right to look. In television, like in theory, it is never a matter of me or you, but of us. Godard concludes:

> On whom does the disappearance of oppression depend?
> On us.
> On whom does the maintenance of oppression depend?
> On us. (128)

Who is this "us"? It is the "us" that would come before or beyond other kinds of collectivity: neither the group of friends, the family, the crowd, the culture, the nation, nor even the whole world. This "us" is an image of the as-yet-unrealized, blocked, and diverted power of television. If everyday practices do not now produce this active "us," perhaps theoretical practices can start the task.

TWO

Image/Machine/Image: Marx and Metaphor in Television Theory

"The whole of life must look like a job, and by this resemblance conceal what is not yet directly devoted to pecuniary gain."—Theodor Adorno, *Minima Moralia*

Of all the economies television is supposed to operate, the most basic one, the one we must continue to call political economy, remains the hardest to see. Whereas television can hardly be mistaken for a purely aesthetic realm untouched by commerce, neither can it be reduced to a gross commercial formula. The televisual morphology of value operates in several registers at once, cross-cutting between long chains of force—money, state power, cultural interests—in the very movement of transmitting its images. If, on one hand, television works at the most global levels of exchange, and on the other hand, at the most everyday levels of ordinary existence, any adequate theory of this system needs a set of mobile abstractions that can recognize links between these disparate spheres. Accordingly, I offer here a map of television's possible economies organized between two conceptual poles called—in highly compressed shorthand—"machine" and "image." Any specific analysis of television must address the problems named by "machine" and "image," and our positioning of these terms determines the definition of that other inescapable term always in play and at stake here—capitalism.

To begin with a simple assertion: television is part of the machinery of global capitalism. The weight of each term and the balance of the sentence depend on the sense of the words "part of": taken at face value, the proposition can be reduced to the simple idea that television is a product of, portrays, and plays some role in capitalist relations. True enough, but nothing has been advanced: although we know that the technology of television developed largely according to capitalist imperatives, it has never been simply a tool of accumulation or just one commodity among others. The relationship between television and capital encompasses a great many figural operations, from microscopic mimesis to general social subsumption. In the televisual nexus, political economy and culture circulate through each other instantly and endlessly.

It is crucial that these figural framings (television as machine, capital as image) do not become one of those superstable theoretical grids so common in television studies, where the critic stacks up "discursive" or "symbolic" or "affective" economies without interrogating the status of the economic model itself. Behind the attraction of economic metaphorics is a systemic impulse, an attempt to link phenomena in terms of an absent or invisible logic of value. Still, the model must always make a fatal choice about its units or its ultimate term: no sooner has "labor power" been rejected in favor of "the signifier" or "desire" than the whole problematic must turn around to confront the truth-claims of systemic thinking and reason itself. (A major strain of seventies theory followed this trajectory: Lyotard is a case in point.) If we want to say that television operates several economies at once, we have to ask not only how that is possible but how we could talk about it.

As a first step, it is important to recognize the ineradicably figural dimension of any theoretical term. Deconstructive criticism has demonstrated how the radical possibility of metaphor cuts through the model of "economy," revealing it as the scattering and gathering of certain kinds of images (or, to use another code, representations). Furthermore, metaphor can be a productive and propulsive device, a built thing, a veritable machine serving the ends of sense. Whenever the relations between knowledge, sense, and representation are at stake, "economy" is not just any old metaphor: it carries in its very figure the axioms of value and structure that are supposed to guarantee the truth-claims of discourse itself. By the same token, "machinery" is more than a handy metaphor to describe economic process; it is the figure of the implacably objective, referring to everything automatic, inhuman, and deathly about social life. How do we proceed with all these images and machines, all these metaphors and economies running through each other? On one hand, the disciplinary discourse on political economy can be read as a shifting composition of concepts and metaphors already caught in the process of making its knowledge visible; on the other hand, the stream of visible images on television can be read as moments of economic circulation, decomposed into abstract markers of value in motion. It goes both ways: any account of "the political economy of television" hinges not only on the value of images but on the images of value.

Little wonder that "machinery" (like "mechanism," "device," "motor," and so on) appears as one of the constitutive figures in the most important interpretive languages, most prominently in those descended from psychoanalysis and Marxism. For its part, film theory has invested heavily in such apparatuses, fusing cameras and projectors to libidinal or cognitive switchboards, so that interpretation becomes the normative prediction of sensory and symbolic output given a certain input. Film machinery itself then functions as the guaranteed connector, transmitter, mediator, and communicator between forces, an object replacing a process without subjective agency or contingent variation. Little wonder again that "machinery" also appears prominently in the critique of such interpretive methods carried out by de Man, Foucault, or Deleuze and Guattari, where the metaphoric distance bridged by interpretation finally collapses and "machinery" (as *dispositif* and *assemblage*) becomes the "literal" blueprint for "immanent" accounts of power. The term "machinic" irresistibly enters our critical vocabulary to account for the constructions of power in an ordered environment. As a result, "writing" and "theory" no longer operate in a poetic, metamachinic space of truth, but become tools and machines in their own right.

One more example: in the midst of doling out "aesthetic worth" to various occupations in the *Critique of Judgement,* Kant castigates rhetoric by calling it the "machinery of persuasion"—no doubt a noisy and nasty image in its time, but nevertheless a ripe one, then and now.[1] As Derrida points out in "Economimesis," the joint dismissal of rhetoric and the machine remains classical: it is the denunciation of a speech without animating intention, of a language running on its own, unmotivated by an internal intention.[2] It is, indeed, the definition of *representation* itself as mechanical, that is, as repetitive, superficial, and disconnected from consciousness. Like rhetoric, the machine is empty, vacant, a pure function; it adds nothing, presents nothing of its own. In its senseless duplications it reproduces and banalizes what might once have been original, creative, or full in the original act of speaking or working. As the obvious conventionality of Kant's phrase shows, machinery acquired its metaphoric senses at the negative pole in a comprehensive schema assigning proper and improper value in commerce and speech. Although related to a certain philosophical attitude toward technics, this sense of "machinery" does not derive from a critique of "science," whether natural or applied. Instead, machinery here signifies *interest*—not only an economic interest that depends on machines instead of craft, but any interest that operates the apparatus of representation as a means of economy rather than expression. Thus at a certain point—dated conveniently by Kant as the end of the eighteenth century—"machinery" emerges as a worldly, public figure; not only a metaphor for the mundane economic world, it is literally a metaphor for ordinary metaphors.[3] In fact, "machinery" can be the most ordinary and inconspicuous of figures, one that labors in language without a hitch: it toils in the background the level of "it goes without saying," among everyday things. For the poets and the philosophers, machinery always designates something "real," not just because it must be object-like, but because it serves the world of interests and economy.

"Machinery" has become a voracious figure precisely because it knows no limiting scale or exterior contrary: it tends to recast its boundaries and operations in each place, determining parts and wholes, causes and effects. The figure of the machine has reversible sides, one side facing economy and conceptuality and the other facing the play of metaphoricity, representation, and appearances. Because it mediates in a given text between whatever is structurally absent in the economy in question and whatever is immediately, automatically visible about its products, its images, the figure of the machine has crowded into all kinds of discourse over the past few centuries, regulating the spaces of expression and action. Now, when economy and image are undergoing a thorough revaluation at every level, the semantic tangle of the machine—which had once distilled the essence of modernity—has been assumed by the screen-spaces of television and computers.

And so the question should not be, where does television fit into the economic machine? Nor, how do televisual images form an economy or a representational machine? But instead, where does the problem of defining television (in terms of visibility and force) intersect a new understanding of political economy (in terms of structure and value)? Three lines of intersection require monitoring. Each line eventually crosses—

not by accident—through Marx, who knew something about all of this long ago. The first line concerns the representation of value in theory; the second, in economy and its history; and the third, on television. After all, if any object of study obliges us to follow several movements at once, it is television.

The Play's the Thing

Enter Derrida, painted full of tongues: "Are not all metaphors, strictly speaking, concepts, and is there *any sense* in setting metaphor against concept?"[4] This rhetorical question is not a defense of metaphors against concepts or vice versa. Nor is it a commonsense plea against a "false" opposition. The question condenses a part of the argument in Derrida's essay "White Mythology: Metaphor in the Text of Philosophy" in which he tracks the longstanding attempts by Western philosophy and science to form concepts through a certain exclusion of metaphor and image, which, since they partake of resemblance and "bad" mimesis, are unreliable bearers of truth. In the passage where this question appears, Derrida points out that concepts, classically considered to be the stable tools of thought, cannot "rectify" or translate a metaphoric language into a purified metaphysical or scientific one: "Does not a scientific critique's rectification rather proceed from an inefficient tropic-concept that is poorly constructed, to an operative tropic-concept that is more refined and more powerful in a given field and at a determined phase of the scientific process?"[5] As he makes clear, there is no sensible choice (where "sensible" joins perceptible and meaningful) between metaphors and concepts, for each has a way of turning toward the other, each a flower to the other's sun. What Derrida describes here as an arrangement of metaphors and concepts in a contextually bound discourse is, in a word, an economy: in any given place, an "inefficient" and badly made unit of writing will be valued less than an "operative," workable one.

"White Mythology" is also one of the few places where Derrida reads Marx without being forced by interlocutors (although he would be the first to point out how fragile this qualification is).[6] The encounter is brief and takes place mainly in the footnotes. Derrida reckons Marx and Nietzsche as the philosophers who draw up balance sheets of "the exchange between the linguistic and the economic," that is, the intersection of *signification* and *value*. This latter distinction, Derrida adds, also marks the difference drawn by Saussure between the systems of semantics and syntax and between synchronic and diachronic models of signifying exchange. One of Derrida's critiques of representation might be summed up through this matrix as the exposure of the irreducible interference between signification and value in the transmission of the written mark through unstable contexts. (See Chapter 7.) By placing Marx close to the Nietzschean characterization of truth as a "mobile army of metaphors" and the Saussurean "discovery" of structure, Derrida gives him a privilege not enjoyed here by Freud, Bergson, Lenin, and others, who are charged with hiding the problem of metaphor in their texts behind a proliferation of metaphors. Possibly, once we agree that concepts and metaphors can form relatively stable sets of "concept-metaphors," a deconstructive reading of Marx could appreciate the care with which the "official" concepts of political economy are freed up by a certain deployment of metaphor.

Enter Louis Althusser, reading *Capital* "to the letter." Beginning with the assumption that the appearance of metaphor in a theoretical text is an indication of a conceptual lapse or difficulty, Althusser locates Marx's "symptomatic" metaphors. Let me quickly summarize a few of them, especially the ones cited by Derrida.

(1) Althusser analyzes Marx's relation to Hegel through the images of "inversion" and "the rational kernel." He rejects the hypothesis of a Hegelian persistence, either upside down or buried deep, in Marx's mature thought.[7]

(2) In his famous essay on ideology, Althusser approves the base-superstructure model insofar as it is a "topographical" image of the structural dependence of ideology on the "economic base."[8]

(3) Elsewhere, Althusser comments at length on the spatial "horizons" and "terrain" of the Marxist "discursive field"; although he finds these images all too "seductive" and phenomenological he retains them as a necessary but temporary moment in the development of a scientific language.[9] He specifies that Marx submits the dialectic to topographical metaphors in order to "recognize that its own figures are prescribed by the material character of its own conditions."[10]

(4) To this he adds a classical description of epistemology as a kind of vision: the changed and "informed gaze" of knowledge sees what the perspectival gaze of empiricism overlooks. Space and vision are of course connected figures here: the critical constitution of the proper discursive field will ensure a kind of structural sight, in which this field "*sees itself* in the objects or problems it defines."[11] Althusser's production of a subject-less historical science repeats the same moves as his theoretical produc-

tion of the capitalist structure itself, which because it can be thought only on the level of concepts, can only be seen in its partial and limited effects (i.e., individual subjects, fetishized commodities, money).

Thus the specific task of historical science is to "read" these elements as figures (metaphors, metonyms, and so on) of the capitalist structure, which, moreover, consists only in these visible traces. "[The] structure, which is merely a specific combination of its peculiar elements, is nothing outside its effects."[12] In order to see all of capital's effects together as a chain of value, precisely as an economy, historical science must discover capital's mechanism for the production and distribution—that is, the *transformation* and *transmission*—of value. A few pages earlier, Althusser cites Marx's basic conceptual name for that mechanism, *Darstellung,* representation, the "key epistemological concept of the whole Marxist theory of value, the concept whose object is precisely to designate the mode of *presence* of the structure in its *effects,* and therefore to designate structural causality itself."[13]

In sum, capitalism's fundamental mechanism, the determining force of the economic instance, can only be grasped as a certain kind of representation called *Darstellung* (which has yet to be defined). Note that what Althusser calls "causality" and "effectivity" is not a one-way, top-down relationship, but a name for the simultaneous interactions of all possible components of the economy.

At the end of his contribution to *Reading Capital,* Althusser finally examines the metaphor of "mechanism" itself.

> Each time Marx presents the capitalist system as a mechanism, a machinery, a machine, a construction (*montage*) . . . or as the complexity of a "social metabolism" . . . the ordinary distinctions between outside and inside disappear, along with the "intimate" links within the phenomena as opposed to their visible disorder: we find a different image, a new quasi-concept, definitely freed from the empiricist antinomies of phenomenal subjectivity and essential interiority; we find an objective system governed in its most concrete determinations by the laws of its *construction* (*montage*) and *machinery,* by the specifications of its concept. Now we can recall that highly symptomatic term "*Darstellung,*" compare it with this "machinery" and take it literally, as the very existence of this machinery in its effects.[14]

To paraphrase, as central images in Marx's text, "machinery" and "metabolism" cross the boundaries of metaphoric representation (being neither representation as "phenomenal subjectivity" [*Anschauung*] nor as "essential interiority" [*Vorstellung*]). "Machinery" and "metabolism" carry the link between visibility and knowledge within their very figure: hence they effect a philosophical representation (*Darstellung*). The exoteric folds into the esoteric—"part" becomes "whole" and vice versa—and the structure is designated completely in its effects.

Whereas all the other metaphors were "images" of the structure in its effects, machinery alone (notice how "metabolism" drops out) is already an "almost perfect" concept, a "quasi-concept," a concept *in effect*. The image of machinery absorbs its conceptual determination (*Darstellung*) and "literalizes" it. For an instant, Althusser appears to have resolved the abstract and the concrete, knowledge and its objects. Machinery is not only figurally adequate to the object "capitalist system" but is also sufficient to "produce the concept" of the structural determination operated by that system. Machinery both represents the force of representation in Althusser's epistemology and deploys the force of representation in the capitalist economy. This fusion of representation and machinery into a single concept-metaphor can be read in two ways.

(1) Since *Darstellung* is the philosophical concept by which Marx thinks the route of value in capitalism—the transformation/representation of particular investments of labor-power, which appear only as images of value (money-capital-commodities)—"machinery" can be both the figure and the concrete mode of existence of *Darstellung*.

(2) Since representation is thus positioned as the structural mechanism of capitalist economy, every instance of value "represents" a mechanical process in a special sense: value is neither "expressed" nor "duplicated," but "constructed" or "processed" at every step, using and remaking the available materials. Recall the French word *montage*, with its cinematic sense of "arranged images." This definition of representation answers the requirements of Althusser's polemic against Cartesian "mechanistic"—unidirectional, as in simple machines—and Leibnizian "expressive"—essentialist and idealist—effectivity.

At this point, still in midsentence, Althusser's "theoretical production" has become an epistemological machine in which all the conceptual working parts automatically duplicate "in thought" the "real" operations of capital.[15] In the face of a perfect and arid symmetry of structures, he escapes into metaphor. "[The *Darstellung*-machine is] the mode of existence of the stage direction (*mise en scène*) of this theatre which is simultaneously its own stage, its own script, its own actors, this theatre whose spectators can, on occasion, be spectators only because they are first of all forced to be its actors, caught by the constraints of a script (*un texte*) and roles whose authors they cannot be, since it is in essence *an authorless theatre*."[16]

The figure has been pushed out the other side. The evacuated theatre is introduced as the metaphor of the structural machine, as if the metaphor of a metaphor could be a concept. As Michael Sprinker has pointed out, this dramatic image brings out another sense of *Darstellung* as the positioning of visible elements in an immanent structure (immanent because its relations of determination are present onstage and nowhere else).[17] Althusser's struggle to give shape and form to his concepts through metaphor reveals a distinctly aesthetic dimension to his theorizing; indeed, the textual clash between "dramatic" figuration and a mechanical (economic, epistemological) structure can be taken as a miniature summary of Althusser's basic mode of presentation.

The whole scenario of the "authorless theatre" is plainly machinic, as well as ideal and imaginary: all its struggles and dramas are "staged" from the start. Nevertheless, circumstances allow for a change of scenery and players. All the authors are gone, but the laws governing action are visible everywhere, from every point of view. Only if these points of visibility could be thought as a whole, as connecting points bearing multiple significations (i.e., determinations), would the absent demiurgic structure present itself to thought. For Althusser, reading the theatre of structural determinations requires a certain blindness he calls "science," a discipline so severe it can only be glimpsed, like Orpheus and Eurydice, when we fail it. Vision proves compulsive, as Althusser well knows; capitalism persists in representing itself and reproducing itself everywhere, foiling any attempt to sum it up in a word or turn of phrase. It offers its own images as its only self-image. How, then, can capital be figured or at least brought within reach of a representation beyond its own representations?

Here we again recall Dziga Vertov's dream of a television that would make the world's economy visible to the workers who produce it. In *Man with a Movie Camera* (1928) Vertov uses images of machines to represent the new machine of images (cinema); together, these vectors of representation form a closed circuit unable to break the spell of visual analogy.[18] But television does not fit this linkage, for it not only manufactures images, but it also assembles and sends them. Its play of representation, its structural drama, and its own rules of visibility can only be understood in terms of capitalism's laws of value.

Marxmachine

Marx's writings, of course, are suffused with metaphors: spatial, visual, organic, machinic. But the reading of Marx that concerns us here is not "literary" or even "literal," but the contemporary reading that restores the concept of circulation to its central position in the Marxian critique of economy. To be more exact, this reading of Marx turns the old conceptual stability of "production" toward its most dynamic possibilities, and traces the movement of value as it threads its uncertain way through every social domain. Marx examines how capital flows in fits and starts, and this description has more than a passing resemblance to a formal description of television as the transmission of images. Indeed the resemblance is intimate: a reading of Marx can show why machinery, far from being inert matter, has always been involved in matters of representation and how the historical expansion of the machine system grants television, at a certain moment in history, new zones of value and new circuits of power.

"Value as such is always an effect, never a cause," Marx explains in the *Grundrisse*.[19] There he struggles constantly with his key notion, labor power, trying to find a way to prevent it from becoming a metaphysical origin of value. He proposes the concept of "value-in-process" to indicate the continuity and restless transformations of capital and to point to the historically specific way in which capital achieves its circumnavigation of the whole social sphere.[20] Each point of capital's itinerary—labor power, money, commodity, machinery, capital—is linked to and formed by the others through specific operations and sets of conditions; each movement between terms is a refiguration and reprojection of value, both an abstract movement of representation and a concrete point of contestation.[21] The formal lesson of the notion of "value in process" should be familiar from contemporary theory: the only possible referent for one term in an economy will be another term in that economy, that is, that reference is (in) motion.[22]

Since capital loves movement, it takes on fantastic and bizarre shapes whenever it is stopped for very long, when it becomes "fixed." Machinery is Marx's most consistent example and metaphor of fixed capital, to the point where it becomes the internal perfection of capital's representational movement. "*Machinery* appears, then, as the most adequate form of *fixed capital*, and fixed capital, in so far as capital's relations with itself are concerned, appears as *the most adequate form of capital* as such."[23] He adds, however, that money is the most adequate form of capital for "external relations," which is why he spends so much time explaining elsewhere how money, as a "form of appearance," conceals the inner workings of capital. In the fundamental distinction between fixed and circulating capital, there is no way to say which is more primary, either phenomenally or conceptually; furthermore, there is no way to maintain that distinction except as a freeze-frame description of a given situation. Marx takes the comparison of machines and money further when he refers to money as "a machine which saves circulating time."[24] Both money and machines hold time as value, but in forms suited to quite different speeds of metamorphosis. Such constructs have allowed capital to rebuild the world as a landscape of choppy time gaps.[25] Today, in the globally mobile sphere of late capitalism, driven by a jet stream of interest, credit, and speculation, each individual capital can withdraw from one location and move to another almost instantaneously, riding out the fast-breaking vicissitudes of regional fortunes and monetary climates, facilitated by the mechanisms of the electronic financial system. The information and telecommunication machinery now encompassing the earth, with its capacity to serve many uses at once, exists first because of capital's imperative to circulate and to change form as quickly as possible. Marx saw these possibilities when he pointed out that the "tendency of capital is *circulation without circulation time;* hence also the positing of the instruments which merely serve to abbreviate circulation time as mere formal aspects posited by it."[26] Capital, in other words, seeks to make each moment of its circulation "ideal," necessarily inscribed and abstract but irreducibly symbolic and translatable, in order to generalize its space of operation. Accordingly, capital employs different instruments—productive and financial—to grind out value at different speeds in different places, each local ensemble always seeking its most efficient gear ratio. Money and machines therefore perform different kinds of integration: whereas the expansion of exchange relations heralds the incorporation of previously distant economies, the emplacement of machinery establishes the socialization of all labor, and points toward the planetary entrenchment of capitalist relations.[27]

To return to machinery as fixed capital: what is symbolic or abstract about that? Here is a power loom, there a factory building; certainly the capitalist bought these things for no other reason than to produce surplus value. But since fixed capital consists of commodities that nevertheless remain in the production sphere, they are not immune to a kind of fetishism. Marx struggles to define it: "*Fixed capital,* actually fixated capital, [is] fixated in one of the different particular aspects, phases, through which it must move."[28] Fixed capital is not entirely itself, not all there, "never completely occupied."[29] Distracted or dormant, maybe, but not dead. Seen in terms of Marx's persistent contrast between "living" labor and fixed capital, the function of machinery in the labor process has a twofold character, corresponding to its place in the microrationality of investment and its definitive role in macrolevel organization of social relations.

First, machinery is a component of the continuing circulation of value. It transfers its value (we will leave aside the question of its price) incrementally back into the products it helps to make, until it has no more value to dispense (obsolescence and final depreciation). We can call this its capital-value loop: it stores and dispenses some previously produced quantity of value. In the second volume of *Capital,* Marx analyzes at length the cost structure of fixed capital in terms of the gradual dissemination of its "fixed" value.[30] The contingent "fixedness" of fixed capital relates to three factors: the durability of the physical thing (its "use form"), its convertibility into circulating capital, and the changing level of available technology. These criteria, which cover both the value of the machine's construction and its situational utility, determine when a machine can be employed productively. Only when a machine can transfer its value to a commodity does it remain part of capital: upon this rule rests Marx's theory of economic cycles, attached to the periodic replacement of worn-out fixed capital (as we will discuss below).[31] From capital's point of view, each machine follows a fatally entropic course, slowed by repairs but hastened by the advent of new and better machines.

Second, and more crucial, machinery exerts a social force on the labor process that cannot be simply quantified. As a powerfully new kind of object, the machine takes on sovereign power, even to the point where it appears to function "for nothing," "like a natural force," becoming a "mighty organism" overwhelming labor.[32] Here the key analogy Marx draws is not between machines and money but between machines and the laborer. (Both analogies, however, describe a concrete mediation.) Under capitalism, the worker and the machine enter into irreversible relations of reciprocal constitution. Both become "effects" of capital, operating on the same plane as "value as such"; unlike "value," however, they are positioned, perhaps tenuously and phantasmically, as "causes" or "use-values" within the production process. As Marx tries to sort out lines of causality between machine and worker, the metaphorics of machinery merge with the metaphorics of the body, to the point where the distinction is both fundamental and indiscernible. Since the production of surplus value can only take place through "living" labor, something about the expenditure of work-time must remain irreducibly organic, unabsorbed by mechanical processes. At the same time, the machine is granted a bodily mass capable of retaining and expending its own energies over time. Thus the line of difference between humans and machines is more analogical than oppositional: the powers proper to the laboring body are transposed onto the body of capital, and vice versa: "[In] the human body, as with capital, the different elements are not exchanged at the same rate of reproduction, blood renews itself more rapidly than muscle, muscle than bone, which in this respect may be regarded as the fixed capital of the human body."[33]

From capital's point of view, this residue of living matter known as the human body can be managed easily enough—its first weapon, of course, is the machine itself. Marx clearly lays out in the first volume of *Capital* the material aspects of a historically original subjection to machinery, in which the modern body is submitted to a new technology of power (i.e., the Foucauldian "discipline"). It should be emphasized that machinery's role in social reproduction is profoundly "ideological" in Althusser's sense. The machinic form of value accomplishes what the exchange of commodities cannot: it constitutes bodies as conscious (self)-representations coordinated through the technical arrangement of economic processes. Marx tells the story this way: "Once adopted into the production process of capital, the means of labor passes through different metamorphoses, whose culmination is the *machine,* or rather, an *automatic system of machinery* . . . this automaton consisting of numerous mechanical and intellectual organs, so that the workers themselves are cast *merely as its conscious linkages*."[34] The worker relays the transmission of value along the same twofold lines as the machine: first as a calculable labor power that receives a wage and buys commodities to reproduce itself, and second as a "watchman" or "conductor" of capital's machinic timetable of acceleration, a more or less efficient switch point for the turnover of fixed and circulating value, "absorbed into the body of capital."[35] This abstraction and absorption of socialized labor power lends machinery further "human" accoutrements. "It is the machine which possesses skill and strength in place of the worker, is itself the virtuoso, with *a soul of its own* in the mechanical laws acting through it."[36] As in so much science fiction since *Frankenstein,* the machine's soul stirs with rap-ture as it receives its human ingredient, "*as though its body were by love possessed.*" (Marx quotes the raucous drinking song from *Faust*, "als hätt' es Lieb im Leibe," to evoke the moment.)[37] While collective bodies are transmuted and transfigured into mechanical systems, the so-called "general intellect"—in the form of institutions of science and knowledge—becomes the index and "organs" of the new social machinery. (Note that Marx's use of the word "organ" appears as another figural crossover from the body to the machine.) Beyond all these acts of submission and service, the final but deferred result of capitalist production is "society" itself, a set of relations played out between moving bodies, appearing to and vanishing from each other at differing speeds, in which the sole task left to human beings is to "renew themselves as they renew the world of wealth they create."[38]

This image of capital as a self-reproducing machinic skeleton reappears, stronger than ever, in Sartre's late work the *Critique of Dialectical Reason*. Describing the situation of the worker at work, he notes first that the machine and the factory only exist as the "dead" labor of previous generations (the "practico-inert"). Whereas Marx's *Capital* provides an account of the socioeconomic structures built out of dead labor, Sartre's *Critique* describes the existential fate of dead labor in the tumble of History. Under capitalism, social being is "crystallized" in material objects and built space that then exert a synthetic force of Otherness over those who follow. Taking as one of his examples a working woman, Sartre identifies a "contradiction which opposes the productive forces to the relations of production," meaning here the confrontation between the practico-inert object and the worker herself. Sartre draws the most extreme conclusions: this encounter "forces the working woman to live a prefabricated destiny as *her reality*," a destiny which arrives from elsewhere as the imposition of an absent human unity. Neither she nor the capitalist "intend" it. He cites a study in which it is discovered that women have fragmentary sexual fantasies as they work at semiautomatic machines, from which he concludes, "But it was the machine in them which was dreaming of love."[39] Because the machine requires a certain kind of half-conscious attention, the rhythms of thought are fit into machine-time. These women's fantasies arise as the clipped and disjointed injections of an objective ensemble of body, brain, and machine. Men, by contrast, do not abandon themselves this way (so Sartre says); presumably they are always active, undistracted, and undistanced, in work as in sex. In either case, however, the machine limits what can be thought and done at the same time, marking out a more or less empty temporal frame that leaves intervals for imaginary work inserted into machinic work. Though Sartre stops short of saying that the machine "produces" the images flashing through the workers' heads, he leaves little doubt that the activities of consciousness are fully captured by the machinery. The mental images are therefore a kind of by-product of the object being produced for commodity exchange. This is not to say that capital can valorize all the fantasies, daydreams, and self-images spun out in the wake of production. Marx recognizes on the first page of *Capital* that loose subjective elements run through economy: there they are called "needs." Sartre indicates that these elements are caught and re-cycled in a dialectic of recognition, representation, and domination.

Sartre's image of the working woman as a mixing vessel for collective fantasy and machinic labor-time raises the spectre of total domination reaching into every corner of subjectivity. Although we do not have to take it at face value, the image usefully recalls a key point made by Marx in Volume I of *Capital:* the introduction of women and children into wage labor is "the first result of the capitalist application of machinery."[40] In the earliest stages of industrialization, the machine baptizes the entire pro-letarian family in the wage circuit. It breaches the existing gendered division of labor and casts all subsequent divisions as instances of direct economic exploitation—struggles over whose work counts as value—both in the factory and in the home.[41] At least since the appearance of capitalism, women's work in the home has been the essential component in the reproduction of labor-power, a structural exclusion from value that makes possible surplus value itself. At the same time, women also enter and leave the wage relation under obvious constraints, on the basis of both socially available life-trajectories and the kinds of work required by capital at a given moment. As the material site of the division of labor, then, machinery has been gendered from the beginning. It requires cer-tain skills that are socially apportioned or, alternatively, a lack of skill that is socially imposed. It may in fact be built to exhaust its workers as quickly as a raw material, using up a particular physical capacity (such as eyesight) before releasing the worker from wage labor (i.e., to run a family). (This is presently the dominant pattern in the Pacific Rim microelectronics industries, the production core of the new information technologies.)

A historical continuity in the gendered division of labor can be traced through the machines operated by working women, from the power looms of early industrialism to the typewriters of the metropolitan–

imperial era offices, to the data-processing and household appliances of our own age. The continuity is reinforced if we include television. The work of Tania Modleski, Gillian Dyer, and others has already shown how television "distracts" the labor and thought of the household worker in ways broadly similar to Sartre's scene: in each situation, the woman finds a way to choose what she cannot avoid and thereby exercises her margin of subjectivity through images.[42]

As the variability and flexibility of women's labor show, the attachment of bodies to machines is not absolute, neither for an instant nor for a life span. The heroically mechanized male worker, familiar from so much early twentieth-century art and politics, was never the ideal for capital. On the contrary, capitalist machinery has always developed so that the cheapest possible work force can be applied. Whether labor power is characterized as strength, care, or intellect, machinery exists to process it. The machine marks and maintains a distance and difference between two forces, one structural and the other subjective. The analytic of machinery remains bound, in the split optic of the Marxian text, to the labor theory of value and a subjective theory of consciousness, as it is expressed in the unclosed gap or fissure between machinic and organic metaphors in the text of economy.[43] This gap survives even in the most dramatic contemporary retheorization of economy: when Deleuze and Guattari redefine capitalism as "a general axiomatic of [the] decoded flows" of labor and accumulated wealth, they carefully distinguish between a "machinic enslavement" that simply incorporates the human being as a "component" of a machine and a "social subjection" in which the human being is exterior to, if not free from, the machine.[44] Without endorsing Marx's historical periodization or dialectical procedures, Deleuze and Guattari remain true to the irreducible play of his conceptual figures.

Through this textual fissure, Marxian metaphorics can lend their theoretical focus to the study of television. The conception of machinery as the body of capital introduces the bodies of humans into the pathways of value and allows us to question how "experiential" dimensions of the world—such as vision and time—can be produced within the circulation of capital.

Television, a Machine for Our Time

A cultural analysis that begins with Marx's account of the capitalist's yet unrealized machinic world will diverge sharply from a discussion that sees capitalist culture only in terms of its commodities, with its themes of reification, alienation, and spectacle. It is clear, at any rate, that Marx's own broad characterizations of culture focus more closely on the state of productive technology than on its products, and more on the differentiated movements of economy than on a dead-end fascination with objects. After the mildly apocalyptic strains of 1960s "consumer society" and "information society" theory died down, several strands of the postmodernism debate renewed the analysis of capital as a formidable and complex ensemble of productive branches. For example, some recent accounts of the geography of capital begin from definitions of fixed capital as built space (Henri Lefebvre, Manuel Castells, David Harvey, Edward Soja). So-called post-Marxist descriptions of "articulated" power networks retain the structural aspects of Marx's analysis of economy but discard the thesis, not necessarily Marx's, that classically "economic" lines of determination cross through every cell of a social space. Any emphasis on the material apparatus of capitalism must raise the difficult question of relations of *force* (domination, discipline, resistance) exhibited wherever the relations of production are reproduced, which immediately transforms the "economic" scene into a political and cultural one as well.[45]

If television is regarded as a nothing more than a commodity plaything or a propaganda megaphone, if its place in contemporary capital can be isolated in a particular sphere of consumption (where anything is possible, even pleasure), then it hardly deserves to be called a machine, and it hardly deserves to be promoted to the status of iconic object and bearer of the zeitgeist. But since we are now in a better position to recognize that capitalism's machinery includes any transfer-point where value can be reconfigured, it will be easier to recognize that television images are themselves always value-in-process, rather than extraneous pretty pictures at second hand, and that this absolute proximity to other forms of capital suggests that television's particular forms of value are central and necessary in the current juncture.

The suspicion that television is more than window dressing for contemporary capitalism has been expressed before. Thus Fredric Jameson's tantalizing formulation, setting video in the historical frame of machinery: "If we are willing to entertain the hypothesis that capitalism can be periodized by the quantum leaps or technological mutations by which it responds to its deepest systemic crises, then it may become a little clearer why video—so closely related to the dominant computer and information technology of the late or third stage of capitalism—has a powerful claim for being the art form of late capitalism *par excellence*."[46] To redirect the question: what is the nature of the intimacy between television and late capital, and what forms could that relationship take? Is television somehow too late to be the darling of late capitalism; is it condemned instead to be its dominant but not emergent cultural form? To show how television has served its historical duty, I will review four different accounts from the hard-economic to the speculative-theoretical.

It has already been pointed out that the depreciating value-loop of fixed capital sets the pattern for economic cycles. Marx saw that periodic replacement of machinery required a large reinvestment in the means of production (Department I). The rate of commodity production (Department II) may undergo variation, but it does not explain the cyclical crises capitalism has undergone since its first full bloom. The technical and economic relation between these departments is known as the "organic composition of capital." (That telling concept-metaphor is Marx's.)

Much of Ernest Mandel's *Late Capitalism* is concerned with the "structure of production" as the relation between branches, for it provides the material basis for his historical schema: an updated version of Kondratiev cycles—long waves of capitalist development and decline, running in roughly sixty-year intervals. (The literature on Kondratiev waves is voluminous, and need not detain us here. It can be pictured as a kind of roller coaster kinetic/potential energy model for capitalism's long-term profit rates and investments.) Mandel attaches great significance to technological turnover. "The characteristic element in the capitalist mode of production . . . is the fact that each new cycle of extended reproduction begins with different machines than the previous one."[47] Each of these changes comes about through a dual accelerated growth in the institutions of scientific knowledge and the capacity of capital as a whole to incorporate new discoveries.[48] Mandel extends Marx's historical account into several additional stages:[49] from the tool to the handmade machine is the first step; from the machine to machines powered by machines is the second, fully capitalist step, which then takes three major shifts: i) steam (the moment of Marx); ii) electric and combustion (when the engines themselves become machine-made); iii) electronic and nuclear.[50] Thus each stage of capital has its emblematic or privileged *power-source* technology that leads the way to an epochal transformation in all other branches of production, including commodity and agricultural production. The capacities and limits of this power-source give shape and duration to the epoch, making possible new zones of profitable production and consumption. In this nuclear and electronic age, Mandel's examples are "jet transport planes, television, telex, radar and satellite communication networks, and atom-powered container freighters."[51] Later he sums it up another way: "This new period [1940–65] was characterized, among other things, by the fact that alongside machine-made industrial consumer goods (as from the early 19th century) and machine-made machines (as from the mid-19th century), we now find machine-produced raw materials and foodstuffs. *Late capitalism . . . thus appears as the period in which all branches of the economy are fully industrialized for the first time.*"[52]

Television is thus situated—but not singled out—as one of the consequential products and the typical consumer good of the third stage. Apart from the fact that it shares with the other examples a global reach, television seems to bear no particular internal necessity to this late capitalist system. It does not express a change in patterns of consumption or in the establishment of a world market for a series of new products (i.e., information and culture). Its proper antecedents are simply all the other consumer goods churned out by capital for the previous one hundred and fifty years. Furthermore, television appears to play no role in the spread of the dominant "instrumental ideology" that Mandel describes in his chapter "Ideology in the Age of Late Capitalism," or in the potentially revolutionary crisis in relations of production that he evokes at the end of the book.

Mandel does give an economic explanation of television, however, in his introduction to volume II of Marx's *Capital.*

> The production of television sets or *films* (including copies of such films) is obviously a form of commodity production, and wage-labour engaged in it is productive labour. But the hiring-out of completed films or the renting of a single television set to successive customers does not have the characteristics of productive labour. Similarly, wage-labour employed in making advertising films is productive, whereas the cajoling of potential clients to purchase such films is as unproductive as the labour of commercial representatives in general.[53]

In an attempt to distinguish between what constitutes "social value" and what does not, Mandel opts for the most orthodox line: the "use" of television is "unproductive" in every form, whether as reproduction of the relations of production, as "cajoling" of consumer desire, or as the essential conduit for the establishment of a worldwide market. The exception of advertising, however, indicates that Mandel grants a certain limited function to those products and services (like consumer credit) that extend the sphere of consumption and hence help alleviate "difficulties of realization" (selling commodities).[54]

Is this line so easy to draw? Only if we ignore the possibility that television—and not just television, but the whole culture industry—does not distinguish, in a way decidable to anybody except the most confident semioticians, between its advertisements for specific products and its large-scale representations of social milieux entirely composed of capitalism's signatures. If, on the other hand, the work of culture is in this sense productive for capital and indispensable to it, television would have to be counted as an "unofficial" conduit of value.

In a liberal defense of long-wave theory, Peter Hall and Paschal Preston have argued the connection between particular technologies and successive economic long waves.[55] Their research centers on the increasingly central relationship of information technologies to economic patterns, culminating in the current fourth Kondratiev wave "carried" specifically by electronics, computing, and telecommunication.[56] Information technologies, defined as all technologies of whatever power source that "record, transmit, process and distribute information,"[57] were secondary industries before the 1940s; only after the immense corporate investment in lab research could they be launched on the international scale necessary to make them profitable. The preconditions for this emergence were a deep involvement of capital in scientific work beyond the stage of the heroic inventor or entrepreneur and the establishment of a new stage of the world division of labor. As a "consumer good" element of this onslaught, television strongly supported the wave at first (1950s–1960s), only to yield its key components in the long run to the "producer good" or fixed capital applications (satellites, surveillance, computer screens, military hardware). As opposed to Mandel, Hall and Preston accord television absolute proximity to the decisive economic circuits of the era, which are simultaneously intrinsic to and a product of the surge of capital. No further comparison or distinction is drawn between the "information" carried by, say, computer networks and that carried by television: having abandoned a labor theory of value, Hall and Preston can not distinguish between these transmissions, nor can they determine whether the modes of transmission and valorization across the range of information technologies have quite different economic or political applications for capital. Still, they place television in a different technological continuum from Mandel's: it appears as the profitable culmination of different strands of innovation that are resolved at a certain juncture. "Information" can at last become a global commodity when gathered and propelled across a geography occupied and reshaped by machines.

A kind of intermediate positioning of television somewhere between machinery and commodity can be found in David Harvey's compendium of Marxist analysis, *The Limits to Capital*. He locates television in a most logical, if vague, economic slot: the "consumption fund," which is defined as "commodities [that] perform in the realm of consumption a somewhat analogous role to that played by fixed capital in the production process."[58] The phrase "consumption fund" occurs most prominently in Volume II of *Capital,* where it designates "means of consumption" that ensure turnover of consumable commodities in the lengthy reproduction equations. Television takes its place alongside forks and spoons, sidewalks, washing machines, even houses: all of these things somehow make consumption possible. It makes a certain obvious sense: without a "consumption fund" popcorn maker, you won't buy popcorn. But this solution solves nothing: the term is hardly useful if it can be so easily extended to cover all public and private space, as well as all those commodities that we don't happen to eat, drink, or destroy right away. Nor does it offer any clue about the crucial questions: how is consumption "produced" by the instruments of consumption? Do different items in the consumption fund (say, a refrigerator and a TV) "produce" different kinds of consumption and different circuits of spending? Harvey's more recent book *The Condition of Postmodernity* answers straightforwardly: yes, "television use" contributes to a necessary increase in demand, promoting a culture of consumerism. But he explicitly leaves aside the analysis of new cultural and aesthetic techniques that have enabled television to perform such a task; after correctly dismissing an easy equation between television and postmodernism itself, he lets the problem fade into the background.[59]

In their impressive synthesis of post-Fordist and French poststructural theory, Eric Alliez and Michel Feher suggest that the mobilization of "information" by capital provides an "economic definition of postmodernism": rather than having an ideological use, information is now calculated in strict exchange-value terms according to "the cost of the information, measured in the time necessary for its formulation and comprehension, [which] must be minimized while its exchange value is increased by the multiplication of references, allowing it to reach a broad public."[60] This new economy can be characterized by its own machine-subject ensembles: the television viewer is now totally assimilated to the "permanent spectacle."[61] The mental operations of "formulation and comprehension" correspond to simple production, the labor of viewing, measured in time; on the other hand, consumption or reception is assumed to be automatic, a function of being "referred" to or addressed as consumers. "Multiplying the references" is the key phrase for Alliez and Feher: it describes a formal, internal transformation of information, in which "reference" is built into each unit so that it can function as a self-sufficient universal commodity. But cybernetic perfection can only be an ambition for a single capital; with many capitals, centrifugal forces will always drive the information commodities toward differentiation and noncommunicating circuits.

Instead of supplying a formal definition for the new postmodern commodity, then, Alliez and Feher in fact rehearse the "lowest common denominator" theory of television programming and information distribution, in which the mass media are blamed for the loss of stable and singular meanings. At this point, they seem to lean much more heavily on Baudrillard (and behind him, Debord) than on theories of post-Fordism. They also seem to borrow a page from Rousseau on the innocence of appetites. As a result, a machine called "television" and a population called an "audience" are equally totalized as "spectacle," an absolute space within which televisual images are supposed to circulate and arrive with cybernetic efficiency and transparency. Nothing is transformed in this production: information and mental labor fuse into a single commodity expended in the white-noise combustion of the spectacle. Like others in the Debord-Baudrillard tendency, Alliez and Feher tell a story in which the image-form of capital achieves a final washout: capital has become homogenous but invisible behind the sheer multiplicity and inherent uncertainty of images. But even if this account were completely accurate, the opposite process must be traced as well, in which images become many different capitals, expanding their repertoire but holding back from total and synchronic inscription. Alliez and Feher find no escape through television, but they hold out hope that there can be an escape from television. At the conclusion of this portrait of a fully instrumental capitalism, Alliez and Feher hesitate a little, suggesting that capital's subsumption of "the totality of time" nevertheless leaves some open spaces at the margins, overlooked but not created by it, waiting to be filled with insurrection. Whatever these forces are, wherever they may appear, they can have nothing to do with the televisual circulation of images and value. Alliez and Feher propose radical refusal as the only gesture of hope.

We can, therefore, outline two poles in the debate over television's work for capital. If Mandel is insufficiently alert to television's figural relation to capitalist economy, Alliez and Feher are oversensitive to it, collapsing all productions of time and value into a single smooth spectacular process without allowing for the persistence of interruptions and flickering metaphysical leaps in the circuit (which are after all what makes culture still valuable). Although television is integral to the distinctive movements of value under late capital, it also drags economy back from the brink of abstraction to the messy realm of collective imagination. Indeed, television can be distinguished from other machines of its age (such as the computer) by the fact that it must pass through the variable times of visibility, that is, it can only perform its tasks for capital in the old, stubbornly slow perceptual and affective time of human subjects. Though television may be part of the new information flow, converging with the others all the time, it always finds itself having to have a "content." Its diffusion may be instantaneous, like the monetary particle-signs coursing through the lines of finance, but its reception as images must still be lived moment by moment.

The Work of Watching

What are television's tasks? What does it produce? Now we must join the two hypotheses proposed so far. First, television works as a machine according to the basic Marxian account, serving as a transfer point between quantities of time already supposed as value, translating between the time of images and the time of viewing (always imperfectly) and thereby motivating further productions and circulations. Second, television appeared at a certain historical moment to incorporate everyday life and culture as "free" time into the body of capital through the mediation of the image. Although neither of these hypotheses takes account of site-specific operations, it must be assumed that every machine will be placed in particular locations ("contexts") and that the system's output will therefore hinge on a number of local factors. At the same time, however, as we have seen, the machine operates as an outpost—the representing representative—of the world capitalist system at a particular moment of its development, integrating local subjective and reproductive flows with overall productive ones.

How does this global machinery make itself visible through televisual images (all of them, each and every one)?

As Jameson suggests, television produces images within a new space and time. The televisual image is not produced "after" or "inside" its temporal and spatial frames; rather, these are working dimensions of the apparatus. The volatility of the televisual image's frame distinguishes it from photography and cinema, the two image-commodity forms corresponding to previous epochal structures of production. Even so, television has proved capable of changing its primary modes of imaging. To cite a familiar example, so-called "direct" transmission or broadcasting of "live" events proved incompletely profitable without greater technical manipulation and arrangement of the event, so that the presentation of "liveness" must be continually reinvented.[62] No matter what formal changes it undergoes, television's basic economic vocation lies in the transformation of material images into units of value through new frameworks of circulation. But before describing this operation, we should recall that "circulation" goes beyond simple movement or transportation; indeed, television's movement of images is best considered part of a larger production process that only becomes visible onscreen.

If the machine system of large-scale industry radically collectivized and redistributed social labor time according to capitalist imperatives, the television system now performs the same function for other segments of time: pleasure time, public or community time, household time, parenting time, childhood time, even animal and vegetable time. In a word, some share of what used to be called "disposable" time is put at the disposal of television, so that non-work time becomes subject to the same kinds of antagonisms that cut across labor time. To be more exact, television's work within capitalism follows two directions at once, corresponding to its machinic attributes.

The first direction, corresponding to the prefix "tele-," involves space: by sending images, the machine gives them form and value in new contexts of potential valorization. Marx observes that the act of bringing the product to market must be considered part of its production;[63] in the case of television, however, the machine brings "the market" along with it. At any geographic scale from a single-channel backwater to a multi-input honeycomb, television engineers a specular market of images. As we saw in Chapter 1, this point applies to state-run systems as well, where the televisual market is simply controlled more narrowly, and therefore deployed less extensively, than the others. At the level of any given system, television captures distance and defines its social territory by grounding itself as a set of material objects: it exists as a vast number of scattered machines, connected by the diffusion of a production occurring elsewhere and everywhere at once. Most of the means of production and transmission (broadcasting facilities, cables, and satellites) remain in the hands of economic and state institutions; but through an arrangement that bespeaks its capitalist essence, everybody else is permitted to pay for their share of the overall machine. In this sense, television can be seen as a continuous extension—through "economic democracy"—of previous technologies of distribution, albeit an extension that alters the composition and strategy of the world market. It would be a mistake to expect television to saturate everyone's lives equally: it can expand only when a reflux of value justifies its efforts.

The second function of the televisual image concerns a transformation in the capacities of capitalism through a new production of time. The most obvious and extreme—though limited—aspect of this change is advertising itself. Several arguments have been made about advertising's relation of time to value on television; I will review two of the most pertinent and suggestive. Nick Browne's seminal essay on the "television super-text" takes the position that televisual time is arranged on two registers: "codes of realistic representation" and the various durations of the working day, week, year, and so on.[64] For Browne, the relation between these two follows a clear logic: the first order of time, belonging to the content of televisual flow, is the calculated bait in the capture of the second order of human (free) time. A familiar dualism arises: the "discursive" or "textual" economy receives its temporal logic from a "general" economy controlled by advertisers and programmers. As Browne presents it, the units of analysis are the visible segments of the schedule; these must be put together by the critic to reconstruct the program, which is the logical sum of the advertiser's and broadcaster's interests. Directed by market research on the habits and tastes of the populace the program translates between the general economy and the textual one. Advertising images—because they participate directly in the production of consumption—are assumed to function one way, having direct and statistically available results, and all the other images are there to keep up the flow and to prop up the attention of viewers, vaguely reinforcing the sales pitch. Sut Jhally carries this hierarchy further, defining *programming* as the "necessary" time the broadcaster is forced by some mysterious social imperative to give up, and identifying *advertising* as the pay-off, the "surplus value" extracted from viewers.[65]

Though both accounts connect the different forms of televisual image with the competition of different capitals, each continues to accept advertising as the primary economic mechanism of television, when in fact it is only one possibility. In other words, these accounts stay close to the advertiser's own version of the story, which is part of every commercial's ideological protocol: the companies insist that they just want to buy slots of time that they hope will be witnessed by a certain demographic slice. We, the audience, are supposed to understand, sympathize, play along. But with the multiplication of channels and the new attachment of VCRs, this arrangement, this pact of complicity, has become more obviously fragile. Witness the frantic attempts by the networks to shore up their crude model of television viewing through more sophisticated statistical methods. (New devices built into televisions look out at the viewers, measuring their presence in the room and their facial orientation to the screen.) Like currency exchange and interest rates, advertising-based explanations are founded in a faith that certain transactions will always come off, that the general equivalent (ratings) really does represent something else (attention, perception, reception and consumption), that lines of cause and effect can be traced from one order to another—in this instance, from the scheduling of images straight to desires and deferred gratifications. Moreover, to regard watching TV as a transaction carried out between economic agents (individual, corporate, or both) is to fall into the same error Marx exposed in the bourgeois economists: reducing the systemic to the subjective and the episodic.

If, on the other hand, television can take or leave that kind of advertising, if television can survive and expand after all empirical guarantees about the viewer's behavior are gone, other forces must be at work and must have always been at work. Certainly, advertisers buy time, but it is *socialized time.* Just as the capitalist buys labor power rather than an individual's labor, so the advertiser buys a unit of social time-power—the hypothetical fusion of "free" time and "free" images calibrated in price according to estimates and averages of productivity and potential return. Television, in its fundamental commercial function, socializes time by sending images of quantifiable duration, range, and according to its own cultural coordinates. By generating a realm of collective, shared time, and by setting standards for the valorization of this time, television advances capitalism's temporal rule: everybody is free to spend time in their own way only because, on another level, that time is gathered elsewhere, no longer figured as individual.[66] As a result, the "costs" of television—if it still makes sense to put it that way—are borne by everybody in myriad ways, spread through all levels of the economy as the overhead of general rationalization and crisis control. We might add that the "choice" of whether or not to watch television and what to watch there becomes part of the way one directs oneself toward others; it is no more a choice than the decision whether or not to work or to use money. Under the general rule of the market, television offers the advantage of turning the subjective thrills of recognition and the jolt of interpellation into commodified moments of choice, letting ideology pass as a matter of taste rather than coercion.[67] Television, by delimiting and monopolizing the time of imagination, allows us to offer up our social lives as free contributions to capitalist power.

Perhaps this is the place to lodge a complaint against a certain use of the word "consumption" in media criticism, especially as in the phrase "to consume images": this is at best an imperfect way to describe an action which cannot even be assumed to occur. It disguises, as the final term in an economic sequence, the uncertainty of a reception, an interpretation, or a production of sense.[68] For Marx, of course, consumption not only leads to production of a new force, but transforms, retroactively as it were, mere individual activity into economic production.[69] This turnaround—which is precisely where all questions of agency in the face of machinery reside, and where social reproduction in the broadest sense occurs—requires the most careful analysis of an interminable process, rather than a hasty metaphorical termination. The "consumption" of television in terms of time "possesses the peculiar property of being a source of value," as Marx says of labor:[70] before there can be any question of what the viewers may get out of the deal, there will already have been an advance, images offered against an expenditure of time, a commitment to television's terms of trade. Conditioned by this preliminary contract, the consumption of television cannot be modelled as an act of reading nor can it be assumed to follow a clear subjective path, whether directed by economic rational interest or transparent desires. As Alexander Kluge has shrewdly observed, this initial expense forces viewers to become desperate "entrepreneurs," rummaging through the images on offer for whatever value they can recover.[71] If we have to talk about consumption at all, it would be more accurate, of course, to say that television consumes our time, producing value and reproducing social relations along the way.

Rather than the "official" time of programming or the aleatory times of atomized viewing, then, the minimum unit of value must be the volatile time of the image—not only the sequences ordered by narrative or direct address, but the fleeting images of channel zapping and quick cuts, approaching an impossible synchrony of maximized returns, a complete equivalence between socialized subjective time and televisual images. Does zapping interrupt the process of valorization, or does it allow for instantaneous increments of transmitted value? Television must always send its images as segments of variable duration, calibrated by the forces of social differentiation and distinction, that will nevertheless always be too short or too long to realize their full potential value. Under these conditions a virtually chaotic aesthetic develops, with new kinds of abstraction, new means of spinning out or freezing up duration in order to allow for maximum absorption of social time. The old dream of a single-channel unitary program—that demiurgic projection of structured time— has always been an ideal construct foiled by its very diffusion. But the differentiation of television by no means implies a perfection of the devices of ideological address; it should be understood rather as a process of abstraction, an original form of reification performed in time rather than through finished things, where relations between people are now absorbed by the passage of countless overlapping slices of images that replace the possibility of shared interests or mutual subjective recognition itself. "Winning time" on television now becomes the most crucial stake in group politics, an acceptance of the cynical assumption that enregistration by the machine will succeed where the politics of representation failed. Such "alternatives" to television, or to its current ideological repertoire, devolve into schemes for occupying as much time as your opponents, setting up shop in the mall of mirrors, which is the preemptive strategy advertisers and programmers have been following all along.

What the vcr makes possible, in fact, is the further ramification of televisual time by altering its speed, and in this sense it retools the televisual apparatus for a new economic cycle. More new machines for this purpose, such as laser disc players, video game consoles, and fiber-optics networks, are already on the horizon. Television's new speeds, however, are both a matter of expanded individual choice and a new zone of fixed capital and image valorization. To use an orthodox Marxist expression, we are currently witnessing the development of relative modes of socializing time, based upon the absolute socialization already posited by the apparatus itself. The potential to change the time scheme of broadcasting by inserting other sets of images makes televisual time more flexible, more capable of capturing and redistributing culture, time, and money in televisual form. The VCR, like television itself, seizes on all kinds of textual events and submits them to reframing and retransmission. In this lies its usefulness to capital, especially on a transnational scale, which can profit only if all culture—high, low, and homemade—reveals itself through localized televisual circuits.

Television's resources for the abstraction of images have hardly been exhausted; each reconfiguration of time and image brings possibilities for a new transduction of value, that is, for a different machinic function. It follows from our earlier discussion of capital's circuitry that each instant is both a sign of value and a movement toward another form. Since television as a whole (geotelevision) may yet become coextensive with the space of capitalist production, each of its visible moments can occupy multiple positions in the overall movement of production and reproduction. Television, in other words, becomes "part of" the way in which value is constructed, distributed, and attached to bodies formed in the general circulation of labor, commodities, and money. It has expanded the zones of value by changing, mediating, that is to say, *mechanizing* the imaginary forces of social relations. When televisual forms no longer follow a single representational logic, a plateau of totalization has been reached: televisual images can adhere to every body in motion, a value marked there in reserve, waiting for the chance to reenter the machinery, whether played out as need or as work. Televisual images do not represent things so much as they take up time, and to work through this time is the most pervasive way that subjects suffer through, participate in, and perhaps even glimpse, the global unification of contemporary capitalism.

At the end of his introduction to the *Grundrisse,* Marx scribbled a little list of things "not to be forgotten." The sixth heading reads: "*The uneven development of material production relative to e.g. artistic development.*"[72] Having noted that there had always been a kind of lag or gap between the realms of political economy and culture, he wanted to know just how one could alter the course of the other. Famously, he never got around to it, nor did he get around to imagining what an art form or cultural practice fully adequate to and coextensive with capitalism would look like, or whether it might be possible for cultural development to be no longer a part of, expression of, or metaphor for economy, but its very mode of visibility.

The next item reads: "*This conception appears as necessary development. But legitimation of chance. How.* (Of freedom also, among other things.) (Influence of means of communication. World history has not always existed; history as world history a result.)"[73] This point—the necessity of relating production and circulation to forms of consciousness and power—also remained largely untouched. For us, the path must be skipped backwards: looking back from the production of a world history by capital, past the legitimation of chance as necessity in our histories and theories of technology and communication, toward a freedom still to be rescued from all the things that obscure it.

PART II   *Commercial Breaks*

THREE   *History, the Eternal Rerun:*

On Crime Story

> The past can be seized only as an image which
> flashes up at the instant when it can be recognized and is never seen again.
> —Walter Benjamin

Is it possible to think about history and television at the same time? Have you ever seen the two of them together? It is one thing to place television in (a) history, to treat television as an historical object belonging to a particular moment; it is another to talk about the way television represents history, how history becomes a set of objects for televisual transmission. Which one frames the other? And what if we cannot assume that these two terms name different orders, an order of forces and events over here and an order of representations over there? How can we place television in a "historical context" once we understand (via contemporary Marxism and/or poststructuralism) that history can be made visible only as a textual production? (That the notion of history's "textuality" is in no way diminishing, simplifying, or debilitating should be obvious from Jameson's *The Political Unconscious* and Derrida's *Of Grammatology*—to cite only two well-elaborated arguments.) Despite these difficulties, we may still reassert the familiar nineteenth-century concept of historical thinking as such, in which the prodigious representational and temporal effusions of television would be viewed as a limited deformation of a larger scheme of events that remains finally comprehensible in outline. But if television participates not only in how history is *figured* but in how it *happens*—thereby mixing the terms, obscuring old lines of sight and making new kinds of events possible—it is not enough to analyze how history appears on television; we must address another problem, which is always there, concerning the fragile constitution of historical sense itself. Here, then, in order to ask about the appearance of history on television, we will have to speak of its apparent disappearance there.

The issue turns on how a new technology of representation dissolves or betrays earlier figural devices in the process of inventing new ones. Although television seems simply to destroy history—through what might be called inaccuracies, indistinctions, and forgettings—it also constructs its own kind of historical material, precisely by projecting new lines of linkage and new speeds of reference. Rather than chart all the ways in which television either cancels or reasserts the possibility of seeing history, I offer a modest demonstration of how one television series—a tenuous narrative here isolated from the programming matrix that carried it—repeatedly encounters blockages that it can "solve" only by breaking its course and starting elsewhere.

Crime Story, a serial broadcast in the United States by NBC from 1986–88, traversed a number of different historical and dramatic situations in its short two-year run. According to its initial press releases, it was designed to trace a decades-long battle between an incorruptible cop (Michael Torello), a liberal lawyer (David Abrams), and a hoodlum-turned-gangster (Ray Luca) from a Chicago neighborhood to Las Vegas and beyond. Many smaller narrative units inhabit this serial story structure, but their relationship to the general plot changes over time, becoming less tangential and more tributary. In broad outline, the Chicago episodes treat the relationship between crime and order in terms of organic social groups: each character belongs to a distinct familial and ethnic milieu, so that conflicts within and between milieux have to be mediated by an outsider, who is in turn caught in another set of conflicts. This interlocking system—in which criminals, cops, and lawyers share the same space—dissolves when Luca becomes a manager for a Jewish organized crime family and when Torello and Abrams move from the city to the federal level of the justice system. At that point, in the middle of the first season and about twelve hours into the series, the scene shifts to Las Vegas.

Crime Story sets out, at least in its own publicity, on a grand scale: not exactly a historical "period" piece that would remain in place, nor a miniseries that neatly crosses and closes down its historical span, but a historical retelling that simply starts "in the past" without any clear destination except, perhaps, the present. It cannot therefore be easily subsumed under the category of "nostalgia film," which Fredric Jameson has identified as a dominant form in postmodern cultural production.[1] At least, it would have to be a different kind of nostalgia from that practiced by cinema, one that takes advantage of a specifically televisual mode of production that allows the historical material of the older narrative forms to be recast precisely as a series of stories whose very shape and scale can change in the telling. It would reflect a nostalgia not only for the objects of a given style gathered into various period ensembles or "moments"— which are typically synchronic frames—but for the dynamic of style itself, the buzz that comes from things happening, replayed as an inexorable process of errant metamorphosis. As a result of this historical drive, *Crime Story* must force itself through several different cataclysms so that it can reset its narrative gears and restock the environment with stubborn signifiers of the past.

From the beginning, *Crime Story* measured time in several registers at once. There is a generational time marked by conflicts within organizations (criminal and legal). On one side, the old ethnic identities of the gangsters are supplanted by the corporate identity of the next generation; on the other side, the old-style cops come under the control of federal technocrats of the RFK stamp. The time scale is inscribed in surrounding spaces, as the dark alleyways and glittering skylines of Chicago give way to the neon frenzy and desert stretches of Las Vegas. (In another code: from Mies to Venturi.) Old, inhabited space becomes new, kinetic space: Torello moves from a high-rise apartment building to a motel, and Luca moves from a neighborhood social club to an immense casino. Of course a whole layer of glaring historicity informs the clothes, the cars, and the background music.[2] In spite of all the momentum built up in the move to Vegas, the official time of the story remains 1963, as if this whole range of uneven developments, ruptures, and displacements could be compressed into a brief fictional sequence. "Our 1963 never really existed," said Michael Mann, the show's executive producer, neatly summing up what goes without saying.[3]

Already in the first season, another kind of time scale—what I call generic time—begins to frame the other elements. At various points, the "story" in *Crime Story* crosses through various postwar fictional genres, allowing their distinctive character types and story patterns to take over and run their course. Generic events—the big heist, the civil rights trial, the car chase, the hostage standoff—are established within a limited rhythm and duration; by the same token, larger generic paradigms—the hardboiled detective investigation, the reporter's crusade, the deposing of a crimelord—can be defined by the way they pace the exchange between transgression and punishment. *Crime Story* cites all of these generic traits and more, treating them as historical artifacts in their own right, a sequence of limit-situations that the main characters live through and overcome on the way to some other fate. Thus there must always be time lags in the operation of a generic presentation: first, if it will work at all it must operate at once, so that its point of departure is as conventional and familiar as possible; then, unfolding, it may offer divergences that break the chain of expectations holding the paradigm together. (This is why the notion of a genre always implies an improbable contract between visible images on one hand and a hypothetical public memory on the other.) In *Crime Story*'s multilayered generic time, historical periods (specifically the Forties and Fifties) are reconstructed through their own narrative conventions, only to be then dismantled. Characters are killed off and situations are wrecked without completing their distinctive destinies, foreclosing certain narrative options when their animating energies, hopes, and struggles have become obsolete.

The shifting from one time scale to another gathers speed toward the end of the first season: as Luca's crimes mount, so does Torello's determination to bring him down. In the season's final episode (broadcast before the network had decided whether to renew the series), the vicious cat-and-mouse game leads to a nighttime shootout on the Vegas strip. But just when the whole story seems to come down to a one-on-one battle to the death, Luca is rescued by his sidekick Pauli Taglia. There is a freeze-frame of Torello on his knees in the street, shooting wildly. Then it is daybreak, Luca and Taglia are in a shack in the desert. Luca, wounded but beginning to relax, notices a marking on the furniture: GROUND ZERO. He shouts at Taglia, they scramble out the door, and begin to drive away— then a white flash on the screen and stock A-bomb footage rolls until the closing credits. This image of the A-bomb blast raises several interpretive possibilities, some of them false starts or dead-ends. All questions about the meaning of the image have to be suspended until we know whether the story will continue.

With the prescribed enactment of justice blocked, events shift to a level beyond the moral economy of the story up until that point. The bomb blast is both an arbitrary, accidental fate and a reminder of some vast and terrible order of events that (for the moment) remains obscure. It breaks several contextual frames at once: the generic traits, the symbolic scale, the contested scene of action. From a crime story to a cynical apocalypse: the series casts a black comic negation over its whole course up to that point.

But how final could any such "conclusion" be? Can this image, because of its "extremity," seal the story? An absolute end would mean that the series halted itself by turning its historical project into an eschatological one.[4] If only the blast is big enough, the story would really be over, a genuine end would be imaginable above and beyond mere resolutions and score settlings. Certain political and religious scenarios would be confirmed as never before. Insofar as any moral reading of this episode, even a cynical or oppositional one, relies on this closure to seal a meaning, the image of the Bomb must also spell the halt of televisual representation: nothing else must happen, no other event or image can join the story and send it in a new direction. Interpretation would have to know how to stop itself at just the right moment, turn off the television, and appeal to some other authority, some other narrative. If the bomb blast seems to insist on the possibility of finishing a story, it does so in the name of something else, something outside the televisual domain, something like a non-narrativizable History. I am not yet speaking of the logic of nuclear deterrence, which as Derrida points out also speaks in the name of something else, "that which is worth more than life, that which, giving its value to life, has greater value than life."[5]

For the image of the Bomb has its own history. It has functioned in the global rhetoric of deterrence as an absolute simulation, a perfect and whole replacement for apocalypse. It is the image of an impossible end, an end without end, an end that waits. The image preserves not so much a memory of a past event (testing) but the prospect of a future one (aggression): indeed, it was not the effectiveness of the bomb being tested in the desert, but the effectiveness of the images of the Bomb. And so, even while they evoke a long tradition of apocalyptic discourse, the images also speak an undeniable realism: we (the audience, the world) need to believe that an atomic bomb destroys utterly whatever happens to be under and around it. Only through that belief and this fear can armament and disarmament take place. And if we believe there is any truth to the nuclear image, *Crime Story* must now be finished. Ray Luca, like Hiroshima, Nagasaki, Bikini, and elsewhere, becomes a sacrifice to the "reality" of nuclear weapons, yet again attesting to the possibility of representing that reality.

If, on the other hand, Ray Luca could survive that explosion, if the image of Luca in one instant can be distanced from the image of the mushroom cloud in the next, if that image does not refer always to the end of all lives and all stories, if it is possible for the show to continue, then televisual narrative proves that it can survive even the Bomb (if only for a second). After all, the image of destruction will always be insufficient to destroy anything: it can appear only on the way to destruction, or on the way toward an end. It is only through certain linkages, especially narrative ones, that this image can come to serve a strategy (like all images, it can never speak for itself). To reproduce this image in a story without end is to reserve the threat of finality within the power of visuality. Nuclear deterrence operates through deferral of an end, just as narrative deferral of closure deters the stabilization of meaning: both share the same kind of inertia.

Yet in an unexpected way, *Crime Story* reinstates a claim to history through its stylized evocation of the end of history. By risking its story in the cultural imaginary of doom, the show reintroduces historical distance at the crucial moment, turning apocalypse itself into an item of nostalgia. Note that the key images of the explosion are in fact "historical" footage. In its day, it was possible for such footage to signify (ironically and iconically) the end of the world (as in *Dr. Strangelove*) or just the end of the story (as in *Kiss Me Deadly*). For us this scrap of footage refers also to that moment—precisely, 1963—when an image of the end could still have been imagined as the final one. Once the apocalyptic tone has been struck and surpassed, the sense of ending becomes merely formal, and the enclosure of the past dissolves into the openness of the present.

Undaunted by Luca's fate, the network (NBC) renewed *Crime Story* for another season. After several episodes, Luca and Taglia are revealed to be alive and recovering from their radioactive burns in Mexico. Luca tells his boss, Manny Weisbord, that the blast has changed him. He is "only looking at big pictures now. International enterprise, that's our future, Manny. Governments become our partners. We go world-wide." Out of the atomic flames, Luca has been reborn as the very soul of neocapitalism. He no longer acts as an individual force; rather, he becomes a nexus, variably passive and reactive, almost an empty relay point in a vast power system, the managing angel. This functional transformation of Luca corresponds to another generic switch. The movement from street hoodlum to organized crime boss goes only so far (as *Bugsy* shows); there remains another story, another tier that reaches from organized crime to multinational enterprise legitimated and served by political power. The site of criminality migrates from urban neighborhoods to enterprise zones to offshore operations, from onscreen to off. Luca and Weisbord no longer just skim the till in Vegas or operate a national telecom bookie scheme: they ship weapons to "insurgents" in Guatemala, bringing back drugs for the American market. The weekly narrative no longer keeps up with the details of the criminal schemes. Now the only course of progress or continuity—and a very slow and stubborn one at that—belongs to the cops. As the story approaches the present, its trajectory begins to lose the sharp turns of historical fiction, taking on the force of an unstoppable fate.

Nowhere is this divergence of history and story more apparent than in an episode titled "Femme Fatale," in which Luca tries to help an agent from the People's Republic of China secure uranium for an H-bomb, in exchange for permission to fly smuggling planes in and out of the Golden Triangle. In the course of the episode, the deal is foiled, severing the expected connections to the historical "facts" of the Chinese bomb and American drug smuggling operations in Southeast Asia. By allowing the logic of episodic narrative to obstruct the unfolding of a more or less "established" history, *Crime Story* refuses to offer a reassuring "secret history" (the way familiar things "really happened") but instead selects and rearranges diverse historical elements in a structure of possibilities, thereby producing combinations that range from the historically necessary to the transitory lost chance. But "Femme Fatale" is overdetermined in another way: the episode has its own generic reference points and visual style distinct from other episodes in the series. It happens that the Chinese agent is a young woman who suddenly appears on Torello's doorstep in distress, shadowed in seductive foreboding. That is the least of the clues: each element of the storytelling apparatus participates in a complex reconstruction of film noir. The first half of the story unfolds through Torello's weary voiceover narration, just up until the point where Luca's plan to hand over the uranium fails, the woman's deception is revealed, and the storyline veers towards an espionage thriller. The logic of conflict shifts all at once: hazy emotional attachments are overwhelmed by resolute national allegiances. More remarkable, however, is the episode's color texture: through manipulation of the light and color levels, the scenes have exactly the look of a black and white film that has been colorized. Neither a simulation of film noir in black and white nor a remake done with the full lushness of the contemporary palette, the "look" of this episode suggests that the representation of history has become essentially a matter of translating images from earlier media technologies into later ones.

In the case of television, such representation can be a matter of re-writing images from one part of the programming matrix into the terms of another, so that images thought to belong to the immediate present (news reports) are displaced into an explicitly fictionalized *and* histor-icized framework. *Crime Story* produces this echo effect by making tele-vision part of its (hi)story. As the second season winds down, Torello orchestrates a televised Senate hearing, where he hopes to embarrass government officials into confessing their connections to Luca. But the wall of complicity appears unassailable, and one witness after another refuses to crack. The déjà vu may be overwhelming—everything recalls the Iran-Contra hearings, detail by detail, which had occupied the screen less than a year before this episode aired. The parallels are played out until Colonel Danz, the Oliver North link in Luca's drugs-for-arms trade, blurts out the whole story. Torello is about to obtain indictments for Luca's gang, and all at once this becomes a utopian version of the 1980s: in the spectacle of a hearing, the bright clarity of the images, and the dis-tilled moment of revelation, the Sixties quiver and evaporate. Suddenly history, or at least the history of U.S. foreign policy, appears disconcert-ingly cyclical: that time Guatemala, that time Laos, this time Iran, or Iraq, or Guatemala all over again. A structure of allusion, operating on the level of images but tagged by proper names, sketches an elliptical politi-cal memory. Except for one new element: the cycle will now be broken, the crimes will be admitted and judgment handed down at last—an imag-inary resolution to real corruptions.

At just this moment, just when *Crime Story* almost produces a tele-visual narrative of historical justice, another kind of televisual history overtakes it, precisely the history of television as a spectacular disrup-tion. The hearing is dramatically interrupted by an announcement: "The North Vietnamese have fired on our ships in the Gulf of Tonkin." Every-body rushes from the room. There will be no climax, no verdict. Torello and his crew look bewildered. "Vietnam?" What's that?

It is not Vietnam that halts the narrative, it is television, or more precisely, a specifically televisual event. In submitting itself to this moment of chaos, *Crime Story* dramatizes the birth of media politics and media history: the original force of television is revealed in the way one media event can interrupt another, the new event randomizing the old horizon of references and suspending the procedures of truth. Now, instead of offering a mimetic proximity to current events, a dense historical distance drops down, punctuated only by television's faulty memory of itself. On that plane, the pre-Vietnam moment is literally prehistoric, before television assumed the task of producing a constant stream of instant history. To situate all of *Crime Story* back then, back when this prolonged televised horror had not yet begun, is to dispel all of its accumulated historical resonance, sending it back to another era. Vietnam, a dreadful future collapsed to the intensity of a single moment, cuts off the narrative drive, stopping it far short of the present and moving the story elsewhere.

Yet the second season does not end here: Luca and his entourage fly to an unnamed Latin American country, where he quickly takes direct control of local drug production, deposes the president, and installs his own puppet leader. Torello and his men follow, seeking a more or less illegal kind of vengeance. The scene is a composite Third World where power is exercised according to different rules—which is, after all, what is supposed to define the otherness of the place. But the change of scenery is neither a "return" to some prior stage of history, nor an escape somewhere "outside" the force field of the United States. On the contrary, this path is the logical opposite of any judicial resolution: now the story follows the genealogy of the "crime," a chase back along the chain of production to expose the general social arrangements that support the criminal enterprise pyramid. A reverse movement like this, however, carries a cost: the characters who perform the "return" become disposable as soon as their purely figural function has been exhausted. Luca and Torello can appear as opposing structural elements only as long as they remain at their stations of individualized power; once they surrender those sites of economic concentration and political command, they no longer serve as significant participants in the "story" they have carried this far. Their fate thus becomes a matter of purely generic interest once the genuine "crime story"—now revealed as the gradual but aggressive creation of a new criminal/capitalist world order—has reached its triumphant completion with the commercial recolonization of the Third World. Any genuinely unclosed historical narrative will always dissolve the privilege of its fictional representatives by returning them at last to our common fate, oblivion and death, so that the drift of historicity can be attached to other figures. So it goes with Luca and Torello: when we last see them, they are fighting hand-to-hand in a plane that crashes into the ocean. Nothing depends on them any longer: even if they were to "survive" this perfect cliffhanger, they would have to be miraculously reconstructed and repositioned before they could again serve as bearers of this story. But they will not survive. The network numbers have long since doomed them.

More explicitly than most, but no more totally than any other, this series projects its historical materials into televisual rhythms. It advances fitfully over the breaks of transmission, turning its moments of suspense and temporary closure into emblems of an uneven historical time. *Crime Story* mobilizes a vast matrix of historical devices—iconic, temporal, textual,—to bring various chronologies into instant adjacency. If on one plane televisual texts are always cutting each other up, on another level they all become figurative extensions of each other. Thus any text duplicates the work of television as a whole, which can only ever produce an image of history as an assemblage of dissembled distances from the instantaneous present. Televisual flux emits a new kind of History—jumbled, familiar, open—which is never yet *ours*.

FOUR   *Mondino, MTV, and the Laugh of Madonna*

> Perhaps all experience that is not a cry of pleasure or pain is recuperated by the institution.—Michel de Certeau, *The Practice of Everyday Life*

> Madonna isn't popular, she's popularized. That's very different.—Jean-Luc Godard

The late Serge Daney, for decades a key figure in contemporary French film criticism and a writer for the periodicals *Cahiers du Cinéma* and *Libération,* no doubt possessed an experienced and discerning eye. In 1987, he wrote that the "prettiest film of the year" was a music video clip called "Mia Bocca," sung by Jill Jones and directed by Jean-Baptiste Mondino. With the air of someone wanting to provoke a scandal among aesthetes, Daney wrote a short paean to Mondino's talent, dubbing him "the ace of hip."[1] A few years later (1990) *Cahiers* ran an approving overview of Mondino's work, together with an respectful interview. The video maker is given the full auteur treatment by the people who do it best, being hailed as "a virtuoso, a poet of the short form in a state of weightlessness."[2]

But is it possible to talk about auteurs of music video, a form in which authorship and ownership are tangled with the privileges of stardom, a form that obscures and overrides the division of labor between making images and making sounds? Hasn't the older prerogative of authorship been usurped by a vigorously commercialized function? Let us make one hypothesis about the case at hand: if there can be music video auteurs, surely Jean-Baptiste Mondino is one of them. We will see shortly that the notion of a video auteur is not an innocent anachronism: it forces us to rethink the web of exchanges that support and propel (music) television.

But first, spare a moment for Jill Jones. Her video, praised by critics, has dropped out of sight. In fact, I have only seen a few seconds of "Mia Bocca," flashed quickly during a BBC documentary about Jones's onetime collaborator, Prince. This brief glimpse was a shot of Jones singing on an empty beach, tinted a striking mustard yellow. Maybe it would make a cinéaste think of Fellini. As far as I can tell—the uncertainty is part of the point—"Mia Bocca" was not shown very often on MTV or any of the other music video outlets operating in the United States. In terms of radio and chart exposure, neither the song nor the album from which it was taken became a big hit. The clip clearly failed in its purpose to promote sales and airplay of Jill Jones's "product." Nor has the clip enjoyed an afterlife through music video retrospectives, which are forever redefining the "greatest videos of all time." Whatever airplay it may have received in 1987, the clip has certainly disappeared since then. How many hours of MTV would I have had to watch in order to be sure it is truly gone? I cannot say: perhaps this video is still in rotation, but like Halley's comet, it is scheduled to return only at some distant date, many years hence, as a totally different kind of artifact. Moreover it is safe to conclude that, along with the obvious megahits and the unseen no-shows, there must be thousands of also-ran clips in the MTV archives that were only shown once or twice, which is to say, clips that only a few million people saw once or twice. The winnowing process is the first technique MTV shares with the rest of television. It is a programmed form of disappearance, immense in scale, from which patterns of repetition can be salvaged only at the pace and the price of lived time. With television, the cost of any kind of knowledge, not to mention certainty, can be astronomical.

It is a small leap from "Mia Bocca" to MTV, the nonstop music video cable channel. ("It's on twenty-four hours a day, just like life," as one of their slogans goes.) In the midst of this endless, incomplete merging of recorded music with recorded images (why incomplete? we will see shortly), it is difficult to decide what the fundamental unit of analysis ought to be. There are two common observations about MTV: each video clip is a little movie, and the channel is nonstop advertising.[3] Neither description hits the mark: music video involves much more than either the rewriting of cinematic codes or the triumph of marketing over all other rhetorics. As we shall see, the clip does not stand against the channel as a part to a whole, or as the finite unit against the infinite flow; on the contrary, each forms a circuit of its own, tracing a path where images both "represent" and "produce" value on the full plane of televisual capitalism.

For critics, the music video has generally been regarded either as the abbreviation and deformation of preexisting codes (especially narrative ones), or as a profuse visual dispersion held together by the integrity of the sound track, which in turn refers to the real-world existence of a buyable commodity (CD, cassette, vinyl). Either way, there are always at least three signifying terms, not two: the video clip includes an image track and a sound track, both of which refer to an absent object waiting to be purchased in the store. (MTV captions each video at the beginning and end to identify the product and its makers: artist, company, and director.[4]) No matter what form the video takes, it connects into other sign chains: to a career (understood as individual biography), an iconography (understood as the historical/traditional archive of images), a contemporary context (understood as a process of linking images from various cultural practices together as synchronic ensembles), and so on. In other words, each clip rewrites the recorded commodity into other materials, through other textualities. From the perspective of economic function, however, the most significant operation is not the conjunction of sounds and images, but the performative distinction between video clip transmission and the commodity object. The video clip must somehow fail to be that other thing, the recording itself, even while giving every appearance of improving on it, expanding it, or giving it away free. Adding images turns out to be a form of subtraction: not only in the realm of sensory plenitude, but also in the mobilization of desire as a temporal vector leading (perhaps) to a moment of exchange in which value is at last realized for capitalist and consumer alike. To the extent that videos have come to occupy the primary sites of music consumption, then, buying a recording becomes a way to buy back the time of listening— which is, after all, one's own free time—from the media industries.

While each clip circulates its call to buy something it can never show, the MTV channel proposes a similar deal, which it renews by bending its rubrics of repetition and redistributing its markers of taste. Its official scope is all-inclusive: it situates cultural events as accents of its own

rhythm, making everything from record promotion to politics and fashion appear as its own creation. But this adaptive framework does not
mean that each video becomes a permutation, let alone an expression, of
some closed set of variants. Like the video, MTV accumulates and circulates images on the basis of a commodified identity (the channel itself);
its ordering logic is different in scale, not in kind. The half-life of MTV
may be longer than the half-life of a particular video, but not by much.
MTV remains subject to the same complex of commercial forces that
produce and dissolve the identity of commodities. Indeed, both the video
clip and MTV, the microform and the macroformat, should be seen as
aspects of a more general process of the 1980s, a shift in the economy of
images in which television sheds the light of its economic logic onto a
number of new cultural surfaces, but only by keeping its formula simple,
its functions narrow, and its variables few.

Now we can return to Mondino. His work in photography and video
illustrates not only the general contours of this shift, but it can also be
read as a running autocritique of it. Mondino belongs to the same Pari-
sian milieu as Jean-Paul Goude and Jean-Paul Gaultier, two notable practitioners of alternative image making. (Goude now directs commercials,
having staged the 1989 bicentennial parade and launched the transatlan-
tic career of singer Grace Jones; Gaultier is a remarkably eclectic fashion
designer, cultural provocateur, and sometime pop singer.) In the late
seventies Mondino began working as an advertising photographer, but
his best-known works are his music videos and album covers from the
late eighties. Out of this disparate and partial set of materials I want to
shape an oeuvre with its own recurring concerns and ways of thinking
through aesthetic problems. As I have already suggested, the idea of
constructing a video auteur is a willfully strategic act. In a purely commercial setting, where artists are supposed to do nothing more than add
style-effects to the presentation of someone else's work, the rearrangement of diverse products under an auteurist framework may bring about
drastic reconsiderations (which is precisely why the theory was developed, to cut a path through the otherwise amorphous and overcoded
industrial output of the studio system).[5] A video that might at first look
like the strikingly new expression of a singer-celebrity, a phase in an
ongoing metamorphosis, may instead resemble an inflection of quite
another aesthetic series, generated by the auteur and insinuated into
every commission, some trace of another expression generally lost in a
rapid flux of competing images and signatures. With his work scattered

across several different media, Mondino will have to be considered something like a postmodern auteur, whose authorial identity consists in the way he "cites" images.

Mondino's work exhibits recurring motifs or components, even as these are partly effaced by the official subject of the image (the singer, fashion designer, or inert commodity). The first such component is "projection" in the most literal sense. Mondino projects one image inside another, so that a figure may become ground or vice versa—for example, Mondino's advertisement for the designer Azzedine Alaïa, where an image of a grinning Asian boy is projected against the body of a model wearing one of Alaïa's trademark skintight dresses. The boy's face takes over the contours of the dress, so that the model's body recedes toward a middle space, no longer foreground but not yet background. The photograph can be read a number of ways: maybe the boy's gaze has hit its object and stuck in place, or maybe the dress is a kind of Medusan shield, capturing the glance of another—even an innocent—by turning it into a stilled image. By mingling two images, the photograph freezes the dynamic of this commodity: as it wraps and presents the ideal any-body (demanding that it be a certain shape) it draws other images as proof of its value. By staging projection, Mondino literalizes the power of images.

Mondino's celebrated clip for Don Henley's "Boys of Summer" (1984) offers a slightly different kind of projection. Now the projected images fill up the living spaces of various characters—a young boy, a teenage girl, and Henley himself—whose expressions and affective states have to be read against a recurring cinematic reference point. Contrasted to the contemporary surfaces against which they are projected (offices, bedrooms, the side of a house), the images themselves have a distinctly 1950s look: a man and woman run along a beach, swinging into a happy embrace, followed, as if one conventional image elicits another, by a different summer scene in which faceless, muscled men jump into the sky. Like Cindy Sherman's paradigmatically postmodern "Untitled Film Stills," these pictures are both arrestingly new and already secondhand. The images begin over and over, countdown leader and all, a repetition so insistent that its associative quality begins to empty out, becoming instead a material notation of collective loss. For it is clear that these images do not belong to the characters alone, but to us as well: at several points the beach shots occupy the entire frame, so that the television screen also becomes a site of projection and our own acts of viewing are drawn into the video's scene of recollection. Film lingers as the stubborn relic of television's historical melancholy. The final trick shot—in which Henley steps away from the back-projected cityscape to drive away, revealing that one urban space is contained within the other—detaches one layer of images from another, breaking the spell of shared visibility that holds the whole video together. The moment is brief: the clip ends with yet another projection figure in which Henley's face in the rearview mirror slides into view, once again insisting on the ineradicable distance between a figure and its fated ground.

In both cases, the multiplication of images within the frame dramatizes the way images are lived as spatial constructs that surround and orient the body. In this sense, Mondino's video clips call upon not only the techniques of still photography, but also the contemporary functions of fashion and architecture. In one set of his fashion photographs, the texture of the image washes out colors and flattens detail: the clothes and models appear already processed by video.[6] Although bodies and spaces may face the viewer, they may also face each other within the image. Mondino's "projection" experiments can be understood as his first attempts to multiply images from the inside: rather than adding one image to the next as in simple montage, or covering one image with another as in superimposition, he lets the "objects" of his images turn into quasi-autonomous images themselves. This creates a profoundly televisual mise en scène: the relationship between things is composed only through the act of transmission. If we consider that the most conventional, even hackneyed way to multiply images within the frame is simply to shoot a roomful of television monitors, each with its own pictures, we can begin to understand how Mondino's images mark out a televisual field in which everything can function as a kind of monitor, no longer glowing from within but deflecting light from an unseen source. Daney spoke of Mondino's clips as a "withdrawal on the image": there is no longer just one image, nor yet many images, but images evacuated by diffusion.[7]

Now the still image reasserts itself as the genuine object of televisual representation: instead of soliciting a specular subject, Mondino's images take the side of things (as Sartre said of Genet) in order to shake off mimetic strictures. His clip for Prince's "I Wish You Heaven" (1987) uses computer animation techniques to let bodies, faces, words (lyrics and slogans), symbols, and objects (apples, guns, guitars) float among and diffract each other, even while everything drifts from the right to the left of the frame, passing through again and again. No background mark or horizon allows us to situate this motion as distance: in its very ideality it can be imagined as both lateral and circular, both endlessly unfolding and forever spinning in place. Two dimensions are relatively stable: the human figures stay upright, and tree boughs dip under the top of the frame, but only Prince's face reaches from the top to the bottom of the frame, offering the closest thing to a cut in this otherwise seamless space. If the drifting movement is circular and repetitive, we may imagine an empty core where the song, like the viewer's desire, eludes figuration (a Lacanian scheme)[8]; if on the other hand, the drift is treated as linear and dispersive, we can imagine the images as enacting the spatialization of the music itself (which is how Jameson describes all of MTV).[9] We will return to the fate of music in video space shortly.

Another opening of an unbroken visual space occurs in what is perhaps Mondino's most rigorous clip, which accompanies Neneh Cherry's "Manchild" (1989). A curtain is pulled back to reveal a shimmering beach scene: an intense blue ocean, cloudy skies, and a silvery strand. But it is immediately apparent that this landscape is a composite, and that the clothesline, the little girl on a swing, and the other figures who soon enter are also separate images scaled and mixed by electronic means. When Neneh Cherry begins to sing, the frame starts swinging in a gentle arc like the girl on the swing; as it reaches the top of each arc, someone or something else comes into view, perhaps a bunch of cherries (a visual pun) or one of the dancers. When Neneh stops singing and begins to rap, the frame settles back into place. As in the Prince clip, figures appear and disappear in varying sizes—there are several Nenehs at one point—generating a lot of motion and activity but without allowing interaction between the planes of images.

Does anything "happen" in this totally reconstructed, purely transparent space? The events recorded here do not emerge from the past but seem to fall back into visibility from a virtual synchrony generated by the technology itself. In this respect, the video shares the aesthetic of fashion stills, which promise never to photograph the past but only the persistence of a perfect present. Mondino's sustained images alter the scene of expression and break with the image/sound organization of standard cinematic and televisual practice. Typically the video clip defers to the rhythms and tonalities of sound in more or less obedient mimicry of the "contents" of the song. The standard industrial practice of MTV is largely illustrative, pitched on a limited range of registers (dominated by performance and fictional narrative). Mondino's clips do not imitate, punctuate, or echo sounds in order to approximate musical forms. His images are objects on the same plane as the sound recording itself, so that one can see and hear what the song and the clip have in common: an inscription of time. As inscribed time, sound too is an image. By giving the video clip its own logic of temporality, which parallels without expressing the temporality of music, Mondino reconciles images and sounds within the purely technical space of production. Where other video clips try to orchestrate synaesthetic affects, the "Manchild" clip proposes an imaginary restoration of a lost harmony between the senses, secured by the recorded commodity and its playback apparatus. When Mondino did another clip for Neneh Cherry in 1991 ("Under My Skin"), he found another way to let images take on the temporal functions of music: the rhythm of the music track makes the image shudder without breaking it, as if the camera lens were also a vibrating membrane.

In the two videos Mondino made for Madonna, "Open Your Heart" (1986) and "Justify My Love" (1990), the projective play of images is equated with the economic processes of stardom. The "Open Your Heart" clip, which has become a defining moment in Madonna's career, offers several kinds of exchange in its peep show setting: voyeurism, to be sure, but marked out as a multiplicity of spectators, isolated from each other but unified for Madonna and for us, men and women whose responses to Madonna's performance range from hound dog lechery and frantic scribbling to impassive calm and vertiginous spinning. As screens inside the viewing booths open and close, the sight of Madonna is cut into slices, each with its own angle and duration. Even the little boy outside the theatre tries his hand at breaking Madonna into her elemental components, framing her playbill image from different angles. Mondino explicitly stages the commercial aspect of this situation: the old man running the theatre, who collects the money and prohibits the boy from entering, chases after Madonna at the end, crying "Come back, come back, we still need you." Her final "escape" with the boy, both of them dressed alike in baggy suits, seems to suggest a repudiation of the adult labor of the stage in favor of childhood, androgyny, authenticity, and nomadic play. (It is also a rather cinematic shot, day for night, again recalling a Fellini hobo setting.) In a moment we will ask whether this apparent closure pieces together a fractured Madonna or builds some other kind of visual site.

"Justify My Love" (which was barred from airplay on MTV)[10] recapitulates the same basic situation, where a series of hotel rooms takes the place of the viewing booths, and a group of versatile lovers take the place of the serialized spectators. But Madonna continues to be the unifying catalyst for us: she makes an appearance in each room, playing out whatever role is called for; if anything, her image is more obviously appropriated for fantasy here than in the peep show. In both clips, however, her departure seals the contract: for the duration of the clip, the image of Madonna will be distributed around the enclosed setting. With this little narrative supplement insuring the fictionality of the entire clip, she seems to choose to free herself and return to a truer (heterosexual? monogamous?) self. What is most striking about these nagging narrative elements, however, is that any explanatory framework is offered at all, as if the presentation of Madonna as image requires some kind of character-based justification. The narrative elements in these videos, in other words, appear to be interruptions in what would otherwise be a pure spectacular display. In terms of the larger enterprise of stardom, Madonna needs moments of narrative in order to collect a profusion of images under the pliable fiction of identity. The restoration of Madonna's margin of subjectivity, her capacity to speak and sing for herself, reenacts the more fundamental hidden moment of the video economy, when the image refers back to the recorded commodity as if it were gesturing toward its true self. In Mondino's dramaturgy, Madonna "herself" exists only to guarantee the exchange from one medium to another, to bind a corporeal referent to a corporate identity, to ensure the translatability between affect and product.

Around Madonna, the questions have swirled: whose desire is at work? whose desire can be expressed? Joel Schwartz, writing in the *New Republic*, offers a stereotyped response: "Everyone seems to agree that there is something puzzling and inscrutable about Madonna, and it is this quality that goes a long way to explaining her cult appeal."[11] On the other hand, Judith Williamson, writing in *New Socialist*, makes it clear who is in charge: "Whatever you think of her sexual style, at least she wields it herself."[12] Since styles and desires encounter each other only on the terrain of images, it cannot be clear "whose" desires are being performed. It's just as wrong to attribute Madonna's sexuality or ethnicity to an intending self as it is to respond to her performances in terms of her inscrutability and inaccessibility. If the pundits of the mainstream press have hurried to take the path of dismissal and denial, another camp of critics (including such figures as Camille Paglia and John Fiske) has undertaken a campaign of beatification, seeing Madonna's every move (literally) as the pure expression of an autonomous will-to-desire, a self-realization of world-historical proportions. It has become increasingly common to say that Madonna's staging of desire serves as a liberating example to everybody else—in fact, Madonna herself uses some of this rhetoric in *Sex,* her book of erotic photographs, in which she offers her personal fantasies as the gold standard of imaginary desires.[13]

Of course, the pro and con arguments overlook the multimedia orchestration of Madonna's selfhood: in the terminology of discourse analysis, Madonna should be seen as the locus, not the subject, of the enunciations gathered under her name. Mondino's role in this ongoing production, then, can be understood as the elaboration of both poles in the myth: the spectacle is affirmed and indeed indulged, then halted by a moment of separation and distanciation. But this final gesture is as much Mondino's as Madonna's—it draws a boundary around the scene of performance, and the final shots belong to his visual architectonic rather than to her personalized narrative. It is not Madonna who is cut loose at the end, but the spectators who have gathered around her. Of course, the spectators do all of the imaginary work, but they cannot be shown: they are scattered without her. By inserting gaps between the star and the various acts of projection, Mondino's clips emphasize the open-ended process of image making: rather than being theatrically self-reflexive or fixated on Madonna's star persona (as so many of her other videos are) these clips dramatize both the uses and the limits of watching. Having done his duty by displaying so many aspects of the Madonna commodity, Mondino begins to wonder if she is dispensable and finishes by subtracting her from the scene, leaving all the spectators to their own devices. With that act of withdrawal, his own role comes to a halt.

Whereas musicians and video directors are capable of thinking through and exhibiting the workings of the promotional system, their products can do no more (at best) than allude to possible modes of creativity outside the channels of commodity value. If we devote all our powers to the extraction of value from the images we buy with our time, the only desires or freedoms we discover will be the ones we have already surrendered. And if we stake our hopes on the image of someone else's escape— even something as joyful as Madonna's burst of laughter at the end of "Justify My Love"—we can be sure that it will not be long before it, too, is drawn back into the spectacular megamix.

FIVE

"Appetite and Satisfaction, a Golden Circle":

Magic and Commerce in Twin Peaks

> Overnight, everything that is primordial gets glossed over as something that has been long well known. Everything gained by a struggle becomes something to be manipulated. Every secret loses its force.—Martin Heidegger, *Being and Time*

For just a moment in April 1990—though it passed too quickly to say for certain—it seemed as if *Twin Peaks* had magically suspended commercial television's innermost laws of motion. The very first scenes, shot with the deliberate deceleration of a suspicious eye and pieced together with a feel for visual distance, promised an immediate departure from standard TV style. By the end of the first two hours, the catalytic mystery—who killed Laura Palmer?—had melted into the atmosphere, pointing questions in all directions. From the beginning, ratings were unexpectedly high: the fact that 35 million Americans, one-third of the nation's viewing audience, watched the first installment was interpreted as the silent majority's declaration of independence from programming formulas. And in one awestruck review after another, the show was described as a "subversive," "surreal" antithesis of the mainstream (i.e., it was not quite a comedy, or a cop show, or soap opera). One magazine (*Connoisseur,* "The Guide to the Civilized World") even declared that *Twin Peaks* would single-handedly change television itself. Later that autumn, when the series resumed and the thrill began to wear thin in the United States, a wave of *Twin Peaks* hype broke over the British press, and most of Europe received its first taste of the show and its p.r. buzz thanks to the Italian media octopus Silvio Berlusconi. (In a symptomatic development, the German broad-caster threatened to sue a newspaper for revealing too much of the plot.) But by mid-1991, the series sputtered to an end in the United States, its audience largely gone, its p.r. sour and its storyline more diffuse than ever. Mark Frost, the show's cocreator, provided an extravagant, bitter postmortem to the *New York Times:* "I don't think it changed television one iota."[1]

What is incredible, of course, is that anyone ever thought that it could do anything of the kind. Yet the idea that *Twin Peaks* heralded some kind of aesthetic revolution in television came into circulation overnight and has not quite disappeared even after the show's cancellation. The pecu-liarity of that idea, at least, ought to be salvaged and examined, like the black box from a plane crash, before the *Twin Peaks* "event" disappears under a second wave of spinoff products, not to mention the gnawing criticism of academic interpreters.[2] It would be pointless to claim that *Twin Peaks* proves the necessary failure of a radical aesthetic: its failures are more intriguing and complicated than that. What can be explored more tellingly are the ways in which the series was thoroughly "tele-visual" to begin with and the ways in which its presentation of images takes place under two rules at once—money and magic.

A Word from the Sponsor

First, a look at economics, lest it be forgotten that television and every-thing on it is a matter of investments and returns—a truism that is becom-ing more true all the time. For obvious reasons, the television production industry was watching the fate of *Twin Peaks* closely. Throughout the eighties, United States networks had been losing their market shares to cable systems and home video viewing. Beginning in 1985 all of the big three (CBS, NBC and ABC) were overhauled by new owners. The founda-tion of faith upon which advertising revenues depend has been shaken repeatedly. Ratings, that precious information commodity upon which networks and advertisers base their transactions, are steadily losing their currency; both sides are demanding new, infallible surveillance tech-nologies of audience measurement. (As I have argued in Chapter 2, ratings represent the means by which the activity of a socialized, serialized viewing audience can be assembled, bought, and sold.) Even on the old terms, the networks cannot always come through: advertisers have to be given free "make-up" time slots whenever promised audiences do not materialize. In short, the old centralization of broadcasting power has been dissolving since the mid-1980s. For the time being, the networks can still attract business by shuttling between sales pitches, packaging access either to raw quantities of viewers or to distinct demographic slices on a national scale. Whereas the former supremacy of the networks corresponded to a modernizing phase of aggregated cultural forms and macrolevel programming strategies, this current, disorganizing phase signals an attempt on the part of a threatened industry core both to secure its monopoly of large-scale distribution and to reposition its expensive cultural products in more flexible but more precisely predictable arrangements. We are seeing the surgical strikes of post-Fordist rationalization carve out new zones of taste from the carpet-bombed terrain of massified culture.

In the spring of 1990, ABC had already boosted its overall standing to a strong second place (behind NBC), in part based on the sudden success of *America's Funniest Home Videos*, a windfall profit machine built on the ubiquity of personal camcorders ready to capture broadcast material from every moment of everyday life. By contrast, *Twin Peaks* seemed to be a deliberate and timely response to the crisis in network television, indicating a tentative acknowledgment that network programming had lost its hegemony and would be willing to compete aggressively by diversifying its schedule. In industry reports ABC began to look the very picture of health, its future rosy and its stock literally going up: "What [*Twin Peaks*] does," said one stock analyst, "is focus investors back onto ABC."[3]

From the beginning, however, it was necessary to focus a reliable audience on the show. ABC scheduled it as a midseason replacement in one of prime time's most competitive time slots, indicating that the network expected *Twin Peaks* to peel off a desirable demographic chunk (especially from third-rated *Cheers*) by virtue of its well-publicized "alternative" credentials. It performed quite well in the spring, awash in free press, and in the fall ABC confidently rescheduled it (along with *China Beach*, a "quality," yuppie's-eye Vietnam drama) on Saturday, the weakest TV night of the week, in the hopes that its new, well-defined, and affluent audience would solidify there. In the event, the show's whole second season went down the tubes, averaging less than half of its audience from the first season and finishing near the very bottom of the overall prime time list (which still amounts to an audience of about 8 million).[4]

Whether the show was canceled because it was badly scheduled or badly produced is not, finally, a very interesting question. Nor is there any point in moralizing judgment, as when a writer in the *Nation* charged that ABC wanted to kill the show because of its "subversiveness" and its uncomfortable "post-Reagan" era "social realism."[5] Recall that ABC was also behind the short-lived *Max Headroom,* another example of a "radical" show cancelled after dismal ratings. It should be clear by now that networks always want success, and that the revolution, any revolution, will be televised if the revenue is good enough—as we saw with the Los Angeles revolts. It is also important to remember that most American television serials are still in production as the season unfolds, and that the feedback loop of ratings, competing shows, and network reaction will direct the course a show takes week by week. Such circling contexts determine the decisions of producers at each step: indeed, every hour of television witnesses the punctual arrival of the economic last instance. But that determination operates only reactively and retroactively. The network paradigm follows a strictly pragmatic rule: everything put on the air should only stay long enough to exhaust the commercial potential of its particular combination of audience segments, which can never be given fully or accurately in advance. By that logic, the "contents" of a program (genre, actors, time slot positioning) function as a cluster of relatively independent "attractions" of uncertain value, a set of traits brought together under more or less original conditions every time.[6] Only when a program's various attractions coalesce in a marketable audience segment will its value be realized.

Within the network paradigm, the brand-name "difference" of *Twin Peaks* solidified too quickly and too narrowly, unable to translate whatever seemed so "untelevisual" about it into profitable terms of trade. That stubborn, unassimilated aspect of *Twin Peaks*—whatever marked its fascination and its failure at the same time—suggests that it falls into the gap between the stratified organization of network television and an alternate construction of televisual time. It is not only that *Twin Peaks* begins and ends without the comforts of beginnings or endings. It was always too early to begin the act of interpreting, even too early to decide what it was "about" in any kind of generic sense. Given the benefit of the doubt, *Twin Peaks* may hint at the emergence of new ways of seeing, listening, and telling that have only become possible with television but do not yet belong to it. Unlike much video art, however, which also points beyond actually existing television, *Twin Peaks* reproduces commercial structures and formulae even in the process of breaking them down into elemental units and recomposing them in mixed and variable forms. Its eventual cancellation need not be considered a punishment for transgression; its very appearance on network television suggests that commercial television can operate with any number of narrative structures, including a series in which time functions not only as the structure of significance, but as the decomposition of significance as well. Before and after all of the temporary mysteries of *Twin Peaks* have come and gone, there remains the one about its own impetus, the mystery of what holds everything together, if not simply the passing of time.

Interpretive Spells

Everything accounted good and bad about *Twin Peaks* will probably be attributed to David Lynch and to the fact that he usually directs films instead of television programs. (In the press reports, cocreator Mark Frost is characterized as no more than a savvy producer.) Perhaps television can absorb only so much cinema before it reasserts its own formal laws. To be sure, films are broadcast regularly, and well-established film directors have tried television before: one thinks of not only Fassbinder, Kluge, and Godard in longer forms but Scorsese and Ridley Scott in shorter ones. From the other side comes a popular tendency to search for American television auteurs, demiurgic producers who, in a farcical replay of the Thalberg style, shepherd a number of shows at once, stamping each with some signature concerns.[7] Rather than simply swallowing cinema in the way that McLuhan and others have described, television reproduces cinematic mechanisms with adoring and brutal efficiency, as though film now retained the thingly craftwork aura it is said to have destroyed in an earlier era.[8]

The question of cinema versus television crystallizes around the use of time (and therefore money). There appears to be a formal indecision between a film stretched out to ten or fifteen hours and a TV series that will unroll for at least twenty hours. In commercial television, the use of time is further complicated by the deployment of commercials, and it is not difficult to see how far dramatic structure has adapted to that time-table. While filming the two-hour pilot for *Twin Peaks*, Lynch described the problem this way: "This business of breaking it all up into eight acts [of approximately twelve minutes each], well, it seemed to fall into place. Now I don't know what the commercials are going to actually do; I've never plugged anything in those holes . . . that would be intense. But there's nothing we can do about it anyway. What you're really making is eight little movies."[9] Unspooling at its own pace amid the clockwork regularity of broadcast flow, *Twin Peaks* avoided both the usual televisual formats (regular breaks and discrete story-tracks) as well as the long-range vanishing point of cinematic closure. Either strategy would offer a kind of formal resistance—in the shape of synchronic or diachronic structures—to the violence of commercial punctuation. But when Lynch saw how his little movies played between the interruptions, he found himself charmed: "It's been a real thrill to watch the show. The commercials are even thrilling. I like to see who's advertising on it. Like Mitsubishi and McDonald's. Big companies."[10] The gaps in his work have been plugged with conspicuously disjunctive material, and Lynch senses that an irregular, nonfitting, or shifting time scale has been produced. Perhaps he felt he had found a way to snag television on these uncertain shifts of tense and place, to strike some friction between a fictive enclave and a giant corporate nowhere. With respect to the corporate control of the medium, that would be no small feat. That is, it would be a great aesthetic trick to find a way of generating something like a dialectical absence, where commercial determinants would be thrown into new relief, violating the customary aesthetic entente holding a series of images in line.

Given that there can be no totalizing representation of the general televisual stream, no substitution of dense parts for far-flung wholes, this alternative productive strategy would be a positional one, clearing a place where the rules keep changing and where no irreversible claims are made on the Real. Faced with the objective necessity of leaving precise holes in a narrative of more or less indeterminate length, Lynch and Frost dropped some of the standard mechanisms of cohesion, letting the holes and the indefinite duration of television itself—its specific, systemic features—become visible through the materials of the story. *Twin Peaks* turns the labor of watching television toward its magical dimension, toward the profuse and effortless schizophrenic effects produced between images, rather than toward the cognitive cutting and splicing construction of meaning and continuity. (In fact, Félix Guattari has named David Lynch as one of the great directors of psychosis.)[11] *Twin Peaks* was made to be read and reread, not only because it promised to reveal everything in the details, but because the details were made to absorb speculation without yielding a full-blown pattern: it is no accident that, as *TV Guide* reported, *Twin Peaks* was the most videotaped show ever on television.[12]

All of these attributes bring about an intensity of the images that is generated by duration, that is, by an extensive projection over time. On commercial television, such a volatilization of visual materials takes place specifically through a decomposition of narrative. In outline, then, the story goes like this: *Twin Peaks* opens with the discovery of Laura Palmer's plastic-wrapped corpse, which sets off a chain of events—investigations, bereavements, schemes—that quickly draw the storyline into branching paths. It would be hard to say exactly when it becomes clear that there is no core narrative problematic: in retrospect, it may seem as if there never had been one. (My own sense is that all of *Twin Peaks's* old-fashioned aesthetic integrity ended with the first commercial break.) Many kinds of disturbances come to light, not only the apparently criminal but a range of others that are never called by name. The problem of viewing becomes a rather complicated process of sorting out lines of causality or zones of effectivity, so that various motor forces—financial, sexual, psychotic, oneiric, occult, or whatever—can be identified and localized. How clearly these strands are ever specified or disentangled remains an open question: the lines of significance and relevance swoop in and out of focus erratically, multiplying possible connections rather than tying off distinct coherences. Insofar as the series refuses both a smooth narrative trajectory and a stabilized recurrent situation, there will be no way to find an interior code that will unify it in a single moment of understanding or judgment. The question of guilt, needless to say, never really surfaces.[13]

Apparently Mark Frost and David Lynch began their plotting with a sketched map of the town rather than a story; maybe this accounts for the way continuities and distinctions are marked by images whose significance depends on which distance they cross, which relations they suggest, and which locations they join. One layer of spatial significance is drawn from that well-worn construct, "small-town America," where everybody knows everybody else and where some quirky local charm is always on display to outsiders. In the 1990s, however, small-town America has already been subdivided into so many competing variations— every corner of the country has been called upon to display its brand of picture-postcard *gemeinschaft*. The Pacific Northwest is now enjoying its turn of stereotyping (as in the films of Gus van Sant and the CBS television series *Northern Exposure*). In the case of *Twin Peaks*, the small-town scale draws an initial horizon around the murder mystery: where everyone is somehow a suspect, everyone is somehow guilty. Once the murder has made the town's organic web of relationships visible and fragile, however, the investigation shifts out of town to the dropout drug runners and those thoroughly corrupt foreign heavies, the Canadians (who apparently can be menacing to the United States only when played as Quebecois thugs). But the more traumatic encounter with the Outside occurs when the townspeople's "evil spirits in the woods" turn out to be some eruption of primal taboos and global dangers, that is, when a traditional, mystical account for things is displaced by an undecidable choice among irreconcilable descriptions (ranging from crypto-psychoanalysis to clairvoyant rationality).[14]

Any sparks of significance are necessarily signalled by visual devices (like cuts and reframings) or aural devices (like refrains and nondiegetic displacements); but *Twin Peaks* emits all kinds of signals, classically realist and otherwise, without recapturing and repositioning them within any single structure, terrain, or procedure of sense. What looks like "hyper-realism" at one point, because it accounts for accidents or idiosyncrasies (the chocolate bunnies, the fish in the percolator, the flickering autopsy lights, the fallen moose head), may become a stylistic signature or an enigmatic clue later on. This degree of aleatory incoherence is not a question of choppy chronology, since the program sets up a fairly consistent vector of linear plot time. But there are few moments of climactic resolution or revelation around which other events will fall into place, receive their meaning, and disappear into the past. Or, in fact, such moments happen all the time, too often, revealing and shedding the false content of the old mystery in order to redraw different rays of significance. Rather than speak of a refusal of meaning, then, we may imagine the *Twin Peaks* storyline as a raw accumulation of referential power, a stockpile of unfolding possibilities where explanations are avoided whenever they would incur a delay, an expense, or a loss of options. We might even say that the scenario itself repudiates interpretation in favor of visceral sensation and magical intervention. For example, in the pivotal scene in the Roadhouse (in the nineteenth hour), Cooper finally calls on "magic" to help him understand the dream in which Laura whispers something in his ear. Then he hears an echo from the dream, the barroom scene freezes, and the dream is replayed. But the dream is not decoded as if it represented its meaning in a distorted form. On the contrary, Cooper simply listens attentively to hear at last what Laura had told him, the "testimony" that her father killed her. In this intensified diegetic instant (which mimics the freeze-frame replay of a VCR) the dream-images are confirmed as already containing their own truth. Magical understanding consists in learning how to attend to images more completely, rather than translating them through the terms of rational analysis. By these means, Cooper is able to effect a temporary resolution and provisional assignment of guilt. Since every "solution" to a mystery not only closes a narrative but also demonstrates a proper reading method for its audience, this solution does no more than affirm the glazed self-sufficiency of images. Meanwhile, as the hours pass, even these hard-won meanings begin to decay, cancelling each other or flaring up in sudden jolts, as more magical images are squeezed out from between superimposed layers of opacity, until only lateral movement between different signifying zones of the story, a slip between any of its virtually unconnected worlds, remains possible—a move well visualized in the final episode, where a puddle of sludge serves as a refracting contact point between the topography of the forest and the folded spaces of the White and Black Lodges.

Even as the narrative line is constantly unravelling, the most pervasive motif and character trait is doubling: from the peaks of the title through a long list of twins, visionaries, doppelgängers, numerous duplicities and double-crosses, up to the sloppy Manichean rhetoric of the final episodes. One turns into two (or vice versa) without any process of gradual becoming. As a rule, women are particularly prone to doubling: women resemble or imitate each other, mingling through their images (Laura, Maddie, Donna); a white American woman disguises herself as a Japanese man (Catherine); another is transformed into a teenager (Nadine); yet another carries with her an illicit past that reverses all of her character traits (Josie). Men, on the other hand, can be either doubled or split: they may undergo a radical transformation (Ben, Leo), suffer a fatal return of the repressed (Doc Hayward), or even appear in two different forms (the giant and the old waiter are "one and the same"). At the core of the mystery, however, is "Bob," who is somehow both a "character" and a double for others at once: an abstract character-function or actant. The identity or role of "Bob" takes several turns over the course of the story, starting with the proposition that he is an individual human being like the others, changing into the idea that he is the subjective projection of someone else (Leland and/or Laura Palmer), leading to the sense that he is a disembodied spirit who inhabits human beings. All of these readings, however, depend on the same visual clue: the appearance of Bob—a scraggly man with long grey hair—within an otherwise "real" physical setting. Bob can be considered a singular human character as long as he appears within the same plane of visibility as other characters, even if that image is situated as one of their memories or hallucinations. Later, however, Bob is repositioned in a secondary plane through a kind of free indirect shot: when Leland looks in a mirror, Bob's face appears. This image can be understood two different ways at once: it may be showing us Leland's "true face," or it may be revealing his self-perception, depending on whether the mirror is for us (objective) or for the character (subjective). The same duality persists through each of Bob's subsequent appearances and prevents our reading Bob as either inner spirit or external symbol. Bob is a double that must be grounded in an act of seeing by both a specific character and the viewer. To complicate matters, we learn that Bob once had a partner in killing named "Mike." Yet Mike never appears onscreen as an image; he is introduced only when a single character (Gerard, the one-armed man), while in a chemically disturbed state, speaks Mike's words. Mike had been Bob's double in the realm of doubles, but now, while "Bob" appears through many different bodies, Mike possesses only one, a mutilated/castrated one at that.[15] In a word, there is no symmetry in all these schizophrenic doublings—which would at least generate an alternate symbolic register or moral code—but only mobile, displaced images and blocked expressions.

Everybody, as the script insists, has secrets. In principle, there are two basic kinds of secret: one lodged in the interior opacity of the psyche, a knowing of the self about itself, and the other hidden within the pair or the group, a knowing among others against others. A secret claims the power of a unique truth, which is broken by revelation and its claim of general truth. On *Twin Peaks,* however, secrets do not work this way. Rather than specifying the identity of a character or the substance of a relationship, secrets reveal nothing but a lack of knowledge and the universal impossibility of saying what is happening or why. The inward knowing implied by the secret, then, defers to the arbitrary incursion of magical interpretation. Whereas the whole rhetoric of secrets harbors the promise of full disclosure within the drama itself, the invocation of magic, by calling upon forces beyond the known relationships between subjects, confesses the incoherence of the situation on its own terms. The greatest disclosure of magical knowledge occurs when Gerard/Mike tells Cooper that he is close to solving the mystery of Laura's death. His pronouncement, "Appetite, satisfaction: a golden circle," not only serves as a clue that points along the course of the mystery but describes the narrative logic and economic equation of contemporary television itself. Agent Cooper, of course, never knows anything consequential except by magical dispensation, since all of his deductive and intuitive methods fail him until the final moment of the whole series, which may now be read less as a fearsome cliffhanger than as the farthest possible point of uncertainty and incompletion.

Twin Peaks offers a mystery that lacks the one crucial generic element: someone who can know the secret.[16] Everyone sees, onscreen and off, but nobody knows. Knowing has been replaced by a gesture toward the unknowable, just as the real has been replaced by no more than a gesture toward the unreal. Stalled in the mood of constant anticipation, time is spun out past the point where there can be any hope of synchronizing the unfolding of events with the process of understanding. For the fictional community of Twin Peaks, as for the provisional community of viewers, the proliferation of secrets ultimately marks the absence of any public knowledge. But the magic of secrets cannot be invoked without giving away its power of cohesion: television constantly reminds us that the price of magical representation is general disenchantment (as the epigraph from Heidegger suggests). The acute sense of lost time and diffused collectivity—which Twin Peaks makes visible through its doubled selves and narrative entropy—may well be a genuine rarity on television, but it is also true that this basic formula of signifying loss and diffusion runs through every span of television, where time is sent and spent without the certainty of sense or the unity of seeing.

PART III *Theoretical Images*

SIX   *The Dangers of Being in a Televisual World:*

Heidegger and the Ontotechnological Question

We hear the Mercedes in immediate distinction from the
Volkswagen.—Martin Heidegger, "The Origin of the Work of Art"

In the revival of philosophy now whipping through the academic avant-
garde, Martin Heidegger has been put to work on a number of fronts,
both hostile and friendly: invoked as a kindly but solemn uncle of pop
poststructuralism, as a sorry example of a philosopher getting mixed up
in politics (when they think they know what they're doing but it turns
out they don't), and, still today, as a stern and pious taskmaster who will
oversee the rebuilding of a rigorous philosophical language. In each case,
Heidegger serves.

To use a Heideggerian language to say something about television,
however, may seem like a forced and painful exercise, a misdirected
interrogation that blunts the precise tools of a rarefied thought. What
could an archconservative philosopher of folksy sympathies, who finds
his lessons in clay jugs and broken hammers, have to tell us about the
immense and uncertain thing called television? In his scattered references to it, Heidegger does not pause for fascination, seduction, or curiosity but acts as if he has always known what to think about it, even
before he chanced to catch a glimpse. In fact Heidegger's thought could

provide the perfect case against television, a thorough rejection in carefully bracketed ontological and ethical terms: television as the almost unmentionable end point in the long decline of Western culture and civilization into falsity, instrumentality, and banality. Though that imperious tone often appears in Heidegger's text, the problem with seeking out a purely negative position is that he refuses to think that way: for him, even the worst thing will still be a thing, somehow present to us and bound to Being. Tucked in the folds of these ontological turns, television can be located in the Heideggerian skein at a complex point just where history and technics, metaphysics and science meet.

To see television in Heideggerian terms, then, involves something more complicated than either an outright refusal or an easy resolution of hostilities under the reassuring wing of Being. In the first place, Heidegger's work submits to questioning all the crucial terms now circulating undisturbed in television theory, especially representation, but also subjectivity, technology, modernity, and (the) world(s).[1] Heidegger, it could be said hastily, distrusts all of these, and in linking them together he proves useful to any attempt to think television's current global dominance, as well as its metaphysical ancestry. By the same token, his work can trip up any thought about television, pro or con, that too easily claims knowledge of its defining terms and their possible meanings. In its concern for the "authenticity" and "piety" of thought, Heidegger's text provides a testing ground for the various arguments (conservative, radical, and otherwise) that television threatens thinking, contaminates the "real world," and interferes with human access to any kind of truth. But to ask questions about the status of "truth" and the "world" in discussions of television, it is not necessary to mimic Heidegger's obedience to the overarching realm of Being. It is, however, necessary to identify the axioms that ground any attempt to assign television an essential (or alien) epistemological and ontological status, as well as to cross-examine all historical critiques of television as an epochal event, that spectacular sickness-unto-death waiting to happen ever since Plato, Isaac Newton, Adam Smith, G. W. F. Hegel, Thomas Edison, and Henry Ford (along with a cast of thousands) paved the way to where we are today. For this job—simultaneously philosophical and historical, but aimed beyond both—Heidegger can offer a number of enduring and trenchant guiding questions.

Another point of orientation: one of Adorno's apt epithets for Heidegger was "agoraphobic." Leaving Adorno's own phobias out of it, we should think about what that word involves and what values are invested in it: fear of open spaces and masses of people, as in the *agora* of Greece—site of commerce and public discourse. To be afraid of exchange, of discussion, and of contact with the multiple is the privilege of sovereigns and elites. *Agora* also happens to be a Hebrew word, a unit of money.

A special difficulty arises in using Heidegger for this job at this moment. No reading of his texts can avoid the growing dossier concerning the nature of Heidegger's links to National Socialism and the Nazi authorities. But no critique of Heidegger should be content with mere denunciation; the complexity of his compromises, theoretical as well as political, must be taken into account. Apart from the crucial fact that Heidegger's political interventions, from the 1933 Rectorate speech to the 1966 and 1969 interviews, were fundamentally premised on questions about the place of science, technology, and the role of the philosopher, there is an additional reason why the recent rash of controversy concerns us here. The debate itself has been staged by its participants as a contemporary conflict between philosophy and the media, in which each side has its own political-economic agendas, discursive protocols, and capacities for social-cultural transmission. In the Heidegger case, antagonisms between the public sphere and the assumed autonomy of philosophy have burst into spectacular and traumatic institutional ground battles. On Heidegger's side, a line of defense has been drawn between, let us say, his image and his thought: while conceding the former to public trampling, the latter is withdrawn, held back, preserved. (Derrida has spoken against any "immediate presentation" of Heidegger's thought, by the press and philosophers alike.)[2] In order for this damage control to find license in Heidegger's thought, most of his partisans have been forced to reconsider and rejustify his political and historical engagements, bringing on a momentary return of a repressed and unwelcome consideration of political "commitment" to the presumably purified soil of existentialism. The media has struck back at Heidegger precisely by spreading the word, his name: from now on Heidegger's image everywhere will precede his thought. The question then arises: where is the place of this kind of philosophical thinking, which locates itself at the end of a long tradition, in the televisual world? What would it look like if Heidegger's thinking (and not just Heidegger, his picture, and his words) could appear on television?

In forcing an encounter between Heidegger's thinking and the visible world of television, there will be a before and an after: first, pieces of Heidegger will be found, cut up, and examined in order to see where the encounter is possible; later, the meeting will have already happened (we can check the tapes) and it will be time to see what remains.

Dasein's First and Last Stand

In 1949 Heidegger delivered a series of four lectures titled "Insight into That Which Is": "The Thing," "Enframing" (later "The Question Concerning Technology"), "The Danger," and "The Turning." He would repeat and expand some of these talks over the next six years. We will read this extended discourse in its original order. Here is the opening paragraph of the first lecture, "The Thing":

> All distances in time and space are shrinking. Man now reaches overnight, by plane, places which formerly took weeks and months of travel. He now receives instant information, by radio, of events which he formerly learned about only years later, if at all. The germination and growth of plants, which remained hidden throughout the seasons, is now exhibited publicly in a minute, on film. Distant sites of the most ancient cultures are shown on film as if they stood this very moment amidst today's traffic. Moreover, the film attests to what it shows by presenting also the camera and its operators at work. The peak of this abolition of every possibility of remoteness [Ferne] is reached by television [Fernsehapparatur], which will soon pervade and dominate the whole mechanism and drive of communication.[3]

This extraordinarily economical passage contains the key themes of our inquiry.[4] Locating itself fully in the moment of its present, Heidegger's text speaks of diminishing dimensions—an encroaching horizon and a falling sky—by listing a series of familiar emblematic scenes. Planes, radio, and film have captured and compressed the various experiences of geographical space, historical events, and organic life cycles (all of which retroactively become recognizable as modes of distance). Formerly—although Heidegger does not put it this way, for reasons to be discussed—each of these experiences would have involved a kind of human endurance, suffering, or what we might call "staying power," a combination of holding steady, holding back, and holding at bay. Now staying power is gone, replaced by the worldly "drawing power" of technics. Information and man alike traverse distances with obscene immediacy, chasing each other into indistinguishability. But of the three technologies mentioned here, film alone makes a truth-claim by bringing its own tools and actions within the field of view, making its work part of the image. (Note that Heidegger either does not recognize or dismisses the fundamentally dialectical aesthetic structure of the estrangement effect, which renders "work" as "image.") Beyond all these, however, at the farthest distance from distance, is television, an apparatus for seeing at a distance that abolishes even the possibility of distance. Thus Heidegger begins his inquiry into the contemporary accessibility of Being by announcing its foreclosure, the coming to domination of a new technical world that threatens to saturate the space of thought with a henceforth uncontrollable hemorrhage of representational operations and obstacles.

Some questions, among others: What is distance, that television could dissolve it? What is time, what is space, that these could be placed in or removed from our presence by a machine? What is world, that television could have one or destroy one? What line of history—perhaps reaching from the pre-Socratics through the whole checkered career of metaphysics and out the other end—has television finally broken? To understand everything at stake in these questions, it is important to reconstruct the arguments and the narratives motivating this seemingly casual mention of television.

For Heidegger "distance" remains a function of a certain mode or motion of presence and hence of Being. "Nearness" characterizes the state of a relationship between Being and a being: the key site is "Dasein," an untranslatable noun that Heidegger uses to indicate an entity—neither fragment nor microcosm—of being that is not yet informed of its Being, "there" but never fully present. "Dasein," as articulated in Being and Time (1927), is a term that allows Heidegger to position and privilege his questioning without recourse to what used to be called consciousness or subjectivity. "This being which we ourselves in each case are and which includes inquiry among the possibilities of its Being we formulate terminologically as Dasein."[5] Dasein, as irreducibly Being-in-the-world, exists only in a setting: this is its existential dimension, necessarily experienced as an ontological dispersion. Therefore it can only be thought through a suspension of self-identity.[6] The in-ness of Dasein cannot be found through self-reflective retreat but only through a kind of diffuse affinity with the existential instability of the setting. This is not to say that the analysis of Dasein finds its consistency through persistent reference to a context of historical reality (as many have assumed, or as Sartre enacts). On the contrary, the version of Dasein proposed by Heidegger seeks to erode the structures of subjectivity posited by Cartesian and Kantian epistemologies (and any historiography that finds comfort in them) by insisting that Dasein can only be sought out by asking what makes it possible at any given moment.[7] That ontological ground, for Heidegger, can be defined neither as "existence" (the route of all humanisms) nor as "essence" (the route of all idealisms); rather, it is to the nonfit and mutual dependency of these two philosophical "solutions" (in the ineradicable "ontological difference" between existence and essence that grounds ontology itself) that Heidegger directs his queries.

To call Dasein "human" would beg the question entirely: it forms the indispensable nexus in Heidegger's argument, a strategic deformation of the available philosophical languages.[8] As *Being and Time* illustrates, the argument of philosophy can continue only after the name of Dasein is granted its fundamental newness. Then, after dispensing with any scientific propositions, Heidegger engages the philosophical tradition as a whole. *Being and Time* is largely concerned with the many pitfalls of Dasein, detailing its manifold authentic and inauthentic ways of being. (Several key passages deal with such everyday activities as chatter, curiosity, and so on.) Heidegger argues that all categorical distinctions between what we would like to call "subjectivity" and "reality" circulate through Dasein, which opens itself to the question of Being by gathering together everything in its purview without immediately imposing any of the "metaphysical" and subject-centered structures of representation. Dasein gathers what it is given: essences strive for existence there, and Being sends its messages there. It is the fundamental "care" of Dasein toward beings that responds so eagerly to the snares of representation. Sending and calling, which appear at this point to be the quasi-divine interventions of Being, will later become the avenue of technological interference with Dasein.

In a series of later texts, Heidegger redistributes the Cartesian subject/object dualism across a number of other terms in order to increase precision or poetic force (the two become the same) in naming the repertoire of Dasein's modes.[9] In "The Thing," a being's proximity to Being is called thingliness, which has to be distinguished as sharply as possible from the everyday nearness of objects brought forward by "immediate perception" or "recollective re-presentation."[10] To think things, Heidegger insists, is to leave "the precincts of representational thinking," which remains snarled in mere objects. "Man can represent, no matter how, only what has previously come to light of its own accord and shown itself to him in the light it brought with it."[11] And where is Being? "Being is farther than all beings and is yet nearer to man than every being, be it a rock, a beast, a work of art, a machine, be it an angel or God. Being is the nearest. Yet the near remains farthest from man. Man at first clings always and only to beings."[12] Unlike both perception and mental representation (which only repeat what is "given" to them), Heidegger's "questioning" or "questing" claims to disclose how that giving or "lighting" comes to pass, or, to put it another way, to ask what it means to say a thing is already there. The thing's obstinate presence, before and beyond any of the inward "metaphysical representations" that seize on it, gives it nearness.

Distance, then, makes sense only as the uncertain range of a Dasein, not as the fixed radius of a subject. (These days people would call Heidegger's account a "displacement of the subject.") Proximity involves neither sensuous experience nor cognitive appropriation. Here again Sartre's "humanized" existentialism provides a contrast: in Heidegger, the senses (especially seeing and hearing) are not in themselves authentic modes of Dasein and do not put things at their proper distance, whereas Sartre's "human reality" is crisscrossed by sensory activity that becomes totalized in the grounding concept of "nothingness."[13] The philosophical dispute between them—whether or not this concept of Dasein is "transcendent"— has never been settled, and it will ultimately depend on whether Heidegger's "thinking" and "asking" turn out to reinstate a "humanist" position after all. (Indeed Derrida has long been troubled on this point: from "Ends of Man" to *Of Spirit*.) The aspect of "distance" relevant here, however, consists in the separation of Dasein's "everyday" spatiality and visibility (the space of objects) from the glowing proximities of Being's "lighting." As long as the structure of Dasein, in which objects and images rear up out of the physical surroundings as discrete metaphysical productions, simply stands in for the perceiving subject, Heidegger has made little headway against phenomenology, for Dasein would only become a better-bracketed metaphysical mediation. To prevent this reduction, Dasein must do more than see things as they present themselves to view: it must be capable of seeing Being by seizing it from the visible world, jolting the scene of understanding in such a way that Dasein itself becomes visible, not merely to itself but to Being. Is it possible to think a purely metaphoric visibility, a visibility without viewers? Reaching the question of Being, the figures of vision that had surrounded Heidegger's account of Dasein's "disclosure" of itself and the world must be cut off from all phenomenological analogy in order to think a kind of visibility proper to Being—its "openness" and "hiddenness"—without falling back on the twin metaphysical scenarios of the viewing subject or an ideal immanence. In *Being and Time,* Heidegger designates this other realm under the sign of "potentiality," which names the way Dasein addresses itself to Being through time. Insofar as this potentiality for Being frames a seeing beyond seeing, it marks a fundamentally original question for Heidegger. Before that question can be fully expressed in the course of Heidegger's writings, however, it changes its scale and its epoch: another kind of potentiality belonging to representational metaphysics has already claimed the world.

The Hazards of Being

The threat to Being changes direction between *Being and Time* and the four Bremen lectures. The earlier work frets over the inauthenticity of mass existence and its capacity to absorb the distracted "concern" or attention of each Dasein. "The Self of everyday Dasein is the they-self [das Man-selbst], which we distinguish from the authentic self . . . Dasein is everyday for the sake of the 'they,' and the 'they' itself Articulates the referential context of significance."[14] Palpable fear of the "they" or the Other is hardly unique to Heidegger: it permeates, at the very least, all the early twentieth-century critiques of modernity (including Simmel's evocation of nervous metropolitan dwellers and Sartre's "pursued-pursuing" consciousness of *Being and Nothingness*). As Lukács says, such questions were simply "in the air" at the time.[15] For Heidegger, however, the question of alienation did not imply an originary wholeness of anything human. Dasein must escape from the initially constitutive pressure of the they-self precisely by resisting the "human" subjectivities on offer. Dasein only "bars its own way" by addressing itself to the trappings of the social world.[16] Thinking and questioning break the spell of everyday Dasein, awakening it to its potential for Being. Thus, while the dimensions of Dasein's task remain marked by everyday "facticity" and the demands of others, the prize is deliverance from Dasein's burden of care. In Heidegger's later work, however, Dasein becomes besieged by more than crowds: history somehow catches up and swamps Dasein in a new epoch of technics.

To explore that threat, Heidegger cannot merely denounce the misleading experience of perception (which stems from his attack on all previous *philosophical representation*), he must account for the contingent way in which things may or may not be present for man's use (which requires an attack on the causalities and instrumentalism of modern *scientific representation*). Both kinds of representation—the first rooted in the doctrine of Platonic appearances and essences, the second in the Aristotelian investigation of causes and principles—forget or miss the "thingliness" and "worldhood" of beings that makes objects "available" to thought or activity in the first place.[17] To explore this problem Heidegger reconsiders the idea of "world." At no point does "world" simply equal the "situation" of Dasein or the generalized context of Being. Heidegger uses the term (in different ways) to register the way in which Dasein grasps whatever surrounds and sets it. In that sense it betrays its Husserlian heritage. Yet because of its traffic with representation, the status of "world" is not above suspicion. On the other hand, in order to grant "world" its full share of Being, Heidegger must make it a repository of its own kind of authenticity. In *Being and Time,* this aspect of "world" concerned the ontic distinction between "present-at-hand" objects (the products of dualistic thinking) and "ready-to-hand" equipment (which conduct Dasein's activity toward things in the world). In later works, the lines of division shift so that the place of "equipment" is taken over by technics, whose proximity to Dasein (i.e., authenticity and worldliness) is much more in doubt.[18] The specificity and utility of "equipment" become the archaic and general simplicity of "things," and the image of a "fallen world of beings" changes into a horrific world of regulated lives and planned destruction. "Authenticity" becomes Heidegger's word of judgment on the things of this world. If we consider the whole "jargon of authenticity" as Heidegger's attempt to reground the worldly contests of meaning and value in philosophical language, the "world" of the Bremen lectures takes a wilder existential ride than the timeless peasant workshop of *Being and Time,* a place where Dasein now finds itself scattered across the world even as it is pressured to fit a smaller subjective slot.[19] The far-flung technical world offers the most ghastly meanings while everyday existence abides in abundant senselessness.

This play of extremes is recapped in "The Thing." The simple jug, useful and thingly, is counterposed to the self-confirming objects and products of science. Like the hammer of *Being and Time* and the peasant shoes of "The Origin of the Work of Art," the jug can, if properly seen, reveal some truth about the Being of beings. Science, on the contrary, betrays a two-level destructiveness. First, it generalizes away from the thingliness of things in the world: "Science makes the jug-thing into a nonentity in not permitting things to be the standard for what is real."[20] Second, science constructs objects of its own that act on the world without heeding their worldly impact: "The [atom] bomb's explosion is only the grossest of all gross confirmations of the long-since accomplished annihilation of the thing."[21] (Later we will ask what the atom bomb has in common with television.) If things have been so thoroughly annihilated, how can thingliness still be uncovered? What labors and contortions of thought are called for? At this point Heidegger raises the stakes, and the gentle consideration of the jug breaks into a full-blown hermeneutic cosmology. "We have sought the nature of nearness and found the nature of the jug as a thing. But in this discovery we also catch sight of the nature of nearness. The thing things. In thinging, it stays earth and sky, divinities and mortals. Staying, the thing brings the four, in their remoteness, near to one another. This bringing-near is nearing. Nearing is the presencing of nearness."[22] All tautologies aside (because Heidegger is always willing to find ontological traces in doubling words), this passage indicates how Heidegger will compensate for his growing distress about the technical world. As his account of contemporary science becomes more complex and nuanced, so too do his interpretive field markers. The simple distinction between "earth" and "world" familiar from "The Origin of the Work of Art," in which a bracketing of worldly representational elements permits access to the earthy truth of things, now becomes a fourfold swirling "ringing of the world's mirror-play" where truthful aspects of things flicker and fade in the course of thought. It seems to be getting harder to find a shred of truth uncontaminated by representational orientations. As a crescendo of ringing and mirroring closes the essay, Heidegger notes that things are "compliant and modest in number, compared with the countless objects everywhere of equal value, compared with the measureless mass of men as living beings." Among the things still out there waiting to be thinged are the aforementioned jug, "the bench, the footbridge and the plow"; the "tree and pond, too, brook and hill"; as well as "heron and roe, deer, horse and bull."[23] Beyond making an advertising plug for pastoral life—in which a string of nouns function precisely as stereotypical images in a unified mise en scène—this claim wants to imply that enclaves of thinking are nevertheless still possible and locatable within and against the encroaching technical world.[24] It is a conservative claim, even within the terms set out by the four lectures. To call it simply "romantic" or "organicist," however, obscures the affirmative gesture Heidegger begins to make. It is no coincidence that Derrida's commentaries on Rousseau in the *Grammatology* are full of such Heideggerian resonances.

The next Bremen lecture has become the best-known statement of Heidegger's "negative" prognosis, published in English as "The Question Concerning Technology."[25] It follows the same general path as the previous lecture. In fact, the four lecture titles themselves summarize the basic points (thing—enframing and mechanization—danger—turning) that Heidegger repeats in marking out the contemporary scene. The second essay, then, must live up to its place in the sequence by making the strongest case for the closure of technology. It begins with an urgent invocation to open "our Dasein" to the "essence of technics," followed by a careful series of distinctions about the historical definition of technics.[26] Heidegger announces that "the essence of technics is by no means anything technological."[27] With this key phrase, he seeks a redemptive redefinition of the problem that returns the danger of technics within the compass of Being. The inclusionary move is made first. All technics as *technē* is included essentially within the Greek term *poiēsis,* as a making that brings forth. "Technics is a mode of revealing. Technics comes to presence in the realm where revealing and unconcealment take place, where *alētheia,* truth, happens."[28] In this "making," technics employs human labor, much as Being uses Dasein in general.

Next, Heidegger draws a crucial distinction opening a number of historical and political issues that he will then try to tame and recoup. Modern technics, along with the sciences it requires, is characterized as a new kind of revealing that "challenges" the world. This challenge receives a special name, *Ge-stell,* which is variously translated as "Enframing" (Lovitt), "installation" (Lacoue-Labarthe), "emplacement" (Weber), and "con-struct" (L. Harries). Each version gives us the sense that this assemblage of practices, apparatuses, and procedures has cut loose from Being, even from "man's" labor, and doubled back, imposing itself everywhere. The term arises from Heidegger's attempts to characterize the way science deals with the real by setting it in place, by ordering and calculating its movements. ("Science sets upon [stellen] the real.")[29] All of these acts of aggression receive special emphasis from Heidegger, each designating a particular way that Ge-stell is deployed. Science is always the heavy net thrown over the world.

Ge-stell thereby includes every objectifying, reifying, subjectifying, and alienating development in the West. At a certain point, Ge-stell even launches itself onto a planetary scale. We would start to call it "capitalism" if Heidegger were not so thoroughly opposed to seeing things in terms of production and history. Among the effects wrought in Heidegger's text by bundling all these functions together as Ge-stell, one deserves special attention: the appearance of the term *Bestand,* "standing reserve" or "standing stock." With this term Heidegger takes an inevitable dialectical plunge: having named the system, he must rearticulate the status of the object within it. The fate of the object, which had enjoyed its own false autonomy under the regime of the *res extensa,* now leads to a kind of disappearance or annihilation beneath the network itself. The only objects of Ge-stell are instrumental processes. Everything else has receded so far from the shadowbox scene of representation that they have become virtual or potential objects only: "Whatever stands by in the sense of standing-reserve no longer stands over against us as object."[30] To be produced by Ge-stell, therefore, is to be inessential and indifferent, no longer present even in a degraded metaphysical form. In an infamous passage from the original 1949 version of the lecture, Heidegger indicates how Ge-stell equalizes and liquidates all of its productions. "Agriculture is now a motorized food industry: in its essence it is the same thing as the manufacture of corpses in gas chambers, the same thing as blockades and the reduction of a region to hunger, the same as the manufacture of hydrogen bombs."[31] In this clever but lame condemnation, Heidegger displays a stunning obstinacy, not to mention a thoroughly reprehensible lack of tact. Most of all, however, he signals his refusal to use either ethical or economic terms of value in his characterization of Enframing. Defying all sense of proportion, Enframing takes on a monstrous and epochal significance. (In a quick outline of the whole history of Being [ca. 1961], Heidegger puts Ge-stell last, beyond even Nietzsche, [American] pragmatism, and "the will to will"—corresponding to the final moment of the "completion of metaphysics.")[32] Throughout Heidegger's examples in this essay, Enframing captures, as its pièce de résistance, what used to be called nature. All natural features have entered the process of calculation, to be left alone or used up according to plan. Rivers are either dammed or left for recreation, while ground is either torn up or left as landscape. The earth, subject to representation, waits stock-still while the frames of a "rootless" reason traverse it restlessly.

Heidegger's discussion of Ge-stell leads us into one of the best-sealed, most irreversible models of modernity ever: we can only say that it has always already happened. Ever since the challenge was put in place (Heidegger does not locate the moment here), it has been too late to explain its appearance, especially not in causal or determinist schemes, which owe their logic to the movement itself. Ge-stell elicits its own apparatus of knowing and doing. Technological activity "merely responds to the challenge of Enframing, but it never comprises Enframing itself or brings it about."[33] As "framing," Ge-stell forces that which is framed to drop out of presence, into the temporal hiatus of the before and after or the spatial oblivion of the "distanceless." As a "revealing" Ge-stell inhabits the "mechanism and drive and scaffolding" [*Gestänge und Geschiebe und Gerüste*]—that is, the assembly [*Montage*]—of technology as its way of working.[34] In fact, Heidegger here uses the very same accumulation of figures to totalize technics that he used earlier to describe the apparatus and motion of television. In this tight verbal concatenation, where machinery, stage, assembly, and Enframing come together, a familiar chiasmus encircles the act of naming the system: it must be shown in two ways at once, both as a technology of presenting and as a presenting of technology.

But now, Heidegger says, this balance has been upset. Enframing anticipates the act of representation; it is properly speaking the global state of representation, reached at a certain moment in the modern era. What can be brought forward into visible presence by Ge-stell are not representations in the Platonic sense, for they are not subject to the rule of ideas or forms. The representations given by Ge-stell are rather emplacements, set-ups, showing no thing "in itself" but only aspects of the ordering, angles, and corners of the framing, coordinates, and quanta of the emplacement. A self-regulating, self-regarding system. In the face of such representations no hermeneutic can refer to an obscured or distorted reality: reference to the real always reasserts the latter's availability as standing-reserve to the system. Representational thinking has rendered all objects—including the subjects of humankind—so present, so much at hand, that none can appear as such. For Heidegger the idea of appearing "as such" was a metaphysical one, implying a certain distance; now even that is gone. In the new space of absolute representation, "man" loses the capacity to recognize the difference between revealing and concealing.[35] At the same time, Heidegger insists, it is not possible to explain the representations of Ge-stell by reference to human activity or instrumental reason: neither one completely informs the unfolding of the representational occupation of the world. Insofar as Ge-stell comes to match, point by point, the terrain of Being and the place of *alētheia,* its own mode of revealing threatens to become coterminous with truth.

That admission propels Heidegger into the theme of danger and a language of the brink, the edge, and the precipice. Technics will teeter there indefinitely. But the danger comes on two fronts, the first hegemonic and the second catastrophic. On the first front, Enframing simply prevents truth from "holding sway" by presenting itself as the only form of knowledge and practice. (Therefore the sly "revealing" of the cinematic apparatus mentioned by Heidegger seems pernicious because it translates a movement belonging to thought into its own fallen language of images.) The unrestrained glare of representation allows for no genuine coming to presence—it is all-revealing with no concealing, all-presenting with no withdrawal, all-signifying with no mystery. On the second front of danger, when Enframing looks ready to complete itself, it turns out that it is not sufficient to sustain a truthful knowledge. On the brink of eradicating truth, it reaches the brink of discovering it: the overriding danger is that it will continue to fail to do so.

Having cast Ge-stell as completely real and worldly, Heidegger cannot afford to reject its representations as simply false or even misleading; on the contrary, he confirms all of them, affirming that the movement of Being—in which "man" is "needed and used"—might still arrive through technics. If Enframing "conceals revealing" then it seems to need only a nudge to tip over the other way, to reveal its concealing. The play of *poiēsis* that had inhabited all previous dispositions of thinking reaches its fatally forked path, "between technē and technology," as Dreyfus puts it, at the point when Enframing oversees all beings from a distance scarcely distinguishable from the nearness of Being.[36] But Heidegger suggests that this outcome was part of the program all along. *Poiēsis* has never stopped tending toward a resolution of truthfulness, and Heidegger admires Western thought for having applied itself so energetically to that task. The longstanding drive to "bring forth" he calls "destining": it is the only concept with which Heidegger will characterize the history of thought from the pre-Socratics to yesterday, and hence the only way to turn the "push" of technics into the ancient constancy of truth. Elsewhere Heidegger finds a way to think this word through Nietzsche: "destining" carries along both the West's irresistible Nietzschean will and an eternal return of the primal same.[37] Whenever Heidegger seems ready to think a historical thought, he resorts to the drifting of destiny. But are the historical dangers of destiny ever defused?

Hardly. Heidegger wants to keep them poised, left hanging in the air as the "constellation of truth," finally unresolvable and "ambiguous."[38]

Far from wishing that technics would go away, Heidegger concludes that its completion is essentially virtual (and virtually essential), that it could even "entrench itself everywhere to such an extent that someday, throughout everything technological, the essence of technology may come to presence in the coming-to-pass of truth."[39] Surprisingly like Marx's dialectic of capitalism and socialism, technics will allow itself to be seen as fully surpassable only after exhausting its capacities. Though art is offered (almost as a reflex) at the end of the lecture as a possible site of confrontation with technics, it is finally no more than an alternate and less dangerous version of the same problem, the same constellation. If art and technics were *essentially* different, one could oppose the other; that is to say, if technics possessed an essence proper to it or a constellation of revealing all its own, then it could prevent or block the modes of revealing that art and poetry allow. But since revealing and concealing happen essentially in the element of thinking, technics can block truth only in the realm of appearances, where its tools rule. Thus at the end of its programmatic assault on what Heidegger calls "things" and "thinking," Enframing finally leaves the destining of truth untouched. It performs its countless global depredations indifferent to the matter of thinking. In this way, the finale of the lecture leaves the "question concerning technology" uncontaminated by technics itself.[40] It is a close call, but no confrontation takes place.

Where, then, does Heidegger ever bite into "that which is"? What motivates Heidegger's examples of Ge-stell, and is he in fact trying to mount a poorly disguised political critique of a social situation that he scarcely recognizes? In answering these questions we might determine what features of Ge-stell are most disturbing to Heidegger, and why television, of all the manifold threats, appears as the most virulent strain of Enframing. After the great levelling campaigns of a triumphant metaphysics, why would television come to epitomize all tendencies of Enframing, mounting to a scale of encompassing that rivals even the question of Being?

End over End

The remaining Bremen lectures, like Heidegger's other texts on technology, do not offer much help in explaining the televisual extreme. Each text does no more than rearticulate the threat of Enframing, marking out an incremental escalation of an endlessly approaching end. Within the destiny of Being, as we noted, Enframing comes last. It gathers the loose ends of metaphysics—death, humanity, experience, nature, history, and will—to reconfigure the whole under the imperatives of planning, calculation, and rationalization. Enframing is bound up with Heidegger's notion of modernity and his efforts to point beyond it, into something we shouldn't be too hasty to call the "post-modern," although others have already blurted out the term in this connection.[41] More to the point, we should follow Heidegger's images of destruction and markers of modernity as they lead to television. The Heideggerian path to television is littered with the hollowed-out shells of metaphysical concepts.

Heidegger chose not to publish the third Bremen lecture ("The Danger") in his lifetime; perhaps it will await his emergence as something he was not in life. Until then, his literary heirs have brought forward several excerpts for the purpose of defending his name from charges of political cowardice, including this elaboration on the earlier remark about the place of Nazi death camps in the sphere of Enframing: "Hundreds of thousands die en masse. Do they die? They perish. They are cut down. Do they die? They become items of material available [Bestandstücke] for the manufacture of corpses . . . Dying, however, means bearing death in its essence. To be capable of dying means to be capable of bearing this death. But we are able to do so only when the essence of death has an affinity to our existence."[42] This small passage signals a point that Heidegger had not made elsewhere and that seems to indicate the lecture's contribution to the longer argument: one of the dangers of the technical set-up is that it changes the way death happens. Of course, death is one of those cherished themes of all humanisms, and in Being and Time Heidegger had made a special point of reorienting it in light of Dasein, so that openness to death becomes a constitutive dimension of authentic existence. To be unable to recognize death as one's own, then, is yet another privation of Enframing, yet another isolation of one's own Dasein from the realm of Being. At the same time, Heidegger's fear of the masses is clearly audible here, mirroring the indifference of Enframing perfectly. As to why this lecture would have been held back, we might note that death was not a preoccupation for the later Heidegger, and that its appearance here—with a new set of charged meanings—would have drawn him into a polemical field he clearly wanted to avoid.

The final lecture ("The Turning") is by far the shortest and least developed of the set. (Heidegger says he published it in its 1949 condition without changes.) The title refers directly to the play of veiling and disclosure that has been identified already with *poiēsis* and *alētheia* (the happening of truth). Accordingly, Heidegger here emphasizes the strength of technology to push itself toward Being, a juggernaut of destiny that man cannot stop. "Technology, whose essence is Being itself, will never allow itself to be overcome by men. That would mean, after all, that man was the master of Being."[43] All that is left for "men" is to let themselves be "used" in the gentle reversals and sudden illuminations of this destiny, and to lend themselves to this turning they need only *think*. Thinking—which always takes place in language—corresponds primally with Being, letting Being enter the world, and thus serves the "restorative surmounting of the destining of Being, the surmounting of Enframing."[44]

Perhaps this is the closest we get to Heidegger's plan of action: do not analyze the situation, but give thought to it—*communicate* with it—so that it may stay with Being. But even here, in the final movement toward a happy surrender to the destiny of Enframing, something blocks the way. "Therefore, as we seek to give utterance to that which is, we do not describe the situation of our time. It is the constellation of Being that is uttering itself to us. But we do not yet hear, we whose hearing and seeing are perishing through radio and film under the rule of technology."[45] Heidegger had just finished telling us that it is futile to characterize the present situation in any historical, psychological, or eschatological terms. Now he reminds himself, if only for a moment, that Enframing is still clamping down on "our" existence and that it is useless to counsel "seeing" and "hearing" when technics has ordered both the world and the senses. He urges just the opposite: do not give in to the temptation to utter what is already being uttered to us. In this reminder he hints at the difference between the constellation of Being and the rule of Enframing: it is the impulse to describe the world—to see it, hear it and position oneself in it—that draws existence into ordering. Enframing conveys a will-to-sense that encloses Dasein's openness.

But the senses, though distrusted all along, are not equally compromised by this enclosure. Though hearing remains essentially bound to language and Dasein, reserved to wait for the call of Being (the "phonocentrism" so often noted by Derrida), it can be captured by vision, which is identified with representation and its elaborate blinds.[46] Seeing becomes the circuit-model of all sense. The worst thing that seeing can do is to hurry hearing along, forcing it to mistake the clamor of Enframing for the murmur of Being. Still, Heidegger recognizes that he cannot help but make a picture of the world in the very act of shouting a warning against all such pictures. Enframing makes vision sweet, simple, and supreme. He loves this trap and makes no move to evade it. Hesitating but rapturous in the face of Enframing, Heidegger recognizes something there that he could not think of resisting: he calls it the "denial" of the truth of Being in the representation of beings as beings, and in the representation of world as world.[47] This denial—"the highest mystery of Being within the rule of Enframing"[48]—tantalizes Heidegger with the spectacle of truth blocking itself, a surplus of representation that sends the whole world spinning.

When Heidegger ends his lectures with yet another reference to radio and film (though without mentioning their future *dépassement* in television), he reactivates a series of arguments and metaphorics concerning the balance of power between images and language in the system of representation. Under Enframing, things and language are formed as pictures and information.[49] In this formation, Enframing supplies the ground upon which "everything that is" can be thought through representation, a projective space arranged under a rule of visibility, where subjects and objects have been arrayed against each other. The rule of visibility is not at all sensuous and remains just as distinct from the "lighting" and "clearing" allowed by *technē* as from the spatial metaphorics or image protocols of texts. Furthermore, the classical schematic difference between the sensuous and the suprasensuous (metaphysical to the core) is rendered obsolete as soon as thought appears solely as a figure etched on a grounding and ordering presence (the "world" of Enframing). As long as there is such a world, the visibility of representation will bear its own ground.

Heidegger's basic statement on the coming to dominance of the visual is his 1938 lecture, "The Age of the World Picture." Though it precedes the Bremen lectures, its conclusions feed directly into the elaboration of Gestell and Bestand: here Heidegger contemplates the completion of representation as the defining moment of modernity, the point at which representation is volatilized in time (i.e., becomes always potential rather than merely present). In a remarkable summary, Heidegger lists the "essential phenomena of the modern age": 1) science; 2) machine technology; 3) the assimilation of art to aesthetics; 4) the definition of all human activity as "culture"; 5) loss of the gods.[50] The rest of the essay articulates only the first point, with respect to the second. (Of the five, only the fourth does not appear to have received an extended elaboration in Heidegger's oeuvre.) Science—defined as the ascent of a methodological "procedure and attitude" over "that which is"[51]—sets itself to the ongoing "explanation" of nature and history. Heidegger also repeats his argument that science belongs to a larger metaphysical development that establishes "man" as a subject. I will explore Derrida's reading of this essay in a later chapter, but for the moment, we need to emphasize just one point: the centrality of the visual dimension to Heidegger's immense generalities. Here is the crucial statement. "The fundamental event of the modern age is the conquest of the world as picture. The word 'picture' [Bild] now means a structured image [Gebild] that is the creature of man's producing which represents and sets before. {The translator notes that Gebild is Heidegger's neologism.} In such producing, man contends for the position in which he can be that particular being who gives the measure and draws up the guidelines for everything that is."[52] In an appendix to the essay, he adds: "When the world becomes picture, the system, and not only in thinking, comes to dominance."[53] In a refrain that should be familiar by now, Heidegger illustrates how the overwhelming, "gigantic" presence of the world-as-picture in fact comes to us as a kind of disappearance, "in the annihilation of great distances by airplane, [and] in the setting before us of foreign and remote worlds in their everydayness, which is produced at random through radio by a flick of the hand."[54] But it is not the delivery of the pictures as such that counts for Heidegger: it is, rather, the submission of all elsewheres to the regime of Everywhere that sets the modern world under a constant shadow of anticipation. The old existential anxiety to see or be seen is transformed through total visibility into a matter of anxious indifference.

In a later text, "A Dialogue on Language" (1959), these issues are raised in an increasingly sly and precious fashion. The two voices elude each other's words and wage a battle of deference. As the Heidegger-naïf and his Japanese doppelgänger discuss language, cinema once again emerges as an agent of Ordering. After the European interlocutor gives a guilty shrug about "the complete Europeanization of the earth and of man," his counterpart deplores Kurosawa's *Rashomon* as a European "technical-aesthetic product" in which "the Japanese world is captured and imprisoned . . . in all the objectness of photography."[55] The passage is striking for two reasons: first because Heidegger specifically extends his earlier characterization of film to the "reading" of a single text, and second because of the cross-cultural comparisons. With respect to the latter, which Heidegger could discuss only in the broadest strokes, it should not be surprising that he was attracted to some of the language of Zen: a residue of his poetic speaking recedes toward its silence. (It is clear that Zen Buddhism, on the rise across the West in the late fifties, is an ingredient in the composition of the Japanese speaker.) Next, in expressing his "enchantment" at Kurosawa's film, the Heidegger-host opens himself to the censure of his companion, who instead recommends the Nōh play as the best cultural expression of a national essence. Both speakers condemn any thought of "realism" as a hopeless longing for presence. Beyond the caginess of the text, however, it is worth noting that in 1967 the editors of *Cahiers du Cinéma* found this passage significant enough to translate and introduce as some kind of philosophical "statement" on cinema. I hope to have indicated already that this is certainly not the case, since Heidegger is always addressing much grander levels of generality. The lesson drawn in *Cahiers* by Patrick Lévy (the translator)—that Heidegger here condemns "objectification"—leads to an avant-gardist question: "Is it possible to conceive of a cinema which escapes objectification?"[56] In the terms of our discussion so far, such a cinema could only be thought on the level of Enframing: that is, at the level of the standing reserve of representation. Such a systematic cinema cannot be conceived as the production of a text or set of texts: it can only be glimpsed when the particularity of this or that cinematic object is surpassed and absorbed by the rules that allowed it to come into being. This surpassing and submerging of the proper space and time of visual objects can be thought, for us, only through television.

Have we reached television, then, as the systemic sum total of death, the world picture, and complete visibility? What about the A-bomb? Wouldn't that be the ultimate threat to everything Heidegger holds dear?

Recalling the potential for destruction that Enframing brings, we can see why Heidegger decided that the Bomb was not such a big deal after all: "For precisely if the hydrogen bombs do not explode and human life on earth is preserved, an uncanny change in the world moves upon us."[57] This uncanniness comes with the whole ensemble of technologies driven by the limitless power (so it seemed in 1959) of atomic energy: from film and television to air transportation and medicine. (Another rare reference to television occurs in such a listing.)[58] The pervasiveness of technics exceeds its destructiveness; that is, having relentlessly redefined the world in its own terms of visible calculation, "destruction" no longer happens.

Heidegger expands the point in the *Spiegel* interview, given in 1966: "Everything functions. That is exactly what is so uncanny . . . [Technology] tears people away and uproots them from the earth more and more. I don't know if you are scared; I was certainly scared when I recently saw the photographs of the earth taken from the moon. We don't need an atom bomb at all; the uprooting of human beings is already taking place."[59] Jean Baudrillard and Friedrich Kittler have said roughly the same thing, but we are now in a position to understand what this kind of post-apocalyptic comment might mean.[60] As essentialist thought attempts to fix a limit on the "planetary catastrophe" of technics, the only marking devices apparently untouched by ordering are themselves four corners of an epochal frame: the "no longer," the "already," the "henceforth," and the "not yet." Throughout his discussion of technics, Heidegger redistributes these markers so that the present moment becomes the fullest emergence of a destiny, a point after which nothing else can happen.[61]

Television, then, is the perfect end point, more perfect and complex than either the Bomb or cinema, a pure will-to-vision that everywhere leaves things ready but unseen. It worlds the world as an englobing, endless series of images: as Heidegger's comment about photographs from the moon indicates (since such photographs are necessarily broadcast), the invisible, pervasive proximity of television races beyond any phenomenology of things or texts. It is not even a matter of form and content—that fine old Platonic division—since television-as-Enframing remains indifferent to what it shows or represents, operating only according to what it could show or represent, which is everything that is. The most potent device of Enframing is, then, literally the frame: the gesture of bracketing that makes something seen at the expense of everything else. For Heidegger, this is the basic act of violence in the modern epoch. (In Derrida's analysis of Kantian aesthetics, the frame [parergon] threatens the assumed integrity of the picture it contains, thereby disturbing the status of the art-object itself.)[62] At this uncanny, gigantic scale, television would initiate countless movements of the frame, sliding over the representational scenery without being reduced to the sequence of its particularities. Still, television would have to sweep along all the bad old functions of metaphysical thinking for local use, to enact and enforce the rules of visibility. In the push to place everything under representation, to make everything calculable, there must be an expansion of the visible forms in which reality is seen as produced by "man." "In that metaphysics perishes, it *is* past. The past does not exclude, but rather includes, the fact that metaphysics is now for the first time beginning its unconditional rule in beings themselves, and rules as beings in the form, devoid of truth, of what is real and of objects."[63] In this picture of control, Heidegger even allows for something that anybody else would have called ideology. "It is part of the essence of the will to power not to permit the reality which it has power over to appear in *that* reality in which it itself exists."[64] If the maintenance of Enframing, then, requires as its single overriding objective the dissimulation of its devices, frames, and techniques, it finally becomes clear why television, in its very ubiquity and randomness, would have to be the indispensable instrument for a total system of ordering: it allows for a continual redistribution of "what is real" in the objective guise of images, through the channels of subjectivity.

Television's Last Word

If Heidegger's thought leads us to think of television in such abstract terms, as something whose logic and function belong to a system beyond politics and economics, indeed beyond any critical reckoning or compromise, how can we explain the fact that Heidegger submitted himself to its apparatus, granting a broadcast interview in September 1969?

Earlier, I cited Derrida's short note cautioning against the "immediate presentation" of thought. As with any such warning, it must make a decision about thought's happening: either there is a flexible relation between thought and its presentation, so that there will be more or less useful and faithful presentations, or thought is that which shrinks away from presentation, or at least from immediacy. These issues are hardly new: we noted already in Chapter 2 how Marx couched his answer in dialectical terms. But after seeing how Heidegger's thought at every step recoils from the bad "immediacy" of a given conceptual language and how his history of Being describes a long encroachment of metaphysical constructions of presence onto the terrain of Being, we can recognize how Derrida's words claim the philosophical prerogative to be *incalculable* and *unwilling* in the face of that which can come and go without a thought: the image.

The question remains: Why, then, submit to the image and its instant transmission and diffusion? Why allow thought to be reckoned alongside everything else, and thereby allow it to suffer the fate of a just-as-instant disappearance?[65] We might answer this in general by talking of the differential speeds of texts and images, and of a will-to-transmission throughout every discursive movement. We can also explain such choices in terms of exigencies and pragmatic considerations (as Bourdieu has done, in connection to Heidegger's early career).[66] Heidegger obviously saw some advantage in broadcasting, but to understand what he thought it could do for him, we need to read exactly what Heidegger wanted to say so quickly to so many.

But first a preliminary remark. The television interview has already been introduced provocatively to the current discussion by Avital Ronell, in *The Telephone Book* and elsewhere.[67] She writes: "[Heidegger] himself got on television and when it was time for ActionLightsCamera, he said something about the relatedness of TV to his thinking."[68] Ronell simply leaves it there. Her statement expresses a desire, perhaps, that Heidegger would have said something on television about his relation to television. It is the sort of thing thinkers are supposed to do: to reflect on the situation and to build that consideration into their responses. (This capacity is, after all, supposed to be the marginal advantage of a *thinking* Dasein over any of the other modes, like a watching Dasein or a zapping Dasein.) But in fact Heidegger does not say anything about being on the air. He does not even mention television. At this crucial moment he shows no sign of resistance to the apparatus, unless that archaic and subterranean ruse called "rhetoric" counts.

Heidegger's appearance on television was carefully orchestrated. As interviewer Richard Wisser testifies, Heidegger screened the questions and prepared his answers in advance. No response from Wisser to Heidegger's answers was allowed. The result was, not surprisingly, something on the order of a stilted dramatic performance between two talking heads, spliced together in the editing room. No banter, no chit-chat, no public intrusion. It is this transcript text, brief (seven pages) but telling, that I want to read here.[69]

What could Wisser ask? Three sets of questions: the first set asks Heidegger to say something about "social change," the second set asks for some clarification of his philosophical texts, and the third (the last question) asks whether Heidegger has seen his teachings carry out the transformation he anticipates.

What could Heidegger say? All he could do is repeat himself, quote himself, summarize himself, complain that he had not been properly understood, and in a pinch, insist that such issues are really much too difficult for "common understanding." In other words, he says nothing philosophically new. He holds back. That is the first striking thing.

But in the course of saying much the same old things, Heidegger cannot avoid throwing in some polemical asides. Two of these concern Marx. It is remarkable that Heidegger immediately responds to the mention of "social" problems by quoting one of his 1929 lectures and then by attacking the Eleventh Thesis on Feuerbach.[70] The second mention comes during a statement about the essence of technology, which Marxism, "concerned with a subject-object relationship," cannot approach. Other comments signal the ways Heidegger avoids or exempts himself from the terms of the questions: these mark, in a way we never see elsewhere, the subtle boundaries between Heidegger's thinking and the public sphere. For example, since he has already defined "today's society" as "modern subjectivity made absolute," a philosophy "that has overcome a position of subjectivity has no say in the matter."[71] This is a doctrine of disengagement, a claim that insight into social existence (with its crude dialectical rules) allows for philosophical separation from its bonds. The withdrawal of thinking uttered here is echoed a moment later, when Heidegger again describes the withdrawal of Being in the face of Ge-stell. The final withdrawal and refusal to answer comes at the end, when Heidegger speaks of a "thinker to come" who will take up where he himself has left off.[72] By invoking the future, Heidegger reinstates a displacement in the present, a distance not yet collapsed by television, the margin of deliverance through which "the saving power" might arrive. This call to the future, like the one he made in the *Spiegel* interview, becomes the only gesture left.

The interview proves not only that Heidegger was utterly traditional with respect to the limits of philosophy, but that he found himself obligated to broadcast his thought, if only to demonstrate and to perform its difficulty. He was no believer in consensual communication and "subversion" is not part of his routine, but he knew he had already become a public image, a famous construct of concrete history and the inflationary speculation of public talk. Mouthing his own words, not to speak them but to place them in the world—which is just the point of televisual discourse—Heidegger chose to make a spectacle of himself. Despite his deft stonewalling and patient self-presentation, Heidegger nevertheless delivers himself over to television, which "needs" and "uses" him in return. Refusing to place his own thought within the epoch of Enframing—that is to say, refusing the dialectic questioning that would force him to reckon his own refusal as one of the ruses of the program—Heidegger, embattled, decides to begin a guerrilla media campaign on behalf of Being, which, having been driven so far from the giddy metaphysical profusion of the technical world that it appears as a withdrawal or even as a negativity, now returns to public space with all the contaminating force of a robust virus. This performance is Heidegger's second great attempt to play at politics by engaging with technology. The first political action began in 1933 and lasted for months and years; the second lasted twenty minutes in the public eye, late one Wednesday evening in 1969, witnessed by an estimated audience of 250,000.[73]

The only remaining question is whether any thinking at all can avoid this televisual fate. In the case of Heidegger, whose philosophical stance is without a doubt the best-defended bulwark against any incursions from either the responsibilities of social life or that errant destiny called history, thinking finally yielded to the laws of immediate visibility, just for a moment, long enough to be captured and sent through the relays of chance that conduct telecommunication. It takes just an instant to show that it can be done. But it would be a mistake to see this moment as a final victory of technics over its last opponent: it is, instead, a final admission on Heidegger's part that confrontation, negotiation, and perhaps even mutual infiltration is unavoidable and that any resistance to the present state of things must always traffic with the forces that rule there. Television, far from abandoning metaphysics or the history of Being, includes all of it: now it becomes a site of negotiation without negation, where the thinking of Being and the presenting of television depend on each other for their uprisings and downfallings, where abyss and ground are alike intertwined in a fleeting figure. Whether it proves to be the last absolute of an obsolete metaphysics remains to be seen.

SEVEN

From Post Cards to Smart Bombs (and

Back Again): Derrida and the Televisual

Textual System

There are many kinds of eyes. Even the Sphinx has
eyes—and consequently there are many kinds of "truths," and consequently there
is no truth.—Friedrich Nietzsche, *The Will to Power*

Preview

As recounted in Eric Barnouw's history of American broadcasting, television had two beginnings, or rather, two ends.

In 1928, engineers at General Electric broadcast the "first television drama production" over the experimental station w2xad. It was called "The Queen's Messenger," a melodrama, shot entirely of facial close-ups from three motionless cameras: the resulting images flickered across a 3″ × 4″ screen, about the size of a small card. Shortly afterward, another drama was broadcast, of quite a different kind: it simulated a guided missile attack on New York City, from the missile's point of view, a slow aerial approach ending in an explosion.[1]

I am tempted to say that these two productions have already exhausted the entire representational range of television, and that television has done nothing since then but pursue the two ends figured here. With "The

Queen's Messenger" comes a promise that television will be the official courier of culture: it announces that television will carry on, and even culminate, the most familiar narrative, generic, and pictorial traditions. With the missile attack, television proves that talking heads and war-heads can offer reinforcing perspectives of the world. Ten years before Orson Welles's radio false alarm "The War of the Worlds," television plays with its own kind of doom: it does not begin with images of destruction, but with the destruction of images—a reminder that the blank screen will always be ground zero.

Today, we can see updated versions of the 1928 experiments all the time: one moment, smart bombs with their video noses fall on Iraq, showing the landscape approach until the blinding moment of arrival—and the next moment, a news dispatch or a sales pitch or some dramatic encounter. The only limit is that, as long as television lasts, it will always cut away from that blank, final moment and return to the traffic of images and sounds, to all the messages carried by all the messengers crossing through its world. When we speak of television, we speak of a world where missiles and melodramas are sent through the same space, the same network of representation, across the signifying chains that link the controlled spread of culture to the spectre of unrestricted destruction. How can we understand this world, its political and even theoretical stakes, unless we continue to try to read some of those messages?[2]

Cards

I will begin, then, with the post card, which will provide a map for reading the televisual delivery system.

Jean-Luc Godard, at the moment when he starts switching between film and television, described his work this way: "To make cinema or television, technically, is to send twenty-five post cards per second to millions of people, either in time or in space, of that which can only be unreal."[3] He goes on to say that nobody has the economic and technical means to send such post cards, so many and so far, except those who are "everybody and nobody" at once, that is to say, corporations, networks, and the State. And then there is the cost of receiving these post cards: the financial outlay for a theatre seat (rent) or a TV set (fixed capital), the market price of spectatorship.

Five years later, in *La Carte Postale,* Jacques Derrida lets the post card, the post, and the card become the organizing figures for a discussion of images, messages, and systems of transmission.[4] At one point, almost as a detour, he describes all of culture as an immense number of postal transmissions, each stamped by authorities and traditions, each cultural artifact "taking a position" by imposing itself or even superimposing itself on the others. Every cultural act thus pays a social and historical price.[5] One of Derrida's words, neither the first nor the last, for this jostling circulation of words and pictures is "telecommunication."

What do Godard's televisual post cards have to do with Derrida's telecommunicated ones? For both, "post card" is another name for an image in transit: subject to regulation, misdirection and profit. Since "post cards" can bear any message, sign or figure, they serve as emblematic frozen moments of a ceaseless transmission of culture. Derrida reads the post card, showing how it bears many duties at once: not only that of carrying its image and message, but also the obligation of a sufficient address, of a legible signature, and of a payment to the delivery apparatus. Along with its senders and receivers, the post card is always responsible to the system that sends it. In fact, it will pay for its own sending twice: once by framing its form and expression so that the system will transmit it (everything must fit on the card, including the address, the signature, the additional stamp), then again by suffering the possibility of failure (or, as Godard puts it, unreality). Everywhere its path can always be interrupted, its image defaced, its message smeared. Insofar as the post card undergoes these necessary inscriptions of sending, it is a telecommunication in Derrida's sense. And insofar as the post card is an image made for unlimited transmission, it is televisual in Godard's sense. Both post cards remind us of the prices we pay (to culture, to the State, to capitalism) for our images and messages.

Obviously, the figure of the post card can go a long way in many directions. Here, the post card leads toward the question of television as a general economy of culture. All of Derrida's cautions about the matrices of textuality take on renewed relevance in the analysis of television— meaning that it cannot be easily defined as a "medium of communication," as a "discursive practice," as "institution" or "apparatus," or even as "text." Its economy is not restricted to language, money, commodities, or images. ("Pleasure" and "reality," two big-money terms in the current manuals of popular culture, will be bracketed off here on principle: they offer reassuring destinations precisely where critical deferral should be sharpest.) Television's limits, in a word, are undecidable: at least they should remain undecidable as long as the study of television keeps itself open to deconstructive questioning. But rather than make deconstruction and television sound alike (which comes out as "slippery signifiers endlessly frolicking"), I want to show how television repositions deconstruction, using Derrida to locate the place of television in that old postal network we call culture, up to and including the possibility of an end to all that, the culmination of all the ages of reason in the smart bomb, which is, as everybody knows, a televisual device par excellence.

Telecommunication

Now what use does Derrida have for this word "telecommunication"? Not only does it appear on the inscribed, inverse side of *La Carte Postale* (something we will return to), but it occupies a crucial position in "Signature Event Context," the essay that closes *Marges de la philosophie* (1972).[6] But this word "telecommunication" depends on and inflects a number of other pivotal words appearing in the earlier "deconstructive" work of the *Grammatologie* (1967) and its contemporary texts.[7] These texts develop a critique of the privilege of "presence" and "immediacy" in such varied discourses as Husserlian phenomenology, Hegelian dialectics, the structuralism of Lévi-Strauss and, above all, metaphysical accounts of language and writing since Plato. For Derrida, "writing" is not a technical appendage of language, distinct and derived from the primacy of speech but a perpetual production of differences ("textuality") that build and inhabit language itself. It immediately turns out, of course, that language is not the only textual system, nor even the primary one: as the general equivalent of signification, "writing" overpowers and undermines the problematic of "language" as it developed from the Greeks to Heidegger. To use a more dynamic figure, writing is how a language *happens* even before we can speak (of) it, and since language happens to be this way, its general relationship to a realm of significance remains unsettled. In the *Grammatologie* we read about the writing of images, experiences, gestures, space, and even cybernetics. "Writing" must be a machine, Derrida suggests—but instead of faithfully capturing spoken language and preserving it for later use, the machine operates in and through every mark, utterance, and thought, always producing an excess (and therefore a loss) of signifying potential that cannot be boxed into the linguistic or semiotic model of the sign.[8] The ideal of the perfectly functioning writing machine is the ideal of all communications theory: a perpetual-motion machine in which expression—the material sign itself, spoken or scripted—would be self-sufficient, fully adequate to its signifying value. But this machine never works, it *plays*—or rather, it works by playing. Whenever writing, possessed by some metaphysical impulse, tries to control its own meanings, or fix a representation of its own reality, or determine its own interpretations, it disrupts the "restricted" economies of meaning and brinks the general economy of *différance*.[9] And this breakdown happens all the time. Any arrangement of signs throws out a restless movement of references, a movement that cannot help but open each text onto the textual system itself (however illimitable that may be).[10]

The status of the "textual system" has been one of the most controversial problems for any historical or formal "application" of deconstruction, since on the one hand any totalizing impulses seem threatened by the microscopic corrosion of textual dissemination, while on the other hand Derrida's refusal to "delimit" textuality to "the text" (let alone the "book") opens the analysis to everything (as in "there is nothing outside the text").[11] This rather too famous comment should now serve as a warning: there was never just a text, or just an image. These things are made possible by, and make possible, other texts. As Derrida put it in 1988, "What I call 'text' implies all the structures called 'real,' 'economic,' 'historical,' socio-institutional, in short: all possible referents."[12] But since all structures of reference are in play as well, the general system of writing can be neither chaotically shapeless nor analytically fixed, but defined only as the contingent disposition of signifying forces as they group and scatter around frames, rules, models, and proper names (to cite only some of the figures Derrida has analyzed). Having stressed the necessity of thinking about all of these possible zones of reference, Derrida nevertheless insists that no rule, no guided procedure, no manner of dialectic can turn "writing" into a concept of totality. There can be no simple opposition between unruly "play" and settled "meaning" in texts, but only "economies" of writing in which the values of sense are articulated. "Play *includes* the work of meaning or the meaning of work, and includes them not in terms of knowledge, but in terms of *inscription:* meaning is a *function* of play, is inscribed in a certain place in the configuration of meaningless play."[13] Here play animates and envelops two distinct processes whose specificity should not be lost in the symmetry of chiasmus. First, the "work of meaning" describes an incessant movement, the action of a mark calling upon something else to give it sense. Second, the "meaning of work" designates a transaction in a specific signifying economy whose balance sheets, where they balance, will count a work as a meaning, as a value. But one never simply moves from an economy of value into a realm of nonmeaning or play: to read in terms of *différance* is to delimit a formation of value by means of a continuous passage through it, out to its aporias, its limits. Deconstruction marks off all movements up to that limit: it is a way of working out the economy of meaningful spaces and understanding the ventilation and regulation of value, its punctuation and puncturing.

With the appearance of the word "telecommunication" in "Signature Event Context," another account of textual mechanics, one pertaining to systems or networks, comes into view. If "differance" is the movement of the text as it tries to pin down—to inscribe—its signification, then "telecommunication" involves a movement of potentially boundless transmission. The writing machine must also be a mobile broadcasting network. Let the word spell itself out: the prefix "tele" makes plain what was true all along, that "communication" is something which is always sent, or emitted, diffused, circulated. The notion of writing as "sending" allows us to imagine a certain temporal and spatial gap in the movement of reference: a sign, even as it refers elsewhere, is somehow "itself" moving (elsewhere). The sign, in other words, communicates nothing but an uncertain movement of reference: we can never be sure where it came from or where it is going. Officially, a sign is supposed to function as a repetition of a certain reference, so that communicating a sign would be a way of reproducing a particular movement of meaning, the *same* meaning available to the one who sends it. (Greimas calls this the sign's "isotopy.") "Signature Event Context" picks apart the ontological possibility of such continuities within any (tele)communication process. Derrida questions not only the identity of senders and receivers ("signatures"), but also the installation of meaning or intention within the sign (an "event"), and especially the stability of all "codes" or "rules" that would regulate writing absolutely ("contexts"). He shows how the very possibility of exceptions leaves its mark on every rule that one might want to set, rendering it incomplete from the start.

To put it in another framework, we could say that the essay cancels, at different points, McLuhan's dictum "the medium is the message": (1) "the medium" cannot be a transparent and homogenous operation outside of effects of writing, for all media are writings; (2) "is," the copula indicating identity, can do no more than graft one term onto another without enforcing an equality or transparency; (3) "the message" cannot remain a singular, ideal entity, for there is never just one message.[14]

In fact, Derrida lands a direct blow against McLuhan at the end of "Signature Event Context."

> As writing, communication, if we retain that word, is not the means of transference of meaning, the exchange of intentions and meanings, discourse, and the 'communication of consciousness.' We are witnessing not an end of writing which would restore, in accord with McLuhan's ideological representation, a transparency or an immediacy to social relations; but rather the increasingly powerful historical expansion of a general writing.[15]

There it is: what is at stake in the complexities of "writing" are precisely "social relations." Writing, not meaning or consciousness, moves through and animates the social text. Furthermore, writing's historical expansion has nothing to do with McLuhan's prosthetic "extension" of the human sensorium. The new technologies have not delivered us to a spiritual transcendence of power relations but have instead actualized, accelerated, and ramified the whole scriptural economy and all its relations of force, its programmings, regulations, and calculations.[16] Telecommunication sends its illimitable texts through a stratified network of differential relays, through the very receiving subjects ("everybody") and sending institutions ("everybody and nobody") evoked by Godard. As with all systems of writing before it, this one is unable to enforce a regime of meanings; yet through certain devices and protocols it has achieved the capacity to circulate texts faster and farther than ever. The acceleration and expansion of the system does not "unify" it; instead, inversely, it makes possible a greater distancing, what Sartre called the "serial absence" of each point to all the others, or what in Derrida becomes the radical and volatile indeterminacy of context.[17]

The absences of agency—of sending and receiving—that surround the mark are not homogenous and strictly formal: they are absences that unfold unevenly and appear contingently. Since the absence of the sender and the receiver to each other is always possible—indeed, these absences, along with the absence of the referent, are the "positive condition" of the appearance of any mark, any writing[18]—we have to expect that different arrangements of senders in general and receivers in general will produce specific kinds of representations, built to endure different kinds of absence and the demands of an expanded iterability. Weaving these distinct absences together, electronic telecommunication transmits a regime of representation proper to our *general socius,* a writing that now crosses through all possible objects and audiences without necessarily representing or reaching any of them. Such a regime of diffusion would bear only a limited resemblance to the system instituted by alphabetic writing, which joined in one signifying unit both phonetic and semantic articulations, thereby inaugurating its rule over all other kinds of linguistic and iconic exchange. The analogy consists in the way the televisual transmission also combines sensory and morphological registers in its text. From image to image, television marks out a space of innumerable viewing acts, graphing an economy of visual/auditory combinations. But it would be a mistake to search for an alphabetic element in telecommunication, that is, a single characteristic term or general equivalent that translates all others. Televisual images and sounds do not derive their force simply by replacing other images and sounds; they do not compose, as alphabetic writing had done, a metalevel of signs. Instead, televisual images and sounds are marked by being submitted, through a mechanism of circulation, to a new rule of visibility, facing the possibility and hence the necessity of new contextual linkages and scenarios. Rather than a graphic substitution, television alters the scope of textual eventualities, opening new tracks of iterability, changing the statutes and the range of the visible.

This would be one way to put it, staying generally within the terms of Derrida's earlier works. All of this comes into focus another way when he starts sending post cards.

Posts

According to Derrida's conceit, part of *La Carte Postale* is supposed to have been written on the backs of many post cards, all of which bore the same image, the same one that now appears on the front cover and again three times inside the finished product. This image reproduces a thirteenth-century drawing of Plato dictating to Socrates, who sits at a desk, writing. It is an old cartoon of deconstruction—but not of deconstruction *avant la lettre,* because there is no such thing. On the back cover there is a signed and dated message from J.D., promising a book that plays with "addresses, postal codes, crypted missives, anonymous letters . . . modes, genres, and tones . . . dates, signatures, titles or references, language itself." A postcard book: text on one side, image on the other. Even inside, one of the reproductions is folded so that it can remain visible whenever the book is open, so that the text always faces, and backs, the image that it designates and that designates it.

Before we open the book to read, then, all these reproductions tell us something: the image is a point of reference with a different status from any of the text's "own" referents: no longer an illustration or an example to be explicated, this image runs alongside the act of reading without directing or exhausting it. And at the same time, no matter how much it swells, the text can never fill up the reverse of the image. What the book immediately gives us to think is the displacement of images and texts, the gap between the picture and whatever we could write about it, the obstinacy of appearances against the waffling efforts of textuality. But it is not as if this image, acting for all images, thereby claims some final primacy over writing. It does not present the truth or even a dirty little secret about the history of Western metaphysics. It makes just one little slip and loses track of the philosophical tradition—proving to Derrida how easy that is and how it has always been possible. Together with its backing text, this image opens onto a deconstructive circuit, a loop of uncertainty about the path of presence in representation, where the thing that is made visible is neither an image nor a text, but the tension between their forces.

Now if the cover manages to make itself a post card and thereby incite speculation about the relations between oral, written, and pictoral representation, the texts inside scatter their own speculations. *La Carte Postale* is a notoriously difficult book to summarize: it makes good on its threats about the instability of its positions, its subjects, its modes, and so on. It also makes many lists of everything it says it is hiding. For the moment, I will simply assemble from the text several fragments or diverging vectors—features of the post card—that together can function as a set of themes or slogans for a discussion of television, held together by the conceptual critique of "communication" already underway. I hope to justify, at each point, the special pertinence of Derrida's text to such study, though it should never be suspected that his book provides a media theory. Everything that it has to tell us about television it says *in passing*, which is why it can say so much.

I will add, as a flat provocation, that *La Carte Postale* is already "televisual" in the sense I am developing here, precisely because it deploys and switches between so many textual registers. Though *Glas* might also be called "televisual," that text resembles nothing so much as the programming grid itself, which the reader must negotiate by scanning and choosing between channels. Though it might be of limited heuristic value to imagine what a televisual book might look like—since the terms cancel each other at so many points—Derrida's many experiments with the "end of the book" have already inspired Gregory Ulmer and Avital Ronell to build their own kinds of transmitting devices.[19]

Like Derrida's other famous coinages (such as "*différance*" and "dissem-ination"), the post card is both offered and withdrawn as a figure for figuration itself. But unlike some of the earlier, linguistically inspired terms, the post card figures the process of transmission rather than in-scription, sending rather than writing. In a word, it is a figure of diffusion. Is it possible to speak of a text or an image being "diffused" without posit-ing a previous moment of stability when it was only just "written"? What happens to the notion of "textuality" if it is cast as a matter of transmis-sion rather than writing down or recording? What are the possible rela-tions or ratios between circulation and production in a textual economy? These are the theoretical stakes when television theorists (since Ray-mond Williams) have wanted to speak of "flow" as a metatextual term for television itself: "flow" would have to be subject to a principle of diffusion that precedes or overrides both the production and the reception of dis-crete texts. Televisual flow could not be a textual object offered up to be read or seen; instead, it is always an entire network of transmissions, both linear and erratic, humming with excess referential power and clattering with unfinished representational frames, whose very law of visibility is that everything can be seen but nobody can see it all. In this sense, "flow" names a given instability that constitutes television in its very mode of appearance, from the scanning cathode ray to the complex potentials of remote-control zapping.

To think television as a post card (à la Godard) means to acknowledge that transmission is the only law of production, and that culture itself is therefore not produced piecemeal but sent through circuits.[20] Further, all of this demands a fundamental shift in our textual ontology, away from the "text itself" (not to mention the "things themselves") and toward a conception of the textual system as an illimitable matrix crossing at variable speeds through all cultural, political, and social dimensions. For Derrida, who had been on the trail of a general theory of transmissions ever since "Signature Event Context" if not before, the deconstruction of writing alone was not enough to open onto this scope. Writing had not yet escaped from the scale of the singular text, no matter how many times it crossed and recrossed its own borders.

With *La Carte Postale* and its related work, Derrida's analysis of "send-ing" (along with its privileged figure, the post card) exceeds the de-construction of writing in two directions: first, ontologically, he looks through Heidegger to find how "sending" is the essential dynamic of representation itself; second, he claims that "sending" initiates another field of work, a "pragrammatology."[21] As Derrida describes it during a discussion of chance and psychoanalysis: "Open to a different sense of the sending (envoy) and of sendings (envoi), pragrammatology should always take the situation of the marks into account; in particular that of utterances, the place of senders and addressees, of framing and of the sociohistoric circumscription."[22] "Pragrammatology" offers us a retrofitted deconstruction adequate to the study of transmissions, granting simultaneous attention to the constraining logics (the forces of programming) and to possibilities of discontinuity between any of the elements (situation, frame, and so on). When the transmissions in question are grouped under the sign of television, it might be better to speak of a "programmatology": an analysis of the controlled diffusion of textual marks, in which television reproduces for itself an uncertainty of contexts and a flexibility of meaning. Programmatology, in other words, takes as its first task the inventory of enforced regularities and calculable slippages within the televisual regime, given that its transmissions deploy many different signifying frames across many different situations. Whenever the question of television's "context" comes up—as it must—the answer must come in terms of forces and determinations. Derrida does not shrink from this imperative.

> If I read in the paper that this evening there will be a performance [*représentation*] of *Psyché* by Molière, or that a given painting represents *Eros,* etc., I understand without the least equivocation and I do not put my head in my hands to figure out what it means. It is enough, obviously, that I have the competence usually required in a certain state of society and schooling, etc. And that the *destination* of the message sent is, to a great probability, sufficiently determined.[23]

Although the subject "I" is not in peril here, its functioning depends on a large, old representational system carrying the weight of a whole cultural determination, an arrangement of destinations premised on each receiver's trained receptivity to the "ordinary" and the "normal." In order to function, then, the logics of sending are bound to leave visible traces, and these traces can be found right there on the post card.

The Stamp

As we saw in the beginning, acts of transmission pay a price: perhaps just a small service charge to the rules of sense, or maybe a large mortgage to multinational capitalism. The stamp commemorates a payment to tradition, to heritage and authority: everyone pays this kind of tax whenever they "do anything whatsoever" (Derrida adds a long list of anythings).[24] Deconstructive criticism often performs this internal revenue service, as a cost analysis of a text's metaphysical debts.[25] On the post card, the stamp is already an image, an official one that carries the most determined kinds of ideological marks. All television everywhere is regularly punctuated by such stamps. In nationalized systems, the State will continue to stamp the transmission with signs of its governance. In commercial systems, the place of the stamp is assumed by advertising itself, which can strike a range of distances from the other messages at hand. (It is also becoming more common for networks to stamp their images with a little logo in the corner.) In either case, the stamp bears the image of finance and the proof of the system's power to exchange one kind of delivery for another, money for messages. Any kind of response—and there will always be a response if a message is delivered—will require another payment, another stamp, a reinvestment in the process.[26]

The Address

Derrida writes, "The essential, if possible, is that the address be unique," indicating the most problematic feature of postal transmission—the place of (receiving) subjects.[27] My remarks will be necessarily schematic. The question of the address bears upon both the "destination" and the "legibility" of the message. Neither can be singular or unique: that is why the post card cannot help but be legible in more than one way and in more than one situation and why the moment of reception is divided in advance and absorbed into the process of transmission, always remaining incomplete. "The condition for it to arrive is that it ends up and even that it begins by not arriving."[28] If destinations could be perfect, and addresses unique, messages too would be perfect and unique, that is, illegible.

Derrida's insistence on the "adestination" of postal transmissions as a condition of their sending has to be read as part of his broader ontological critique, here and elsewhere, of "communication" and "representation" as the impossible conveyance of a value of "presence" through a "medium" or post. Since diversion and interruption are always possible, no message can ever arrive fully; which is to say that no message can ever be made visible as a message without chancing itself.[29]

The notion of "address," then, marks a complex intersection of representation and subjectivity. This crossing provides the terms of Derrida's reading of Heidegger's essay, "The Age of the World Picture," on the delimitation of "the epoch of representation in modern times." Assuming that such an epoch can be marked off, one of its consequences or permutations is, for Derrida, "the world of the mass media": a nightmare regime of "calculable and representable subjectivity," the "inverse of the democratic and parliamentary ethics of representation."[30] As soon as subjectivity has been inserted entirely within the order of representation (a punctual historical event, according to Heidegger, as we have seen), the notion that representation makes objects visible to subjects doubles back on itself, leaving subjects open to representation in turn. Here is the scene: caught in the act of representing themselves to themselves, "modern" subjects place themselves in the "open circle of the representable," in a "shared and public representation." Thus a subject is defined as "what can or believes it can offer itself representations," that is, as something formed by the imperative to be an image, in order to receive images.[31] "Address" includes both vectors of representation, enunciation and perception, by which subjectivity addresses itself to and is addressed by the world. Just as subjectivity organizes itself as an object of self-knowledge through its representing activity, so too representation is organized through subjects, rendering each series of images limited and calculable. (Hence the Heideggerian problematic, where "representation" as the overriding, encompassing historical phenomenon owes its existence to a prior ontological, nonsubjective "destining" or "sending," a Big Bang of Being.) Derrida is not so sure about origins; he is more interested in ends. As he draws it out, the program of representation regulates itself as an ensemble of sendings that traverse from the offer of singular and distinct subjective identities to the multiplication of forms of representation necessary to service them all. The concept-metaphor "sending," then, shakes the enclosure of the representational/subjective matrix and allows for an analysis of the composition of the field as a function of stronger or weaker distributions of force.

Television would be the place where the positions of "calculable subjectivity" and images as "profoundly calculated approximations of verisimilitude" (in Godard's phrase from *Passion*) are finally combined into a single differential circuit of representation. Television's "calculation" does not consist in the perfectibility of its programming but in the thoroughness with which it translates values into representational terms, so that all traffic (of politics, aesthetics, desire) passes through the televisual post. Television makes representations visible and accessible to each other and makes a profit only when that visibility can be approximated, calculated, programmed. Addresses, or what used to be called subject-positions, in fact function as the transfer points of this network, where the representational forces of selves, others, and objects negotiate. This relay of representations is just what Raymond Williams described as televisual "flow": now this term should be taken as a figure, not only of an observable televisual text (the phenomenological moment, though inadequate, remains inescapable) but also of the absorption back into the televisual network of all subjective centerings. There can be no flow of televisual representations without an ebb of subjective ones.

To find another set of coordinates, we can look back to Althusser's great essay "Ideology and Ideological State Apparatuses." The word "telecommunication" appears precisely where the concept of "interpellation" (hailing) is introduced.[32] "Interpellation" is supposed to confirm the subject in its identity and its place through the receipt of messages. Althusser writes that "[the] practical telecommunication of hailings is such that they practically never miss their man."[33] But—and here is the moment of slippage in Althusser's text—what if one misses? What if, in practice, an ideological sending does not arrive? What if the target turns out to have been someone else? And what if a message reaches, "practically" but not by design, the wrong man, the wrong woman? *How could it miss?* In Althusser, everything depends on the correct functioning of interpellation, its unerring aim: it is interpellation that "always already" forms individuals in and as subjects.[34] But if ideology can miss, it must have been unstable as sign and as event, it can never simply be the transmission of a meaning to the subject. Indeed, ideology neither hails nor nails the subject in place, since both terms only appear on the occasion of a telecommunication. Althusser's concept can only be made rigorous by Derrida's postulate of misdirection, which operates at a different level from the Lacanian/Althusserian postulate of misrecognition. At this level, ideology must be conceived as a mass of sendings or a flow of representations whose force consists precisely in the fact that they are not perfectly destined, just as they are not centrally disseminated. Far from always connecting, ideology *never does*: subjects look in on messages as if eavesdropping, as if peeking at someone else's mail. (This is also always the route of desire, which, as everybody knows by now, never comes.)

To express it in a formula: ideology requires a short circuit between the singular and the general, so that the *reception of a representation* becomes a sending back—a *representation of a reception*.

The "Material Support"

A post card must, after all, be made of something, for references alone aren't always solid enough. As Derrida says of his cards, "The cardboard . . . preserves, it resists manipulations; and then it limits and justifies, from the outside, by means of the borders, the indigence of the discourse."[35] The card is already a functional item, a thing designed for efficiency; the place of the public and the private messages are drawn openly on its two faces. But, Derrida says, "a certain form of support is in the course of disappearing"[36] and with it the spaces of differentiation.

The material change from cardboard to electrons introduces a specific history. Reading a long excerpt from an official report, Derrida is struck by the postmaster's ambition to extend the function of the post to a pure mediation between "THE population and THE Administration," that is, to achieve "omnipresence."[37] The postal system's tendential movement toward an instrumental totalization brings, as its reciprocal motion, the abstraction of all transmissions. As soon as the card is threatened by electronic transmissions, it must remake itself increasingly on the data-processing model. In submitting all previous forms to the same general law of transmittability, television behaves just like the postal network: it does not simply "transport" previous forms (theatre, film, radio) but rather translates and recombines them. This shift to a new technology is not just a matter of changing delivery speeds but, in the case of television, a dual process of *de-materialization* (everything decomposed into a single electronic stream) and *de-literalization* (suspension of all codes under a general rule of visible writings).

The televisual system dreams, if it does, of an immaterial world.

The Postal Axiom

A final word: "Above all, say or think nothing that derails, that jams telecom."[38] With this mock imperative, Derrida sums up everything that programmatology would want to reveal and unravel. (It is the closest thing to a political plan of action in the book.) When it comes to telecom, we can imagine a more Weberian Derrida than before: a Derrida who sees rationality closing in and shutting up. "No, I don't have a big hypothesis about the conjoint development of capitalism, Protestantism, and postal rationalism, but all the same, things are necessarily linked."[39] Which is just the point: he does not try to "explain" the emergence of such linkages but to demonstrate how they cross through anything we might want to say about them. To link, to repeat, to send: Derrida goes through the motions, bristling at the thought of being drawn into the network and knowing it has already happened anyway.

Telecom can be taken in a number of ways—as the mission of Being, the horizon of sense within non-sense, the final destination of everything, or as the immense extension of a system, economic on all levels, whose global logic can be glimpsed in the smooth but crackling flow of televisual images, bombs on this channel, messengers bearing news on another. There can be no question of "ending" television: it has already demonstrated perfect mastery of all discourses of the end, all apocalyptic gestures. We can only imagine the end of television as the continuation of everything on it. Jamming telecom would require a signal of its own, neither negative nor irrational, but one that disintegrates the circuits and postpones any final accession to the program.

EIGHT *Ineluctable Modalities of the Televisual*

> . . . contemplating under Eros the feat of prose ab-
> stracted to a point where no image track occurs.—William Burroughs, *The Ticket
> that Exploded*

Gilles Deleuze and the Natural History of Images

From the start, Gilles Deleuze announces that his books on cinema—
Cinema 1: The Movement-Image[1] and *Cinema 2: The Time-Image*[2]—should
not be mistaken for a history of cinema. And, although he does not say it
as clearly, he also refuses to offer anything like a "film theory," if by that
we mean an interpretive framework for the analysis of cinematic texts.
What his books declare, then, is a "philosophical theory" of images that
understands cinema as a kind of thought in its own right. Deleuze is not
interested in how films *work* but in how they *think*. The project may be
more difficult to locate on our intellectual maps than this description
suggests. Deleuze does not want to treat films "as if" they are philosophical texts, since that way of putting it already privileges philosophy as the
only discourse capable of formulating thought. Nor does he want to
isolate films in a sterile formalism of aesthetic devices. His books, on the
contrary, classify cinema's thoughts according to its own specific preoc-
cupations and problematics. Deleuze claims that his texts serve as a
conceptual "illustration" of specific films, as opposed to theoretical read-

ings that only offer analogies between cinema and some other discourse (such as linguistics or psychoanalysis).[3] Nevertheless, Deleuze cannot escape the temptations of either history or film theory, each having already entered the hall and taken a seat before he got there. As always, his inclination is inclusive: Deleuze finds ways to incorporate the most diverse materials into his patient philosophical spadework, acting as a friendly host who secretly sets out to have his way with everything he touches.

In this spirit—a poststructural pragmatism—I want to use Deleuze to explore the components of the televisual electronic image. It will not be a simple task, however, to locate this image in the massive typological and protohistorical edifice Deleuze has built. The conclusion to his second volume just barely reaches the moment of video before closing down in a mood of vague expectation. It is clear from his closing speculations that video cannot provide the model for an understanding of television, just as cinema cannot finally include all other kinds of image as logical extensions of its laws. When Deleuze claims that television's image "remains so regrettably in the present unless it is enriched by the art of cinema," he does not so much disqualify television from his study of images as indicate an unsolved problem, for it is by no means obvious how images can "remain" in the "present."[4] Indeed this comment suggests that television exceeds, without entirely including, the work of cinema. Television is both more profane and more profuse than cinema or video. The study of television cannot then proceed entirely through a series of great works or emblematic moments; it must be forced instead to explain the modulation between its interminable present tense (which has to be maintained by specific kinds of images) and a fleeting capacity to achieve other kinds of time, based, like cinema, on the fundamental characteristics of its machinery.

In terms of Deleuze's own project, however, television remains an animal that cannot think for itself, however much it scavenges from cinematic ideas (not to mention other fields of thought). If we were interested in proving television's aesthetic worth, Deleuze's negative remarks might be discouraging. But there seems little point in concluding that television is indifferent to thought or in forcing Deleuze to say that television might be as profound as cinema; we can take and leave his tangibly cosmopolitan tastes while still affirming that television produces its own kind of image-thinking. After all, "cinema" has been for a long time more a category of taste, evaluation, and marketing than a term designating distinct practices or operations. Even in Deleuze's usage, "cinema" designates a radical program of "aesthetic research" carried out by a small fraction of filmmakers. Although adjacent to this ongoing practice, television can only be specified within different coordinates: its systematicity—social and temporal—alone defines it. Its intricate stasis of instantaneous multiple transmissions, its tendential synchrony, its impure and inaccessible "present": these are powers that the cinematic image does not possess. And while television blocks the temporal complexities of cinema, video already surges onward without any guarantee that its discoveries will be passed back to its ancestors. Together, television and video come both before and after Deleuze's cinema. They are the unthinking and not-yet-thought image-regimes that oversee his project from the outside. It would seem that only the exteriority of television allows us to think cinema as a history and film theory as a historical discourse in the first place.[5] It can be no accident that Deleuze will locate the fundamental moment of crisis in cinema at a point just when television appeared on the scene.

Deleuze assigns a new set of coordinates to the perennial question of television's relation to cinema. No longer a matter of aesthetic demarcations, the issue here turns around two distinct axes, extensive and intensive. The first axis—the properly discontinuous or circuitous historical vector—indicates to what extent cinema prepared the way for television, projecting and subdividing a space of images and linkages that would be rearranged under new laws of transmission. Alternately, we might ask whether cinema has not always been compensating for its incapacity to transmit images—if, in other words, the dream of television as simultaneous inscription and diffusion has not haunted all cinematic forms from the beginning. Along the second axis—the intensifying vector—cinema's linkages or relays cluster around two mutually reinforcing functions: the formation of subjectivities along with the projection of visible spaces in an "assemblage" of images with changing external limits and variable densities.[6] Since television arrives after cinema has already broken up the strongest relays between subjectivization and visibility, it never takes up the problem of such linkages. Television refuses the modes of relationality and combination with which cinema continues to experiment, to the point where the necessity of linkages between images is itself suspended.

Deleuze, then, offers another way to pose the question of Derrida's "textual system," except that now many of the problems are simply cancelled out. Instead of a deconstructive wrestling with the inevitability of representations and subjective recenterings, Deleuze can easily grant that representation "happens," but only in a kind of meteorological sense, as the movement of an unstable mass of force from one pressure zone to another. It would not be the concept of representation, its ontology, or its truth-claims that matter but the mapping of energies and actions that might be released with any given set of images. Both critiques have abandoned the search for a "ground" outside the commerce of representations, but each understands the constraints of textual programming in different terms. For Derrida the problem is recognizing the guiding hand of logocentrism with its covert essentialisms; for Deleuze the problem is identifying the mixed forces at work in each textual ensemble, which may or may not adhere to the classical binaries of metaphysics. (As this all too quick distinction suggests, any extended comparison of the two thinkers would have to be triangulated through Nietzsche.) Whereas Derrida proves useful in recasting the whole scenario implied by the concept of "communication," Deleuze serves on a somewhat different front, where a descriptive, evasive cartography takes the place of deconstructive reading and where "communication" is no longer a stake to be won or lost. But in the present context, we need not decide between the two, since each way of thinking can generate an image of "television" that does not rely on empirical or psychological essentialisms.

When Deleuze opens the archive of cinema, he discovers that its philosophical dimensions are given from the beginning: if the camera apparatus is supposed to duplicate human visuality, it faces a paradoxical task—how can it replicate a properly continuous movement by breaking it into frozen singular images? In specifying the terms of cinematic thinking, Deleuze warns against two false problems, that of the "realism" of the image and that of the unique or autonomous "perception" of the viewer. Both refer the definition of images to values and processes outside the cinematic situation. To forestall these theoretical temptations, Deleuze turns to Henri Bergson and elaborates his key concept, "the movement-image," from Bergson's *Matter and Memory* (1896).[7] There are several components to a definition of the movement-image. First, "images" are always relations of visibility rather than freestanding pictures or representations. In general, visibility becomes possible when there is a movement from the worldly aggregate of matter to a particular body possessing the capacity for memory. Memory makes it possible for a body to organize the images that pass through it in terms of its own interests and actions. This alteration and reconfiguration of images occurs through one of three mental "powers": the *concept* that translates, the *percept* that contracts, and the *affect* that expands the force of a particular image in relation to the image of oneself.[8]

Just as Bergson understands human memory as part of the open universe of images, Deleuze will begin his analysis of cinema from the scandalous premise that the "viewers" themselves must always be considered images on the same plane as the filmic ones. There is no radical disjuncture, but only various types of movement, between the time and space "onscreen" and the time and space of spectatorship. Thus any contiguity or contact between images—the seen and the seeing—passes through a specific "kind" or type of manufactured image, a "cinematographic concept" whose many forms and permutations Deleuze will classify and describe.[9] At the same time, these relations of visibility can be reconstructed and charted only after the movement between images has passed: the gap between them may be spatial (say, the space of a theatre or the space of montage), but it requires a function of time to connect the points, to give the movement its chance to pass from one body to another. The two primary terms, then, will be movement (the spatial quality of an image-construct) and duration (time treated as a quality of image movements): together they articulate a Whole. The status of the Whole is in turn determined by the parts it allows to take shape as visible images.

Why does Deleuze resort to this Bergsonian language? The simple answer might be, to put phenomenology into reverse, spewing the inward out, forcing consciousness to become a wandering orphan among the things called images.[10] Whatever activities had been assigned to the mind and body—its inward "perception" and "affection" as well as its agency, "action"—now can be formulated as cinematic movement-images (whose three basic varieties bear those designations). (The most important bodily activity—thought itself—must await the crisis of the movement image before it can occur as such in the cinema.) In Bergson's discrediting of so-called natural perception and the ensuing exposition of a dynamic world, Deleuze finds a plane of relations consistent with his repudiation of all depth-hermeneutics. "Physical" and "psychic" realities must be seen in a constant process of combination.[11] What Bergson allows Deleuze to do, surprisingly, is totalize the field of images all the more completely, unhindered by the necessity to refer all images to a single point of reference (the ideal viewer, or Deleuze himself). Before embarking on his immense accounting of cinematic images, he rules out from the beginning several models and premises of contemporary film theory. There is no spectator's dialectic in Deleuze, no duality of projection and introjection, no axiology of experience. Remarkably, there is also no emphasis on "desire" here: coming from a coauthor of *Capitalism and Schizophrenia*, this absence does not mean that the idea has been written out of the account but that it has been written in at the most fundamental level. Whereas "desire" used to be expressed in terms of audiences, now it must be posited as the unifying force of the entire cinematic plane.[12]

Everything passes through the eye and the brain, which are nothing but contingently self-privileging images, really just angled movements, sites of constantly cycled actions and reactions.[13] The "viewing" image's privilege consists in a single aspect—that any movement through it involves an interval, a pause, between touching one of its facets and reaching another. (In the language of *Anti-Oedipus*, this would be called a "conjunctive synthesis.") The deflection of movement that occurs through the "living" image is the basis of subjectivity and the beginning of affect: but instead of allowing that image to assume sovereign powers, Deleuze argues that it constitutes nothing more than a second system of reference alongside the first one (the illimitable Whole of images), both of which belong to the same dynamic plane. Here he glosses Bergson on the two systems of reference:

> The thing and the perception of the thing are one and the same thing, one and the same image, but related to one or other of two systems of reference. The thing is the image as it is in itself, as it is related to all the other images to whose action it completely submits and on which it reacts immediately. But the perception of the thing is the same image related to another special image which frames it, and which only retains a partial action from it, and only reacts to it mediately.[14]

The image "in itself" moves like an atom, striking and colliding with other images in the "objective" universe. The living image then enters that flux by cutting, framing, and selecting other images in accordance with "needs and interests" it develops by virtue of its bodily existence.[15] Thus while the two systems of reference occupy the same space, each is irreducible to the other. (This is how Bergson and Deleuze refuse the Kantian hierarchy—but not the duality—between things and subjects.) Since neither philosophy nor Bergsonian psychology can become the image of all images, Deleuze's account of cinema has to ride a line between textual formalism and affective positivism. His descriptions of particular films can only be "pragmatic" (a central and radical notion for Deleuze and Guattari), that is, confined to an essentially descriptive level, against which all general topographies of the Whole will always be "indeterminate."[16]

Cinema catches Deleuze's eye because it begins without prejudice to the subjective point of view. Its mechanical "duplication" of natural perception cannot help but be unfaithful, opening onto "vast acentered and deframed zones."[17] All processes of reproduction and simulation belong more to the first system of reference (things as movement) than to the second (perspectives as duration), television just as much as cinema. The apparatus itself promises unique and instantaneous access to images that, in their very mechanical randomness, do not appear to have been filtered through a subjective screen, yet are not valorized as more "truthful" for all that. The camera, in other words, makes it possible to lose objects in a nonconscious circulation of images, to snatch things from the universe of intentional gazes. Only images taken in this way can be composed into sets having a mobility beyond that of subjectivity. Deleuze excludes, therefore, noncinematic images where movement is too premature, too much a part of a subjective function of selection. He cites the long exposure photograph, which compresses the random instants of the photographic still through a certain length of time. But a better test case would be the electronic image, where the speed of the apparatus allows for a different kind of movement in the image. Although there would still be a mechanical randomness, there would be no partition of movement into sections or segments. In the electronic image, the indistinction between object and image dissolves into continuous movement, allowing time to pass in a newly automated consistency. (These themes will be taken up later.)

Alongside the Bergsonian scheme Deleuze places Peirce's classification of signs, which are arranged in three tiers: immediate apparence (firstness), dual relationality (secondness), and abstraction (thirdness). When Peirce's terminology is turned toward Bergson's system, semiotic terms come to qualify not meanings but perceptions. With this combined arsenal of terms, Deleuze sets out to present all the possible combinations of movement-images under the sun of visibility, from so-called things to so-called consciousness and back again. Rather than rehearsing all of these categories here, I want to note something else in Deleuze's account, namely, his resolute refusal to be drawn into the swamp of linguistic-based semiotics, into the interminable debates about visual language, and so on. His instinctive cringing from that kind of work does not prevent him, however, from appropriating its vocabulary from time to time to name some zone of his great plane of images. More to the point, we can recognize in the levelling operation waged through Bergson and colored by Peirce the same impulse we see throughout *A Thousand Plateaus,* where Deleuze and Guattari provocatively redefine language in terms of its indirect coercive force, and narrative as nothing more than second-hand "hearsay."[18] Language, then, would have nothing to do with the transmission of a signified content (as we heard Derrida argue above) but instead assembles and regulates signifying regimes, stitching bodies and enunciations together. Instead of a lock-up in the prisonhouse of language, Deleuze and Guattari portray an endless parole: speaking itself appears as a way of serving a life sentence of obedience. With cinema, it would have to be the same thing; instead of resemblances or laws of signification, Deleuze speaks of variable links between ever-changing elements. Thus, no representation, only images in conjunction at different angles and speeds, intersecting aspects of bodies in motion.

The movement-image, however, forms a definite historical force that exhausts all its options within a few generations. It begins with the near-miraculous simultaneity of Bergson and Lumière, and it comes to an end as soon as the circuit of movements that it had allowed has broken down. As Deleuze explains in a *Cahiers du Cinéma* interview about the first book, "I believe that all images combine differently the same elements, the same signs. But any combination is not possible at any moment: for one element to develop, there must be certain conditions, otherwise it is left atrophied or secondary. There are therefore levels of development, each as perfect as it can be, rather than descendants or filiations. In this sense that it is necessary to speak of a natural history rather than a historical history."[19] Under the initial disposition of cinematic elements— the camera shot and the editing cut—Deleuze identifies three basic types of movement-image (perception-image, affect-image, action-image) that are arranged in four varieties of combination or montage. Each montage belongs to a national cinema and a philosophical perspective.[20] A montage develops from a particular attitude toward the material image, an attempt to arrive at different kinds of Wholes from the same given capacity of capturing instants. Thus Griffith's organic realism must use images of the same substance as Eisenstein's staged dialectical conflicts, Renoir's measured exploration of psychic intensities, and Murnau's stark spiritualism. Each option occurs as a distinct activation of the terms of the movement-image.[21] What they have in common, and what in fact defines the entire regime of the movement-image, is the way in which sequences of images are supposed to extend into the responses emitted by those living images called spectators. (I would call these "subjects supposed to see.")[22] Deleuze's keyword for this extension is "sensory-motor link": the phrase recalls both Freudian and formalist postulates assuring that a given construction of images will produce a given reaction. But Deleuze would not say that the response is produced—since perception itself is only activated *as* an image, the sensory-motor link crosses back and forth through a set of references as its immanent principle of unity, its "plane of consistency." It motivates the structure without emanating from a single source.

All of *Cinema 1* rests on the assumption that the sensory-motor link actually works through the movement-image, that is to say, that certain images draw out others reflexively, even up to the climactic "completion" of cinema in the Hitchcockian "mental image" (where an "idea" takes the form of a third image in order to relate two other images).[23] Perhaps the best indication that the sensory-motor link defines the regime of the movement-image is that Deleuze scarcely critiques the idea in the first volume.[24] At the outset of the second book, however, as soon as he has to explain how the order established under the movement-image disintegrates, he must reinvent the concept and apply it retroactively. This shift of thinking is all the more striking because it permits the relation between the two books to be posed in the grand-scale language of his earlier historical thinking, so little in evidence here.[25] Although the movement-image names something more than a discrete era of film history, it has to be posited in those terms first; only later does it become possible to identify what other dimensions it crosses. Throughout Deleuze's richly textured taxonomy, where the shining singularity of each film or director still stands within a rigorously delimited slot, the movement-image attaches to such a vast number of image-sets and worlds that it cannot simply define a proper space of cinema but extends to an entire historical dynamic or wavelength. With its dual reference systems and self-sufficient rules of justification, with its economic cosmology and ergonomic microscopy, the regime of the movement-image is above all one of "reterritorialization": not a general loosening of energies but a strident reclamation of images from both the dazed modern subject and the dispersed social machinery. Like money and words, it works as a general equivalent; also like them, the movement-image can never be isolated from the relations that support it. (Deleuze even reinforces the monetary comparison by naming the two basic processes as reversible formulas—SAS' and ASA'—that recall Marx's circulation models in *Capital*.) The function of the movement-image is everywhere connective, joining images of an "any-space-whatever" to another image elsewhere, across co-efficients of organized time. Each of the idiosyncratic Wholes of the great directors testifies to the same problematic or abstract goal: to splice together objects and subjects in a common milieu of images—a spatial resolution of incommensurable temporalities.

In Deleuze, it becomes possible to ask if the movement-image might have existed in multiple forms beyond cinema. Not to say that cinema simply infected everything else with its logic, but that something like a movement-image surfaces in a range of activities sharing the same abstract (acentered, variable) relations of exchange and mobility. Bergson serves as a native guide in period costume along one such track and stands alongside other contemporary "discoverers" of the movement-image: Einstein and his Special Theory, Cézanne and the early avant-gardes, John Dos Passos, almost-forgotten experimenters in aesthetic cognition,[26] George Herriman, Coco Chanel, Henry Ford,[27] Le Corbusier, and so on. With all of these figures and many more besides, one of two reciprocal movements takes place. Variable elements are brought to bear on a single image that expresses them, or else a single image is varied, multiplied, and distributed throughout the world. Of all the movement-image franchises, however, cinema completes its circuit of reterritorialization most rapidly, returning to its most stable state or simplest formula—the action-image—and repeating it endlessly. Working up its own world of situations and actions, cinema clears a gridwork of formal grooves for its images to travel. That solidification and stratification lets cinema regulate the unpredictable worldly connections that it opens; in effect, it becomes possible for cinema to be constituted as one more machine among others, with the movement-image as its staple commodity.[28] (In this sense Deleuze proposes his own version of the "Culture Industry" thesis.)

For if the ensemble of movement-images defines a set of Wholes constructed according to common axioms of visuality and movement, then the breakdown of that set must bring a cataclysmic reorganization, a massive deterritorialization of the zones enclosed by the movement-image. That reversal forms the familiar two-way hinge between *Cinema 1* and

Cinema 2: not only does the sensory-motor link in cinema become un-coupled, but the time-image emerges within a new state of disorganized exchange networks. Deleuze himself offers a simple two-ply account. "We hardly believe any longer that a global situation can give rise to an action which is capable of modifying it—no more than we believe that an action can force a situation in disclose itself, even partially."[29] At this moment the rational orchestrations of the movement-image cannot find any point of liberating release. Belief—as a power of perception obeying memory—now finds it easy to entertain new kinds of disjunction, dislo-cation, and faithlessness among images. New indiscernible Wholes blur the outlines of the old ones.

The second volume describes this much different kind of regime, where the unity of cinema itself (and much else besides) has been cast into doubt. Deleuze appeals to the "soul of the cinema," its "will to art" as it pursues the kind of thought of which it is capable; this soul, how-ever, scarcely rescues itself from the commercialized juggernaut of the movement-image and the temptations of stratified constructions. To move beyond the movement-image, then, becomes an act of ambiguous rebellion, a refusal of a major power in favor of a minor one (to use another Deleuze/Guattari opposition). This gesture of refusal takes the most errant shapes, although for Deleuze each replaces the spatial-temporal complex of the movement-images with new geometries of con-struction. Images reassert themselves within a distinct temporality, an inhuman universe of time, refusing to be reduced to subjective reference points.

Before following Deleuze any further into the crystal palaces of time-images, I want to reintroduce the question of television, video, and "the electronic image." For if the first part of the twentieth century proved to be a generalized era of reterritorialization under the dual forces of the movement-image—centrifugal one of inclusion under the sign of gener-alized visuality and the centripedal one of subjectivation under the sign of centered visibility—then the time-image must not only effect a deter-ritorialization, but its features must surely be registered in other realms. If, in other words, the auteurist cinema of the postwar era runs against the tide of the movement-image, then so does the television system. The routes of deterritorialization differ in each case, but the two-edged histor-ical framework obliges us to recognize how the powers of the time-image moved into and beyond the cinema, joining a larger, epochal disposition of forces. The radical difficulty in reading Deleuze's second volume will be to see the same short-circuiting force of the time-image elsewhere, in perhaps less auspicious and admirable forms.

Beginning with the inaugural steps taken by Italian neorealism, the support-struts of the American action-image are kicked out, its causal schemes disassembled, and a new element added to the available repertoire of images: the "direct image of time." With a few strokes, Deleuze ingeniously sketches the salient points of neorealism: characters now stand outside events, as spectators in their own right, and narrative takes shape as a *balade,* a voyage and a ballad at the same time.[30] An autonomous "pure optical and sound situation" appears, no longer driven by actions that would tie all its images together. In the vacuum left by the loosened sensory-motor link, cinematic *description* becomes possible. For Deleuze, these developments stray from any careful demarcation of real and imaginary. "[There] is no longer even a place from which to ask" about the distinction, he says.[31] From these initial efforts of postwar disorientation, more follow: Welles, Robbe-Grillet, Ozu, and most centrally, Godard. The latter attempts a special kind of break with the old regime: an autocritique—maybe even a show trial—of the image and a confrontation with its clichés. Since the clichéd image bears the simplest possible sensory-motor links, it becomes Godard's target and weapon all at once.

But none of these images can prevent the reappearance of the movement-image and the reassertion of its two-dimensional force, which appears poised to overcome any film from within at any moment and tighten up its slackened strings of sense. In response, the time-image multiplies its dimensions and layers in order to liberate time from the movements that occupy it and to allow time to form more complex figural "thoughts." Thus the autonomization of sound disengages another "outside" from the realistic synchronies of the image, just as the autonomization of the camera's motions shows how the apparatus itself emits thoughts.[32] Whereas action and perception were previously threaded by a single automatism, now the gap between them is wedged wider by new circuits of the Whole: the crumpled temporalities of the "recollection image" (including flashbacks), the obscure flights of the "dream image," and the encircling approximations of the "world image."[33] In all of these innovations, a "direct image of time" folds out of a stream of movement-images and disorders it by following an "aberrant" and incomplete course. Montage (in the sense of "assembly") becomes a "*montrage,*" a "showing" of images in their singular duration, opticality, and sonority, rather than as raw materials that construct a movement.[34] The "falseness" of the time-image ends up as the only way to tell the truth about cinema's rules of construction.

When Deleuze speaks of an "indiscernibility" between real and imaginary, he wants this zone to be considered an aspect of the object-character of the images, not as the putative confusion of some viewer. The power of indiscernibility developed by the postwar cinema pivots on a structure he calls "crystalline time." A crystal-image always implies two sides, actual and virtual, put in constant correspondence and mutual usurpation, "a double movement of liberation and capture."[35] Coruscating objects, having lost the grounding continuity of action, vibrate in the time of potentiality. Crystalline structures branch off as soon as the image registers the splitting of a present moment into the past and the future, the simultaneous projection of a now and gathering of a past. That gathering occurs as memory, the accretion of subjective reflexes within time. "It is we who are internal to time, not the inverse . . . Subjectivity is never ours, it is time, that is, the soul or the spirit, the virtual."[36] The crystal-image, then, does not bring forth recollections or dreams, nor does it represent time, but it fluctuates between its two temporal aspects, its present actuality and its past virtuality. Deleuze gives the Bergsonian terms for these aspects: "Peaks of present" and "sheets of past."[37] Their only point of encounter is the screen, that is, the brain.[38]

All of these new image-forms should be strikingly familiar once we strip off the cinematic allusions, once we stop reading Deleuze's concepts as brilliant and beautiful descriptions of Resnais or Welles and notice that simultaneous peaks of present and virtual loops of returning past occur in everyday segments of television. It may well be true, however, that these crystalline structures remain transparent, glassy and glossy, emptied of the chromatics that tint the great works of cinema. As we have seen, Deleuze attributes to the highest cinema a capacity for thought, a means of forming concepts that had gone unrealized in the ascendancy of the movement-image. But thinking is precisely what has been lost by these new televisual images: the force of the images is insufficient to break with organic movements and unable to produce a shock that would open the possibility of thought.[39] That kind of shock had been possible under the movement-image as the "spiritual automaton" of newly mechanized vision that jolted its audience into reaction. But this automaton became the achieved solidification of sensory-motor links and was immediately incorporated into commodity culture. The avant-garde failed to safeguard its discoveries.[40] Now, with the time-image, another kind of shock can happen; or rather, two versions of the same disturbance, one totally identified with the schizoid flow of television, the other duplicating that flow in order to think about it. Both forms of shock stay within the automatic ticking of dislocated images; both imply an outside "world" marked only by the cracks between images, not a world that fills and upholds images in themselves. For Deleuze, again, Godard presents the best example of a cinematic practice that confronts the formal emptiness of the shock, rather than merely celebrating it as an estrangement device. What Godard offers is a concept of the cut itself as the interstice between images, as the upsurge of a power of difference in the ruins of the old logics of sense.[41] For its part, television offers disjunction as part of its apparatus: the more complex the televisual system, the greater its powers of dispersive flux.

Is it possible to think a cut in itself? This is the ultimate question Deleuze extracts from Godard and turns into the final decisive question of his own work. And it is the minimum necessary question for any global discussion of televisual flow. The "irrational" cut in Godard's films can be granted its full import: it spurns all syntax and figurality between images, it draws attention to the possibility that the two images being joined are of *different kinds,* it deplores closure as much as it distrusts the openness of a projective rational totalization, and it brings the noise of sound to the pitch of a perpendicular interruption. (Deleuze accounts for dislocated sound by dubbing it a "sound image" [*image sonore*].)[42] But the televisual cut seems invisible and silent, squeezed on both sides by the most stratified, most regulated blocks of images—yet only the cut allows us to recognize the flow in the first place. Already in *Anti-Oedipus,* Deleuze and Guattari had theorized the relation of interruptions and flows as the serial linkage between machines.[43] A drastic rewriting of the notion of televisual flow would have to account for the multidimensionality of cutting and for the persistence of visual forces beyond syntax and interruptions. Or we could insert quite different terms—using neither "ideology" in the classical sense nor "discourse" in the Foucauldian sense—by recognizing that the limit-question for television can never be "what will it refuse to show?" Instead, the question becomes "what will television refuse to cut, or cut between?" An image, cut or combination would be "impossible" only if every possible linkage had been fixed in advance—but they never are.

Deleuze recognizes that the "electronic image" implies in its very structure the possibility of the most radical cuts: the integrity of the frame is at last violated and images can now surge up from any part of the screen.[44] The image never fully appears because it is always cut laterally anyway, since strips of blackness persist, forever unlit, while tracks of luminosity sweep past.[45] Even granting that television offers visual resemblances or approximations, televisual cutting still has nothing to do with the "grafting" of codes, the so-called polysemy or intertextuality with which so many cultural critics are anxious to credit it; cutting never brings a complete translation or exchange between codes but only a scattering, a dispersal, a deterritorialization of codes.[46] On a television network, through the syntax of sponsorship and corporate identity, those codes can reterritorialize themselves again in new locales, drawing together a set of linkages, warding off semantic contaminations, claiming temporary property rights over a zone of signification. In that sense, cutting is also a fundamental operation in the capture of time. It isolates discrete sites in which codes can be modulated and multiplied in increasingly narrow variations, even while being deployed across longer spans of time. Since instantaneous cuts "connect" boxed-in quantities of movement only in this very special sense, reading a series of cuts in terms of an intelligible sequence will recuperate only a part—the programmable part—of the whole assemblage.

Now, before we turn to these televisual matters in the next section, one major question remains to ask Deleuze: what, finally, is the historical status of the time-image? Already I have suggested—staying generally within the Deleuzian framework—that while the movement-image was a properly cinematic concept, its lineaments extended in a number of directions. As industrial product and mechanized optic in one, the movement-image fulfills Debord's definition of the image as the highest stage of commodity reification. With the time-image, however, we face a gradual dissolution of that logic in the remotest artworks and the most everyday image-flows. The spectacle, if we keep the word, undergoes the same cutting that the movement-image had. If it no longer assumes a direct extension to the spectators, that is because images have achieved an unexpected new level of totalization. No longer functioning according to the spatial imperative (to be seen, to make something visible), images now switch into another register, directly intermingled with the temporal fluxes and turnover times of economy and information. The appearance of the time-image presupposes the generalization and concretization of movements carried out by the previous regime. Now, zig-zagging through the well-programmed machines with their well-worn physical and ideological automatisms, the time-image offers a respite from the heavy-handed representational blows of the movement-image.[47] At one end, a refusal of sense for those who throw away their time in reckless abandon; and at the other, suspension of sense for those who try to look for a meaningful world anywhere on television, even for just a moment. For, as we will now see, television produces a time-image the moment it has been turned on—which is to say, regardless of whether it is turned on for anyone in particular. Televisual time is already in the air, lofted in the world's atmosphere and running rings around earthly existence. No longer the core of psychic life or the continuum on which everything finds its place, but time as the infinitesimal fissuring of an interminable present.

Aloft in the Stilly Light

To catch television in flight, a conceptual filter has to be held up against the glare of images. So far we have been following Nam June Paik's intuition—shared by many critics since—that the fundamental concept of television is *time*.[48] It precedes and envelops any semiotic: As the previous chapters have argued, time is the substance of television's visuality, the ground of its ontology, and the currency of its economy. Television has been analyzed as a machine for the prodigious regulated construction and circulation of time. Its limited morphology of representation obeys strictly temporal constraints. There is a structuring movement of flow and segmentation, certainly, but also speeds of transmission and diffusion, intensities of filling and draining that alter images as if from within. An adequate conceptualization of time as an open-ended process of composition and decomposition is a precondition for any homology between televisual images and exchange value, not to mention any discussion of how television's systemic *visuality* accounts for the contingent subjective processes of *visibility*. Time must be theorized at the greatest level of generality without taking for granted that it bears sense, narration, or discursivity.

A basic proposition: Time moves in two directions on television, toward the still and toward the automatic. By "still" I mean the breaking of one movement of images (matter in motion) by a kind of mechanical movement (inscription). The still depends upon a subjectivizing formation, a provisional image of subjectivity, for its linkages. By "automatic" I mean the extension of a movement by another kind of mechanical movement (illumination and scanning). The automatic is that which generates an autonomous series and requires no interval to pass through a subjective formation. With television, the mechanical movements that break up the instantaneous and charge up the continuous are in fact inseparable. Neither kind of time necessarily allows the appearance of a visible image—television does not always produce one. Nor are these concepts bound to an idea of perception: both the still and the automatic can occur at speeds separated from human existential reality—indeed, that is the whole point of trying to think about them. Still and automatic time constitute the intensive and extensive limits of the apparatus itself, and depending on which kind of time is assumed to be dominant, television will take on quite varied characteristics. What some descriptions of television register as fragmentation, reification, and formal heterogeneity can be more fully grasped in terms of diffracted slices of still time, and what strikes us as television's compression of distance and presence is perhaps better understood as its capacity for automatic time. These are not the same vectors circumscribing cinema, cybernetics, photography, or print, although television can intersect all of these. Every process of recording and inscription enfolds a certain temporal mode, each with its specific forces of retention, transportation, and repetition.[49] With television, all discursive forms and figural strategies draw upon the forces of the instantaneous and the automatic in order to generate distinctive temporal shapes approximating narration, distance, and even history.[50]

The temptation to read some kind of invariable "content" into temporalities is strong. Let me cite two strongly suggestive examples. In a brief essay titled "TV in Two Parts," Hal Foster names "two ultimate (?) 'forms' of capitalized time" on television: "the fetishistic and the fluent," the fragmentary and the flowing.[51] What Foster wants to identify—in a brilliant shorthand borrowing modernist and psychoanalytical terms—is not so much the geometry of televisual time as a particular logic of consumption: on one hand, severed instants that seem to trap and burn off desire in a high-speed combustion cycle; on the other hand, sustained images that seem to loosen viewing time into an ambient sensory emptiness. However apt these characterizations may seem—and I will allude to Foster's terms as I go—it is worth wondering if these kinds of time will always bear these functions. As I suggested in Chapter 2, the link between television and contemporary capitalism is extremely mobile: the circuits of valorization trace countless configurations of time. By the same token,

May Ann Doane's tripartite distinction between temporalities of "information, crisis and catastrophe" designates an easily recognizable scheme in our current televisual system—where events are defined by different transmission times—but there is no reason to suppose that other systems, in other places and historical moments, will not have found various ways to rescale, reverse and rearrange these categories.[52] If what counts as "information" or "catastrophe" has to do with different rates of presentation, we may expect television (and the systems joined to it) to invent new ways of storing, altering and restaging events, so that "information, crisis, and catastrophe" may become consumer options rather than modes of dissemination still obeying the temporality of some Real.

Still and automatic time operate as thresholds in an alternating current: the instant disrupts the continuous and vice versa. In film, the simplest kind of interruption is a "cut," recalling the snip of scissors and the handmade splice. On television, the cut has been overtaken by the "mix" or the "switch," which makes every change of image an occasion for potential displacement. (Deleuze names a cinematic variant: the "irrational cut.")[53] It does not matter who makes the mix or the switch; the point is that mixes and switches can always be made and that every image "begins" and "ends" that way. Although we can only talk about "seeing" what happens as a mixture of still and automatic time, the mix or the switch structures seeing. It marks the place of the virtual world of images, and the switch may or may not break, connect, rupture, blend, close, or open.

Hence still time is not a moment of capturing a picture and making an object of it, as in photography. Televisual stills are created by switching away from a picture, pushing past one toward another, by halting a movement or adding a different one. And these stills do not add up or follow one another: each turns over and disappears from view. Meanwhile, automatic time appears when an image is switched on and left running, so that it is no longer an image *of something*: it is the time of the camera's relentless stare, persisting beyond the movements of objects and scenery that pass before it. If still time slices off images and designates them as past, then automatic time opens onto an anticipated future: it is an image waiting for its event to happen.

At the extreme, still time could be achieved only as a series of pure instants, without any relation whatsoever, like a bottomless trash pile of snapshots or postcards. And—here is first paradox—this pure still time would have to be moving so fast across the plane of transmission that images would have no time to drop their loads, to deliver messages, to enter into syntactic or narrative chains. They could not be, strictly speaking, discernible. Baudrillard has spoken of television as a "succession of instants,"[54] but this is only part of the story: such a succession posits a viewer, any viewer, for whom this randomness could be registered (for example, that newly born mythical figure, the zapper). Even in the high-speed switching of zapping, however, a sheer succession of instants would invert the formula and make something visible: namely, the apparatus and its matrix of virtual temporalities. As television extends the range of its virtual images, diegetic or discursive time unwinds under a new pressure to sum itself up at every instant. The "moment" can no longer afford to be simply an incomplete part of a whole; now every instant can be placed in a number of different series which expand the parameters of the image's outside totality or world. (Recall that, for Deleuze, an accessible Whole was the absolute presupposition of the movement-image.) Jean-Luc Godard has commented on this possibility. "If you watch three television programs, even for ten minutes, this doesn't give you three times ten equals thirty minutes, but perhaps three hours, sometimes thirty hours, sometimes even three thousand hours . . . [Zapping] escapes these three thousand hours to reduce them to one true minute."[55] The important point about zapping is not that it gives the viewers a new way to chase their pleasures across the channels. In fact, zapping draws on a force already built into the televisual image from the start, a cleaving force that refers the image not only to the innumerable points of visibility called viewers but also to other streams of images, unseen, which nevertheless share the same moment and which always stand ready to emerge into a new present. If, recalling Foster, we think of these images in terms of capital, the instant image can be seen as a tentative response to this threat, a way to economize on the time costs of meanings and desires. It floats images at the smallest possible exchange rate, saving expenditures to maximize distribution.[56]

Conversely—and here is the second paradox—automatic time, the unending effusion of visuality that might have seemed closer to the steady gaze of the eye, eventually leads away from the fits and starts of perception toward an implacable and unplaceable collection of spatialized data. Automatic time runs through the operations of video scanning, where a field and a frame become flattened surfaces for gathering, arranging, and combining sets of images. On a continuously modulated screen surface, layers can be superimposed and blended, allowing the eruption of new

spaces out of the middle of previous ones.[57] Changing camera angles
becomes unnecessary, for the field of objects itself can be adjusted or
moved by the camera's processor (as in computer-guided animation).[58]
Continuous time allows for the loosest possible attachment to the image
as expression and the greatest possible imposition of a total temporality,
thereby replacing a logic of subjective visibility with an environment of
machinic visuality.

Bounded by these abstract limits, everything else, all actually existing
television, is constructed by combining forces of stilling and extending
time. In fact, the practical range of any given system may be quite small:
where traditional representational tactics still hold sway, still and automatic time will only appear in muted, tendential forms. Even so, North
American television, as the dominant international form, has developed
at least a rudimentary repertoire of time-designs. Still time, the flurry
of instants, occurs most commonly on music videos and commercials.
Rapid or meandering images, with unpatterned or erratic framings, offer
fleeting glimpses of things, a collection of scenes and objects that neither
compose nor contain one another. In those cases, however, the rapid
flight of images is reined in by the presence of a single commodity (or, in
the case of music video, an autonomous, automatic sound-image) that
serves as a separate referent or interpretant for the entire set. It should
not be surprising that the still, in this dissipated form, has been reasserted
as the most direct presentation of commodities, especially those most in
need of imaginary differentiation or ideological tinting (pop singles, fashion clothing, automobiles, political candidates). Since a stack of instants
does not present a thing but a proliferation of aspects of things, still time
lends itself well to repetition and rhythm. In its fastest state, the instant
image constitutes the minimal unit of televisual aesthetics, the smallest
interval for the activation of sensory-motor reactions, and the most intense fusion of subjectifying and objectifying image making processes.

At the other end, automatic time belongs to a specifically televisual
epistemology, occurring most often in nominally "live" televisual situations: sporting events, televangelism, air raids, and to a lesser extent,
various direct address presentations, such as State of the Union speeches
and emergency bulletins. Automatic time is pitched at the level of the
pure event, the direct, the scene that speaks for itself. A number of critics
have commented on the ideological uses of "live" television (see Chapter
1); the significant point here is that automatic time does not necessarily
take on the trappings of nowness or "real time"; it maintains its own

consistency and control by limiting when and where internal switches can occur. In fact, the "live-effect" can only be produced by a certain pattern of switching away from and into automatic time, often using two series of images that confront each other as "simultaneous." The presentation of "presence" always refers elsewhere for confirmation, even if it is nothing more than the little word "LIVE" electronically pasted over an image. At one extreme, the sudden and sustained irruption of automatic time on television (the emergency broadcast) constitutes a new kind of microhistorical event, a disruption of everyday existence with far greater capacity for provoking general terror than car bombs or Scud missiles.[59]

If there is a universal archetype or ur-form of mixed televisual time, it must be "the news." Every national system has a news broadcast, and now with CNN, every system can have the same one. News offers itself as the most immediate, most disjointed production of a world assembled by a constant vigilance, where all rays of representation leave and return to a single point, that is, the newsreader's face. (Here, like much of television, faciality remains a central signifying paradigm.)[60] The basic range of time is deployed, zigzagging between still instants and automatic continuities. The mode of presentation can perhaps best be grasped as the inverse of the theoretical language called "overdetermination": instead of combining and multiplying relations between images, television news disconnects and abandons them.

Nevertheless, neither still nor automatic time can reach a final end point or fulfillment, where each would finally become the other—though video art offers much more extreme if fleeting possibilities. (Nam June Paik came to video because he found the temporal disciplines of zen too boring.) Fredric Jameson has made the suggestion that we should pay attention to the way video temporality allows for the simulated appearance of "fictive time" on commercial television.[61] To pursue this idea, we would have to imagine all of television's programs (including series, serials, and even broadcast films themselves) as spectral islands of residual visibility floating along a homogenous, imperceptible layer of time. Simulated fictive time can be posited only on the ground of an absolutely mechanical present tense, always occurring elsewhere first—a temporality that is, precisely, the metaphysical center of television understood as communication, representation, and visibility. Commercials, announcements, and station breaks, in the service of that present tense, mark out fictive time by retroactively dividing it into subcontracted zones. Fictivity, narrativity, even associability are nothing but local effects allowed by (rather than threatened by) the differentiation of time. Insofar as all television has been programmed by rules of segmentation and scheduling, brand-name and generic rules of drama develop within general guidelines regulating the consistency, repeatability, and interruptability of a time scene/scheme. (Hence sitcoms and series tend toward features of still time—interchangeability and repeatability—whereas serials exhibit a more automatic form, linear and incomplete.) I would revise Jameson's account only to point out that simulated fictive time can no longer be considered filmic, since it must already be suffused by the imperatives of transmission, caught in the grid of distinctions and the gearbox of speeds that drive televisual programming. It is not "things" or "situations" that are reproduced, represented, or even simulated, but the archaic speeds of their appearing.[62] Or, put another way, from the perspective of overall programming, it does not matter what visual scheme operates within each slot, as long as some power—a network, the state—can claim to control the series of switches. This is why every staging of the present tense calls most directly on the political and economic concentrations of power that make television possible. Since the opposition between the fictive time of segments and the equally fictive real time of the apparatus occurs at the simplest level (the differentiation of representational forms), it does not correspond to the crossed vectors of still and automatic time, which constitute the plane where all kinds of time are produced and circulated. What appears "fictive" after a single switch may become instantaneous after several; what arrives as "live" may be switched across a couple of instants to become something more remote and uncertain.

Again it is worth saying something about video cassette recorders, if only to forestall the objection that the vcr changes everything. As I suggested in more technical terms earlier, vcrs do nothing but extend the range of still and automatic time, offering an additional loop of flexibility in the circulation of images, bringing new speeds and greater turnover. When it is not opening its own automatic time during recording or playback, the vcr machine allows its own kind of instantaneous switching, where images can be slowed or virtually stopped. Since a videotape contains images only in their decomposed linear state—as a series of spatialized instants—it does not escape the boundaries of the still and the automatic. By permitting another form of tactile participation with the apparatus, video allows people to operate another series of switches, a privilege bought with more time, money, and subjective attachment. The fundamental question is economic: who profits from this new and immense expansion in the volume of overall televisual time? The answers have been clear: paranational electronics manufacturers and entertainment conglomerates, who are integrating vertically as fast as possible. The VCR and all of the newer systems testify to the deliverance of the televisual system from the demands of solely representational unities in favor of multidirectional technological solutions.

With the ongoing distribution of video cameras and recorders to larger segments of the world population, it becomes even harder to imagine that there will be a single ramified televisual "system." But that is precisely the concept I want to retain by speaking of time, of its speeds and linkages. Although, to be sure, television is unevenly distributed throughout the honeycombed cells of global culture, we cannot speak of autonomous enclaves of video. Even when video images do not share the same screens with television broadcasting (as in a museum), they take the latter as their raw material or point of cancellation; there is no point of exteriority from which video could escape television.[63] (Deleuze might say that there are countless points from which video could "falsify" television by disturbing its habitual patterns, but this is a different enterprise indeed.) In an immediate technological and spatial sense, video images never stand alone but are always strung out on lines leading back to ordering processes of commercial television (no matter who runs it). Rather than providing a unitary "language" of video, then, television can assert its rights of translation over any image-production whatsoever—"translation" in the sense of having the power to alter and inflect the textual framework through which a set of images might be understood.

As it spreads into a world of its own making, television, like all other kinds of writing, develops its own analytic of the Real, which it alone makes visible and which it alone maps. Once still and automatic time are recognized not as forms of experience but as television's tools of "analysis"—its methods of construction and breakdown—then its images do not need to be interpreted as much as located in their diverse sets and series, in their sectors of distribution and valorization. Every kind of analysis can be defined by sets of elements—characters, situations, drives, things, languages—which are arranged in various permutations and pushed toward limit-cases. With television, the limit was given from the beginning: the impossibility of connecting and communicating its singular components into a single absolute world. Every transmission makes a gesture, a feint really, toward this transcendent impossibility. (Recall Lacan's comment about impossibility and the Real, quoted here in the preface.) What we get instead are myriad projected encirclements, various ways in which a particular assemblage of images posits a complete world in order to claim dominion over other assemblages of images. In that operation, television uses the techniques of still time to trace unstable relays leading across a social-cultural space that never solidifies, bound by its very diffusion, composed of serialized viewers and incomplete imaginary triangulations. Still time does not form a geometry of relationships: its instants may repeat or interfere with each other without generating a common charge. Automatic time, on the other hand, opens a distanceless conduit to any elsewhere: it forms a hollow world, its surface seen only from the inside.

One time-speed scatters, the other encloses, and both override the point of conjunction where watching television would take on the temporality of some other action—work or play, remembering or forgetting, contemplation or distraction. As a result, its currents of time are still clogged by the rattling chains of representation, with links broken or missing, yet carried by the velocity of televisual circulation. The dynamics of causality, sequence, and logical order are subjected to the demands and exigencies of more abstract temporalities. Of course, nothing prevents television from transmitting the most severe formalisms or didacticisms, except that such constructions will always be underwritten and overwritten by the rules of economic valorization. Any radical intervention aiming at a momentary unification or transgression of televisual images would face yet another paradox: should television be drawn back into the order of representation, there to answer for its apostasy from "reason" and "truth"? Or, on the contrary, is it possible to understand television's heterogeneity in terms of an overall strategy, where the whole dissemination of images ultimately and doggedly "represents" the reality of a dissimulated state of power? In order to propose this kind of hypothesis, the old terminology of reflection (where the superstructure mirrors the base) would return, with the proviso that this kind of representation has become general and immanent in the domain it claims. Television would "reflect" the global situation in the same way the stratosphere reflects signals back to earth, a concavity where rays cross and scatter.

If this metaphoric description does not quite work, it is because it requires a totalizing framework specifically prevented by the instantaneous and automatic speeds of the apparatus itself. Television establishes the mechanics of a global representation without being able to perform it, just as capitalism itself has put in place the means of exploitation without being able to crank it up everywhere. But if, from time to time, a sudden show of force is required, that can be arranged: if anyone doubted the strength of television's brutal superimposition of economics and ideology, it is there for all to see in the quick switch from video-guided missiles hitting Iraq to the CNN reporter in Atlanta reading the incoherent official script of legitimation to a watching and waiting world. As I have been suggesting, the switching and mixing does all the work, organizing actual images even while it "represents" nothing in the usual sense. The Futurists, as Benjamin reminds us in the artwork essay, would have regarded such switches as objects in themselves and no doubt found them beautiful.

It is tempting to regard this expansive visual network as the culmination of the surveillance system Foucault traced to the nineteenth-century Panopticon. No doubt video, coupled with computers, has made it possible to manage massive spaces visually (or, as with the Rodney King tape, to make the agents of control visible as well). But even if the Panopticon still seems to be a good metaphor for all the electronic data banks and security systems ringing multinational capital, it does not clarify the necessity of new distributions of culture carried out through television and its newer extentions. For if telecommunications in general is pursuing a logic of ever greater diversification and differentiation, there can be no panoptic focal point. How can this matrix be understood in terms of power? Deleuze has suggested that the panoptic disciplinary systems have been thrown into crisis, giving way to "societies of control" populated by amorphous capitalist enterprises. There is a corresponding shift in figures: as rigid discipline spreads out and becomes flexible control, the "enclosed" subject becomes the "indebted" subject.[64] Here, then, we can recognize the prototypical television viewer: in exchange with the screen a revolving debt is incurred, one payment is dispensed while the other is held back, so that an obligation and an interest are set against the future. Above and beyond the work we perform by watching television every day, there is still the promise to return. For debt is above all a model of temporal orientation. It persists because the debtor has promised a reciprocal action, a service for a service. When television is no longer offered as a single expressive event (the voice and visage of Authority), each act of viewing becomes charged with the responsibility of fabricating its own present tense, affirming the basic transaction while watching for a message, waiting to see what comes next. The televisual bargain will last, moment by moment, image by image, as long as we feel we owe something to television, whether it is the solemn duty to find sense in what we see or the sweet burden to pursue our pleasures there. Whereas automatic time demands that we keep watching, still time demands that we keep switching; driven by these two pressures, the image onscreen extends its claim over other images, near and distant, already past and yet to come.

But if we insist on the possibility of seeing the future anew, delivered from the constraints of this unbearable present time, our eyes ought to be trained not on television but on the active and critical powers of thought.

NOTES

Preface

1   Jacques Lacan, *Télévision* (Paris: Seuil, 1974), 9. I have slightly modified the translation appearing as "Television," trans. Denis Hollier, Rosalind Krauss and Annette Michelson, *October* 40 (Spring 1987): 7.

2   Michael Speaks has, in an as yet unpublished study, argued that "architectural thinking" is a way of constructing images of space no less decisive than built space itself. My use of the notion of "theoretical images" is meant to complement his position in architectural theory.

3   George Gilder, *Life After Television* (Knoxville, TN: Whittle Direct Books, 1990). This peculiar text, with its dramatic predictions, its free market animus toward television, and its Federal Express advertising, deserves an analysis I cannot provide here. It is becoming more common to hear business ideologists champion telephone-based communication systems as an effective way to erode the "liberal" media system.

One. The Outbreak of Television

1   Pascal Bonitzer writes: "The image of television . . . is not in itself an image: it is an image of images. It reproduces and diffuses all images . . . obliging them to pass by the program grid, by this special regulation of time, this comic homogenization of events which is its specific work. The Audiovisual . . . is this double phenomenon: the disparity but also the homogenization of images in a continuum." "Les Images, le cinéma, l'audiovisuel," *Cahiers du Cinéma* 404 (February 1988): 17–21. As images of television go, this is an excellent one; it is nevertheless only one possible image ("television" as transcendence and unification).

2   For an evocative treatment of total "telereality," see Paul Virilio, "La lumière indirecte" *Communications* 48 (1988): 45–52.

3   Rudolf Arnheim, *Radio,* trans. Margaret Ludwig and Herbert Read (London: Faber and Faber, 1936; reprint, New York: Arno Press, 1971), 229–30.

4   Dziga Vertov, *KINO-EYE: The Writings of Dziga Vertov,* ed. Annette Michelson, trans. Kevin O'Brien (Berkeley: University of California Press, 1984), 56.

5   Jean-Paul Fargier, "Le Cinéma plus l'électricité," *Cahiers du Cinéma* 406 (April 1988): 56–7. Fargier endorses Vertov's idea that television would overthrow cinema by making "direct" representations possible. See also V.I. Lenin, "Report on the Work of the Council of People's Commissars (December 22, 1920)," *Selected Works,* vol. 3, 512: "Communism is Soviet power plus the electrification of the whole country."

6   Jean-Paul Sartre, *Critique of Dialectical Reason,* vol. 2, trans. Quintin Hoare (London: Verso, 1991), 438. Henceforth cited in the text as CDR II.

7   Sartre describes the phenomenological dimension of the practico-inert as a return of dead praxis "from the outside" to direct living praxis. "Destiny" therefore takes on a specific sense: it is "the future inscribed in the practico-inert," or, to put it in another code, the investment of our possibilities in the objects surrounding us. Jean-Paul Sartre, *Critique of Dialectical Reason,* vol. 1, trans. Alan Sheridan-Smith (London: Verso, 1976), 828; see also 259. Henceforth cited as CDR I.

8   See Sartre, CDR I, 270–76 (about radio), 277–93 (about the market), 642–54 (about the Top Ten). For a nondialectical account of television in terms of seriality, see Arthur Kroker and David Cook, *The Postmodern Scene: Excremental Culture and Hyper-Aesthetics* (New York: St. Martin's Press, 1986), 270–72.

9   Although presented in the specific language of my discussion above, these three components bear an intended resemblance to Fredric Jameson's definition of a *medium* in terms of "three relatively distinct signals: that of an artistic mode or specific form of aesthetic production, that of a specific technology, generally organized around a central apparatus or machine; and that, finally, of a social institution." *Postmodernism, or, the Cultural Logic of Late Capitalism* (Durham: Duke University Press, 1991), 67. In the following pages I hope to show how, with television, some of these signals become rather less distinct.

10 Raymond Williams, *Television: Technology and Cultural Form* (New York: Schocken, 1974). Henceforth cited as *Television.*

11 Williams, *Television,* 14.

12 For some play on these words set in a discussion of these issues, see Barbara Herrnstein Smith, *Contingencies of Value: Alternative Perspectives for Critical Theory* (Cambridge, MA: Harvard University Press, 1988), 122.

13 Williams, *Television,* 24.

14 Ibid., 25. Williams's emphasis.

15 Roy Armes, *On Video* (New York: Routledge, 1988), 61. Since much of the information in the following pages has been presented in a number of sources, I will cite these sources only for specific details. Besides, the history and mechanics of television are practically the stuff of legend.

16 For more on the contrast between alphabetic writing and television, see Chapter 7 on Derrida.

17 Brian Winston, *Misunderstanding Media* (Cambridge, MA: Harvard University Press, 1986). For a more sophisticated discussion of the issues involved here, see Wiebe E. Bijeker, Thomas P. Hughes, Trevor J. Pinch, eds., *The Social Construction of Technologi-*

cal Systems, (Cambridge, MA: MIT Press, 1987). In the essay "The Social Construction of Facts and Artifacts," Pinch and Bijeker propose a "social constructivist" account, in which groups, technical problems and solutions are mapped as "molecular" constellations subject to various pressures. Another essay in the same volume, Steve Woolgar's "Reconstructing Man and Machine: A Note on Sociological Critiques of Cognitivism," argues that technology has to be seen as a site of continual negotiation over the status of "man." In rather different terms, this idea will be raised in Chapter 6.

18 Ibid., 54.

19 *World Radio and Television Handbook* (Copenhagen: Billboard, 1991), 353.

20 Williams, *Television,* 28–29.

21 As the debates within the music industry show, digital technology can replace "high fidelity" analog equipment simply by claiming its own standards of "fidelity." For a discussion of the analog/digital distinction, see Anthony Wilden, *System and Structure: Essays in Communication and Exchange,* 2d ed. (London, 1980).

22 Eric Barnouw, *Tube of Plenty,* rev. ed. (New York: Oxford University Press, 1982), 78.

23 Joseph H. Udelson, *The Great Television Race: A History of the American Television Industry 1925–1941* (Tuscaloosa: University of Alabama Press, 1982), 31. This is undoubtedly the best history of the early experiments and regulations that guided the development of television. Though Udelson champions some of the lone inventors of television, it is clear from his evidence that corporate investment shaped the establishment of the system from the beginning.

24 Ibid., 51.

25 John Hanhardt, ed., *Video Culture: A Critical Investigation* (Rochester, NY: Visual Studies Workshop, 1986), 18.

26 The key text on the theoretical significance of sound recording and film is Alan Williams, "Is Sound Recording Like A Language?" *Yale French Studies* 60 (1980), 51–66. Williams makes special reference to Godard.

27 Keith Geddes and Gordon Bussey, *Television: The First Fifty Years* (London: National Museum of Photography, Film and Television, 1986), 5; Armes, *On Video,* 56–57.

28 Armes, *On Video,* 57–8.

29 For more information, see Armand Mattelart, Xavier Delcourt and Michele Mattelart, *International Image Markets: In Search of an Alternative Perspective,* trans. David Buxton (London: Comedia Publishing Group, 1984). The authors point out that television has become the dominant channel for the distribution of United States audiovisual products, representing a new alliance between satellite-broadcasting companies and film producers (78–80).

30 Winston, *Misunderstanding,* 89; Armes, *On Video,* 76.

31 For a popular account of this history, see James Lardner, *Fast Forward: Hollywood, the Japanese, and the VCR Wars* (New York: New American Library, 1987). For a theoretical and historical account, see Jane Gaines, *Contested Cultures: Image Properties in the Industrial Age* (Chapel Hill: University of North Carolina Press, 1991).

32 For a discussion of this phenomenon, see Sean Cubitt, *Timeshift: On Video Culture* (New York: Routledge, 1991), 21–43. Unfortunately, some of Cubitt's appropriations of poststructural theory are premature. Despite a reference to Derrida's *Grammatology,* he likens the videotaping of television to the writing of oral speech: "Through video, television can cease to be a slave to the metaphysics of presence" (Cubitt, *Timeshift,*

36). I try to show in Chapters 2 and 7 why this would have to be considered a radical misunderstanding.

33 John Fiske, *Television Culture* (New York: Methuen, 1987), 311.

34 A wealth of information on video is available in Manuel Alvarado, ed., *Video World-Wide* (Paris: UNESCO, 1988).

35 Williams, *Television*, 145.

36 Raymond Williams, "Means of Communication as Means of Production," in *Problems of Materialism and Culture* (London: New Left Books, 1980), 55.

37 For a review of the literature on the topic, see David Buckingham, "Television Literacy: A Critique," in *Radical Philosophy* 51 (Spring 1989): 12–25.

38 Bertolt Brecht, "The Radio as an Apparatus of Communication," in *Brecht on Theatre*, trans. John Willett (New York: Hill and Wang, 1964), 52. See also Brecht's "Radio as a means of communication," trans. Stuart Hood, *Screen*, 20, no. 3/4 (Winter 1979/80): 24–28, where Brecht takes the position that radio was invented as a "means of production" before it had the raw material to work on. Like Williams, Brecht believes that radio could become a two-way communication. Now, under television's ascendancy, radio can begin to offer some kinds of local, alternative broadcasting space.

39 Williams, *Television*, 30.

40 Ibid., 86.

41 Ibid., 92.

42 Ibid., 105.

43 Ibid., 118.

44 Raymond Williams, *Towards 2000* (London: Chatto and Windus, 1983), Chapter 5, "Culture and Technology."

45 For an account of this important project, an experiment in collective organization and public access politics as much as video production, see Dee Dee Halleck, "The Wild Things on the Banks of Free Flow," in Doug Hall and Sally Jo Fifer, eds., *Illuminating Video: An Essential Guide to Video Art* (New York: Aperture, 1990), 259–66; and Dee Dee Halleck, "Watch Out, Dick Tracy! Popular Video in the Wake of the Exxon Valdez," in Constance Penley and Andrew Ross, eds., *Technoculture* (Minneapolis: University of Minnesota Press, 1991), 211–29.

46 That separation, at least, is not up for flow: wavelength bands are closely regulated by governments; to "step on" sovereign frequencies is tantamount to an incursion of airspace, although the United States has yet to admit guilt over the Television Martí broadcasts to Cuba.

47 I am summarizing data culled from the *World Radio and Television Handbook* and Philip T. Rosen, ed., *International Handbook of Broadcasting Systems* (Westport, CT: Greenwood Press, 1988). Ownership of television sets, on the other hand, is still a matter of class privilege throughout much of the Third World. In one of the strongest African systems, Nigeria (with 34 stations) there are 10 million sets (approx. one for every 10 people), more than South Africa; in Zaire, by contrast, there are 20,000. Mozambique, in 1990, still had only 35,000 sets, and a weekly total of 24 hours of programming. (For more on the Mozambique situation, see the final section of this chapter.) The effects of underdevelopment are always more visible in the production sector, but poorer Third World countries like Mozambique and Tanzania refuse to spend large amounts of foreign exchange capital for broadcasting facilities, well aware

of the continual outlay of further capital it would require. Analogies to the infamous Nestlé baby food operation in the early eighties come to mind: the cultivation of dependency. For essays on the topic, see also Cynthia Schneider and Brian Wallis, eds., *Global Television* (Cambridge, MA: MIT Press, 1989).

48   The relevant statistics can be found in Tapio Varis, *International Flow of Television Programs* (Paris: UNESCO, 1985).

49   The word has also broken into French theoretical language: see Marc Vernet, "Incertain zapping" and Dominique Chateau, "L'effet zapping," in *Communications* 51 (1990). Both see zapping primarily as a rebellion against advertising; Vernet even cites a J. Walter Thompson study as his primary evidence, where zapping and its cousins "flipping" and "grazing" pose a threat to the stability of the ratings system. Since ratings are basically the media oligarchy's convenient fiction, these terms and their assumptions about attention spans and viewing habits have no theoretical weight.

50   John Ellis, *Visible Fictions: Cinema Television Video* (London: Routledge, 1982), 112–26.

51   Ibid., 122–23.

52   Jane Feuer, "The Concept of Live Television: Ontology as Ideology," in E. Ann Kaplan, ed., *Regarding Television* (Frederick, MD: University Publications of America, 1983), 15–16. This is perhaps a good place to note the persistent use of gerunds in the titling of books on television: watching, reading, understanding, misunderstanding, regarding, opening, illuminating, viewing, etc. Evidently the noun "television" remains impervious to these verbal assaults. It is worth noting also that most of these books are anthologies, short essays having become the main academic currency in this and other contemporary fields of scholarship.

53   Ibid., 16. In "Crossing Wavelengths: The Diegetic and Referential Imaginary of American Commercial Television," *Cinema Journal* 25, no. 2 (Winter 1986): 51–64, Mimi White pushes the point farther, linking flow (understood as a phenomenological artifact) to the creation of an ever more self-referential "world" of television. Fascination becomes a more total mode of absorption into an image-track than anything cinema could do. Rather than scrapping the "address" model of textuality, White insists that it can work *en bloc*. Again, we see that the theorizing of flow as experience leads critics to interpret television's formal diversity as an ever more complete subjective enclosure.

54   Rick Altman, "Television/Sound," in Tania Modleski, ed., *Studies in Entertainment* (Bloomington: Indiana University Press, 1986), 39–54.

55   Tania Modleski, "The Rhythms of Reception: Daytime Television and Women's Work," in Kaplan, ed., *Regarding Television*.

56   Williams, *Television*, 77.

57   John Fiske and John Hartley, *Reading Television* (London: Methuen, 1977). It is striking that a book claiming that television is "oral" as opposed to "literary" would use the word "reading" in its title.

58   John Fiske, *Television Culture* (New York: Methuen, 1987).

59   Stephen Heath and Gillian Skirrow, "Television: A World in Action," *Screen* 18 (Summer 1977).

60   Ibid., 15.

61   Ibid., 56–58.

62   I borrow the term of Jean-François Lyotard, whose essay "The Tensor" thoroughly

deranges the semiotics of subject-effects. See *The Lyotard Reader,* ed. Andrew Benjamin (Oxford: Basil Blackwell, 1989), 1–18.

63   Stephen Heath and Gillian Skirrow, "An Interview with Raymond Williams," in *Studies in Entertainment,* ed. Tania Modleski (see note 53).

64   Ibid., 9–10.

65   Ibid., 15–16.

66   Stephen Heath, "Representing Television," in Patricia Mellencamp, ed., *Logics of Television* (Bloomington: Indiana University Press, 1990), 279.

67   This text and several others by Godard comprise a special issue of *Cahiers du Cinéma* 300 (May 1979). For more on Godard's Mozambique experiences, see his *Introduction à une véritable histoire du cinéma* (Paris: Albatros, 1980), 56, 209, 245.

Two. Image/Machine/Image

1   Immanuel Kant, *Critique of Judgement,* trans. J. H. Bernard (New York: Hafner Publishing Company, 1951), 171–72.

2   Jacques Derrida, "Economimesis," trans. R. Klein, *Diacritics* 11, no. 2 (1981): 3–25.

3   Raymond Williams, *Keywords* (New York: Oxford University Press, 1983), 201–2.

4   Jacques Derrida, "White Mythology," in *Margins of Philosophy,* trans. Alan Bass (Chicago: University of Chicago Press, 1982), 264.

5   Ibid.

6   For some of Derrida's comments on Marx and Marxism, see "Politics and Friendship: An Interview with Jacques Derrida," in *The Althusserian Legacy,* ed. E. Ann Kaplan and Michael Sprinker (London: Verso, 1993), 183–231; *Positions,* trans. Alan Bass (Chicago: University of Chicago Press, 1981), 60–67; "Some questions and responses," in *The Linguistics of Writing,* ed. Fabb and others (New York: Methuen, 1987), 254; and the peculiar cutting job on *Capital* performed in *Dissemination,* trans. Barbara Johnson (Chicago: University of Chicago Press, 1981), 31–34.

7   See Louis Althusser, *For Marx,* trans. Ben Brewster (New York: Vintage, 1970), esp. 93–104; and in *Reading Capital,* trans. Ben Brewster (London: Verso, 1979), 37, 153.

8   "Ideology and Ideological State Apparatuses" in *Lenin and Philosophy,* trans. Ben Brewster (New York: Monthly Review Press, 1971), 135.

9   Althusser, *Reading Capital,* 27. Althusser's footnote reads: "I retain the spatial metaphor. But the change of terrain takes place *on the spot:* in all strictness, we should speak of the mutation of the *mode* of theoretical production and of the change in function of the subject induced by this change of mode."

10   Louis Althusser, "Is it Simple to be a Marxist in Philosophy?" trans. Grahame Lock, in *Philosophy and the Spontaneous Philosophy of the Scientists* (London: Verso, 1990), 215.

11   Althusser, *Reading Capital,* 25.

12   Ibid., 189.

13   Ibid., 188.

14   Ibid., 192–93.

15   Ibid., 56.

16   Ibid., 193; translation modified. See Louis Althusser and others, *Lire le Capital* (Paris: Maspero, 1968), 71.

17   Michael Sprinker, *Imaginary Relations: Aesthetics and Ideology in the Theory of Historical Materialism* (London: Verso, 1987), 290–92.

18 See Jean-Louis Comolli, "Machines of the Visible" in *The Cinematic Apparatus*, ed. Teresa de Lauretis and Stephen Heath (New York: St. Martin's Press, 1980), 121–42.

19 Karl Marx, *Grundrisse*, trans. Martin Nicolaus (New York: Vintage, 1973), 673.

20 Ibid., 536; see also Antonio Negri, *Marx Beyond Marx*, trans. Harry Cleaver, Michael Ryan, and Maurizio Viano (South Hadley, MA: Bergin and Garvey, 1984), 114–15.

21 The indispensable texts on Marx's "economic text" remain Gayatri Chakravorty Spivak's "Scattered Speculations on the Question of Value" in *In Other Worlds: Essays in Cultural Politics* (New York: Routledge, 1987), 154–75; and Michael Ryan, *Marxism and Deconstruction: A Critical Articulation* (Baltimore: Johns Hopkins University Press, 1982), especially chapters 3 and 4, 65–102.

22 See also Alain Lipietz, *The Enchanted World*, trans. Ian Patterson (London: Verso, 1985). Lipietz argues that "perceived relations in economics" are not extrinsic to Marx's theory of value, but rather its singular object. For Marx's comment that ideas about economy are "merely the expression in consciousness of the apparent movement [of the laws of production]," see *Capital: Volume 3*, trans. David Fernbach (Harmondsworth: Penguin, 1983), 428.

23 *Grundrisse*, 694.

24 Ibid., 671.

25 It should not be forgotten that time is in fact the "substance" processed by capital into a new and quantifiable stratum; or better, it is that which is "captured" in the moment of exchange, when a potential force is rendered actual: "having acquired labor capacity in exchange as an equivalent, capital has acquired labor time . . . in exchange without equivalent" (*Grundrisse*, 674).

26 Marx, *Grundrisse*, 671.

27 Ibid., 712.

28 Ibid., 620–21.

29 Ibid., 623.

30 Karl Marx, *Capital: Volume 2*, trans. David Fernbach (Hardmondsworth: Penguin, 1978), 237–43. Cited in the text as *Capital II*.

31 Karl Marx, *Capital: Volume 3*, 370–71.

32 Karl Marx, *Capital: Volume 1*, trans. Ben Fowkes (New York: Vintage, 1977), 512; cited in the text as *Capital 1*. See also *Grundrisse*, 693. In a long note in *Capital I*, 493–94, Marx argues the need for a history of human technology to parallel Darwin's history of "natural technology, i.e., the formation of the organs of plants and animals." He goes on to say that "technology reveals the active relation of man to nature, the direct process of the production of his life, and thereby it also lays bare the process of the production of the social relations of his life, and of the mental conceptions that flow from those relations." Note—among other things that could be said about this rich comment—that Marx here describes the materialist analysis of technology as a visual act, rather than stating a law of determination.

33 Marx, *Grundrisse*, 670. For other bodily metaphors, see also *Grundrisse*, 701, and *Capital I*, 286.

34 Ibid., 692; emphasis added to latter phrase.

35 Ibid., 674. See also *Grundrisse*, 705 and *Capital I*, 285.

36 Ibid., 693. Emphasis added.

37 Ibid., 704. Significantly, Marx uses the same quote in *Capital I* to describe the process at a higher level of abstraction, i.e., the absorption of labor power into capital itself,

which becomes "an animated monster which begins to 'work,' 'as if its body were by love possessed'" (*Capital I*, 302). This startling citation also appears, in roughly similar terms, in the draft chapter "Results of the Immediate Process of Production," *Capital I*, 1007, and in connection with *money* in *Capital III*, 517.

38   Ibid., 712.

39   Jean-Paul Sartre, *Critique of Dialectical Reason*, trans. Alan Sheridan-Smith (London: Verso 1976), 233.

40   Marx, *Capital I*, 517.

41   See, for example, Christine Delphy, *Close to Home: A Materialist Analysis of Women's Oppression*, trans. Diana Leonard (Amherst: University of Massachusetts Press, 1984).

42   The work along these lines is already extensive and rich: see Tania Modleski, *Loving with a Vengeance* (New York: Methuen, 1984), and the articles collected in Helen Baehr and Gillian Dyer, eds., *Boxed In: Women and Television* (London: Pandora Press, 1987).

43   For a rather different account of this fissure, see Donna Haraway, "A Manifesto for Cyborgs: Science, Technology and Socialist Feminism in the 1980s," in *Socialist Review* 80 (1985). I would stress that this metaphoric pair can be mobilized within capital's own techniques of labor organization and ideology: it can hardly point the way back to some lost authenticity.

44   Gilles Deleuze and Félix Guattari, *A Thousand Plateaus*, trans. Brian Massumi (Minneapolis: University of Minnesota Press, 1987), 453–58. For more on Deleuze, see Chapter 8.

45   See R. Panzieri, "The Capitalist Use of Machinery: Marx versus the 'Objectivists'" in *Outlines of a Critique of Technology*, ed. Phil Slater (London: Ink Links, 1980), 45–63.

46   Fredric Jameson, "Surrealism without the Unconscious," in *Postmodernism: or, the Cultural Logic of Late Capitalism* (Durham: Duke University Press, 1990).

47   Ernest Mandel, *Late Capitalism*, trans. Joris De Bres (London: Verso, 1975), 110. Of course, Marx had famously stated: "It is not what is made but how, and by what instruments of labour, that distinguishes different economic epochs" (*Capital I*, 286).

48   Ibid., 249–50.

49   Marx, *Capital III*, 173–74.

50   Mandel, 118.

51   Ibid., 119.

52   Ibid., 190–91, his emphasis.

53   Marx, *Capital II*, 45; his emphasis.

54   Mandel, 390–98.

55   Peter Hall and Paschal Preston, *The Carrier Wave: New Information Technology and the Geography of Innovation 1846–2003* (London: Unwin Hyman, 1988).

56   Ibid., 164.

57   Ibid., 5.

58   David Harvey, *The Limits to Capital* (Chicago: University of Chicago Press, 1982), 229.

59   David Harvey, *The Condition of Postmodernity* (Oxford: Basil Blackwell, 1989), 61.

60   Eric Alliez and Michel Feher, "The Luster of Capital," *Zone* 1/2 (1987): 331.

61   Ibid., 348.

62   See Jane Feuer, "The Concept of Live Television: Ontology as Ideology," in *Regarding Television*, ed. E. Ann Kaplan (Frederick, MD: University Publications of America, 1981).

63   Marx, *Grundrisse*, 635.

64 Nick Browne, "The Political Economy of the TV (Super) Text" in *Television: the Critical View*, ed. Horace Newcomb (New York: Oxford University Press, 1987), 588.

65 Sut Jhally, *The Codes of Advertising: Fetishism and the Political Economy of Meaning in Consumer Society* (New York: St. Martin's Press, 1987).

66 Marx, *Capital I*, 451: "The socially productive power of labor develops as a free gift to capital whenever the workers are placed under certain conditions, and it is capital which places them under these conditions. Because this power costs capital nothing, while on the other hand it is not developed by the worker until his labor itself belongs to capital, it appears as a power which capital possesses by its nature—a productive power inherent in capital."

67 For further discussion of the concept of interpellation, see Chapter 7.

68 For an extravagant example, see Beverle Houston, "Viewing Television: The Metapsychology of Endless Consumption," *Quarterly Review of Film Studies* 9, no. 3 (Summer 1984): 183–95. Houston characterizes television viewing as a search for the plenitude of a nurturing presence lost since infancy. Hence, "all of television's spectators [are put] into the situation provided for the feminine in theories of subjectivity as well as her actual development and practice in patriarchy" (189). I would argue that such a conclusion, in which television and "the feminine" are alike reduced to a set of necessary affects associated with "consumption," should be regarded with skepticism.

69 See especially Marx, *Grundrisse*, 90–94.

70 Marx, *Capital I*, 270. To illustrate the analogy, I should quote the passage at length. "In order to extract value out of the consumption of a commodity, our friend the money-owner must be lucky enough to find within the sphere of circulation, on the market, a commodity whose use-value possesses the peculiar property of being a source of value, whose actual consumption is therefore itself an objectification [*Vergegenständlichung*] of labour, hence a creation of value. The possessor of money does find such a special commodity on the market: the capacity for labour [*Arbeitsvermögen*], in other words labour-power [*Arbeitskraft*]." Hence the peculiar property of watching television is that time enters into a cycle of value without being treated as a commodity by those who spend it. The networks, then, appear to act as brokers who make value as if from nothing (see note 66): they simultaneously "buy" (with images) and "sell" (as ratings) this socialized time. It should be remembered that this commercial system is undoubtedly limited, historically and geographically; as soon as it becomes more technically and economically feasible, images will not be offered without direct lines of return, i.e., having viewers pay for one kind of time (image time) with another (money, i.e., labor time).

71 Alexander Kluge, "On Film and the Public Sphere," trans. Thomas Y. Levin and Miriam B. Hansen, *New German Critique* 24–25 (Fall/Winter 1981–1982): 206–20, esp. 210–11.

72 Marx, *Grundrisse*, 109.

73 Ibid.

Three. History, the Eternal Rerun

1 See Fredric Jameson, "The Existence of Italy," *Signatures of the Visible* (New York: Routledge, 1990), esp. 217–29; also "The Cultural Logic of Late Capitalism" and "Nos-

talgia for the Present," in *Postmodernism: or, the Cultural Logic of Late Capitalism* (Durham: Duke University Press), esp. 19–25.

2   On-screen music offers a different twist: when Luca and Abrams listen to Miles Davis in a club, they do not hear the late-bop Miles of the early sixties, but the wrinkled electric Miles of the late eighties, who happens to be right there in the smoky lounge, looking even more like a time traveller than usual.

3   "'Crime' Pays on City Streets," Kay Gardella, *New York Daily News*, August 20, 1987. Mann is best known for the television series "Miami Vice," which introduced the word "nihilism" into the lexicon of television reviewers, and the film "Thief," another allegory of crime and capitalism that exposes the anarchist underbelly of the American Dream myth.

4   For more on apocalypse, catastrophe and television, see Patricia Mellencamp, ed., *Logics of Television: Essays in Cultural Criticism* (Bloomington: Indiana University Press, 1990), especially the essays by Meaghan Morris, Margaret Morse, Mary Ann Doane, and Patricia Mellencamp. See also Joyce Nelson, *The Perfect Machine: TV in the Nuclear Age* (Toronto: Between the Lines, 1987).

5   Jacques Derrida, "No Apocalypse, Not Now (full speed ahead, seven missiles, seven missives)," trans. Catherine Porter and Philip Lewis, *Diacritics* 14, no. 2 (Summer 1984): 30. Also see "On an Apocalyptic Tone Recently Adopted in Philosophy," trans. John P. Leavey, Jr., *Oxford Literary Review* 6 (1984). There Derrida raises the question that an apocalyptic horizon hangs above the "program" of the West.

Four. Mondino, MTV, and the Laugh of Madonna

1   Serge Daney, *Le Salaire du zappeur* (Paris: Éditions Ramsay, 1988), 136–40.

2   Thierry Jousse, "Forme brève," *Cahiers du Cinéma* 434 (July/August 1990): 82–84, and "Entretien avec Jean-Baptiste Mondino," 84–89.

3   See the MTV special issue of *Journal of Communication Inquiry*, 10, no. 1 (1986), especially the articles by Dana Polan, Virginia H. Fry and Donald L. Fry, and Margaret Morse; E. Ann Kaplan, *Rocking Around the Clock: Music Television, Postmodernism, and Consumer Culture* (New York: Methuen, 1987), and Andrew Goodwin, *Dancing in the Distraction Factory: Music Television and Popular Culture* (Minneapolis: University of Minnesota Press, 1992). Goodwin's book offers the best overview of the various critical approaches to music television.

4   Shortly after the completion of this essay (December 1992), MTV began to credit directors as well. Speaking for his employers, Kurt Loder of MTV News gave two reasons for this decision: directors not only deserve the credit, they deserve to get "big bucks" for their work. MTV has not, however, begun to apply directorial credits to older clips. Their affiliate VH-1 began to append directorial credits to new videos in January 1993.

5   The classic reference is Peter Wollen, *Signs and Meaning in the Cinema* (Bloomington: Indiana University Press, 1972), 74–115. See also Fredric Jameson's discussion of cinematic auteurs in the context of modernism in *Signatures of the Visible* (New York: Routledge, 1990), 198–201.

6   See *The Face* 90 (October 1987), cover and 90–95.

7   Daney, *Le Salaire du zappeur*, 139.

8   See Jacqueline Rose, *Sexuality in the Field of Vision* (London: Verso, 1986), 184–88.

9   Fredric Jameson, *Postmodernism, or, the Cultural Logic of Late Capitalism* (Durham: Duke University Press, 1991), 299–300.

10 Sales of the "Justify My Love" videocassette may have reached 500,000 copies, which amounts to millions of dollars in net returns. It would be interesting to know if the record company thought that airing the clip would have brought in more money in record sales.

11 Joel D. Schwartz, "Virgin Territory," *New Republic*, August 26, 1985, 30–32.

12 Judith Williamson, "The Making of a Material Girl," *New Socialist*, October 1985, 46–47. See also Williamson's "What men miss about Madonna," *Guardian*, August 2, 1990, 28. The relevant anthologies are Cathy Schwichtenberg, ed., *The Madonna Connection* (Boulder: Westview Press, 1993) and Adam Sexton, ed., *Desperately Seeking Madonna* (New York: Delta, 1993).

13 For a variety of responses (mostly skeptical) to this claim, see Lisa Frank and Paul Smith, eds., *Madonnarama: Essays on Sex and Popular Culture* (Pittsburgh/San Francisco: Cleis Press, 1993).

Five. Appetite and Satisfaction, a Golden Circle

1   William Grimes, "Welcome to Twin Peaks and Valleys," *New York Times*, 5 May 1991.

2   Including the prequel film *Fire Walk With Me*, which turns out to be an attempt to start over and rewrite the television series in filmic terms. *Twin Peaks—Fire Walk With Me* thematizes its emergence from television at the beginning and continues to cut blue television static into its intense montage sequences, along with spacy references to electricity and buzzing shots of utility poles. To say that the film "explains" the course of the television program, however, would be a mistake: by the very terms of the media, the film was bound to reframe and refocus what appeared on television as narrative diffusion. The suspension between, for example, diegetically positioned individual delusion and collective involvement in magical forces is almost completely eradicated, in favor of characterological explanations.

3   "Twin Peaks caps ABC season," *Broadcasting*, 23 April 1990.

4   In June 1993, the high-culture cable channel Bravo began airing the series again, setting it amongst its usual fare of operas, imported British programming and international art films. This fate proves that some television shows may need several rerun cycles before they find an appropriate niche, although that settling-in process may be financially ruinous.

5   "Twin Peaks, U.S.A." *Nation*, 11 June 1990.

6   For Jameson's very suggestive uses of this Eisensteinian language, see *Signatures of the Visible* (New York, 1990) 212–14, and *Postmodernism, or, the Cultural Logic of Late Capitalism* (Durham, 1991) 190–92.

7   See for example Randall Rothenberg, "Yesterday's Boob Tube Is Today's High Art," *New York Times*, 7 October 1991.

8   As Ingmar Bergman puts it: "The most fantastic thing about the camera and the film is that, technically, it's exactly the same as it was in 1895 in Paris at the Grand Café. And you know, when they edit a video film, they're sitting in a kind of submarine . . . You can't feel anything, you can't take the film out and touch it and look at it" (*Guardian*

Weekly, 18 November 1990, 15). Also, of course, Walter Benjamin, "The Work of Art in the Age of Mechanical Reproduction," in *Illuminations,* trans. Harry Zohn (New York: Schocken, 1969).

9   Howard Rodman, "The Series that Will Change TV," *Connoisseur,* September 1989.

10   Richard Zoglin, "A Sleeper with a Dream," *Time,* 21 May 1990.

11   Félix Guattari, "La machine à images," *Cahiers du Cinéma* 437 (November 1990): 71.

12   To give an obvious example: several important scenes were shot with dazzling strobe lighting, which can be easily tamed by a vcr's slow-motion replay. The television critic for the *Los Angeles Times* also explained how the video replay of an apparently horrific scene revealed an entirely opposite, kinder and gentler reading.

13   For some comments on the "morality" of *Twin Peaks* in the context of contemporary America, see Kathy Acker, "On Top of a Peak," *New Statesman and Society,* 11 May 1990, 42–43.

14   Susan Willis has remarked suggestively that *Twin Peaks* can be read as a failed First World attempt to produce "magical realism."

15   In fact, the matter of Gerard's lost arm involves yet another interpretive bubble. When Cooper asks Gerard what was tattooed on his arm, Gerard becomes distraught, and says one word—but because of his fraught pronunciation, this word could either be "Bob" or "Mom." Uncertainties like this have to be left alone—they are gifts. (And I have been unable to find agreement among my friends who have watched the scene.) Supposing that the missing arm is understood as symbolic castration (just for a minute), the reading of Gerard/Mike's desires, as inscribed by the tattoo, is caught between classical Oedipal and homosexual scenarios. Since the body is shared by two "characters," perhaps both are equally true.

16   For a discussion of detectives in terms of the Lacanian subject supposed to know, see Slavoj Žižek, *Looking Awry: An Introduction to Jacques Lacan through Popular Culture* (Cambridge, MA: MIT Press, 1991) 57–63.

Six. The Dangers of Being in a Televisual World

This essay is dedicated to Dallas Denery.

1   See Samuel Weber, "Upsetting the Set Up: Remarks on Heidegger's Questing After Technics," in *Modern Language Notes* 105, no. 5 (December 1989). Following Weber's lead, I will largely use "technics" whenever referring to Heidegger's word *Technik:* it has the additional virtue of recalling Lewis Mumford's great historical work, *Technics and Civilization.* "Technology" will be used in a more general sense, outside the terminological web of Heidegger's text. I thank Professor Ken Surin for bringing Weber's essay to my attention.

2   See Jacques Derrida, "Comment Donner Raison? How to Concede, with Reasons?" in *Diacritics* 19, nos. 3–4 (Fall–Winter, 1989): 4–9. Of the professional philosophers' treatment of Heidegger's texts, Derrida speaks of a "fictive immediacy destined to mask other theatres"; although the press "lacks the place for a patient analysis of this problem" it has managed to disrupt that philosophical stagecraft.

3   Martin Heidegger, "The Thing," in *Poetry, Language, Thought,* trans. Albert Hofstadter (New York: Harper and Row, 1971), 165. Hereafter cited in text as "Thing." Also "Das Ding," in *Vorträge und Aufsätze* (Pfullingen: Neske, 1954), 163. Henceforth cited as

VuA. My emphasis, translation modified. The phrase "the whole mechanism and drive of communication," translates "das ganze Gestänge und Geschiebe das Verkehrs." (Hofstadter translates it as "the whole machinery of communication.") Suffice to say here that "mechanism" mediates and compromises, in a classical way, the philosopher's investment in the ideal of "communication." But Heidegger's phrasing is more peculiar: "Gestänge" denotes bars, rods, or transmission shafts; "Geschiebe" is a pushing or shoving motion; "Verkehrs" has the sense of "traffic" and "intercourse" as well as "communication," the latter of which is more commonly rendered as "Mitteilung." All in all, a much more dynamic sentence in German, suggesting both a movement and an apparatus.

4   For contrast, compare this passage from Theodor W. Adorno's *The Jargon of Authenticity,* trans. Knut Tarnowski and Fredric Will (Evanston, IL: Northwestern University Press, 1973), 76. "[The] routes between the whole and the atomized individual subjects are shortened, as if the two extremes were near to one another. The technical progress of the means of communication runs parallel to this. These means—especially radio and television—reach the people at large in such a way that they notice none of the innumerable technical intermediations; the voice of the announcer resounds in the home, as though he were present and knew each individual." Adorno compares this occlusion of mediation in the media to the "second-hand primalness" of the Heideggerian and National Socialist jargon, where community is falsely produced as part of economic planning.

5   Martin Heidegger, *Being and Time,* trans. John Macquarrie and Edward Robinson (New York: Harper and Row, 1962), 27; also "Introduction to *Being and Time,*" trans. Joan Stambaugh, in Martin Heidegger, *Basic Writings,* ed. David Farrell Krell (New York: Harper and Row, 1977), 48. The quotation is taken from the latter translation.

6   Heidegger, *Being and Time,* 346.

7   Heidegger, *Being and Time,* section 75, 439–44.

8   But see Adorno's attack on the notion of Dasein in *The Jargon of Authenticity,* 113–16. Adorno asserts that Heidegger's attempt to separate Dasein from consciousness simply "transforms a bad empirical reality into transcendence" (116).

9   Frank Lentricchia has argued that Heidegger "defies the normal capacities of discourse"; it could be presented another way: that he seeks a careful alteration of it. See *After the New Criticism* (Chicago: University of Chicago Press, 1980), 81 ff. Lentricchia's essential thrust concerns the "ahistoricality" of Dasein, which is to say, the incompatibility of Heidegger's existential analytic with the language of historical representation. No doubt Heidegger would have been glad to hear such a verdict.

10   "The Thing," 167.

11   Ibid., 181, 171.

12   Martin Heidegger, "Letter on Humanism," in *Basic Writings,* 210–11.

13   See Martin Heidegger, "The Origin of the Work of Art" in *Poetry, Language, Thought,* 26; also Jean-Paul Sartre, *Being and Nothingness,* trans. Hazel Barnes (New York: Washington Square Press, 1966), 51.

14   *Being and Time,* 167.

15   Georg Lukács, *History and Class Consciousness,* trans. Rodney Livingstone (Cambridge, MA: MIT Press, 1971), xxiv.

16   *Being and Time,* 167.

17 For this distinction, see George Steiner, *Martin Heidegger* (New York: Viking Press, 1978), 28.

18 See Hubert L. Dreyfus, "Between Technē and Technology: The Ambiguous Place of Equipment in *Being and Time*," in *Tulane Studies in Philosophy* 32 (1984).

19 Indeed, Heidegger reserves some vitriol for the very idea of discussing "value" in connection with Being. See "The Word of Nietzsche: 'God is Dead'" in *The Question Concerning Technology and Other Essays*, trans. William Lovitt (New York: Harper and Row, 1977), 103–4. (Henceforth cited as *Question*.) Also "The Age of the World Picture" (discussed below) in *Question*, 142. Clearly, Heidegger's reluctance to consider value is an index of his unwillingness to grant any place to economics in the various histories and destinies of Being. This is in turn an indication that none of his categories can be easily translated into a Marxist lexicon, although many have tried (Gianni Vattimo and Kostas Axelos, for example).

20 "The Thing," 170.

21 Ibid.

22 "The Thing," 177.

23 "The Thing," 182.

24 See the "Conclusion" of Michael E. Zimmerman, *Heidegger's Confrontation with Modernity: Technology, Politics, Art* (Bloomington: Indiana University Press, 1990) for a discussion of Heidegger in the context of "deep ecology." (There is no doubt a New Age Heidegger waiting in the wings.) Zimmerman provides very useful bibliographic material, as well as an overview of Heidegger's writings on technology.

25 "The Question Concerning Technology" in *Question*.

26 *Question*, 3–4, translation modified. See *VuA*, 13.

27 *Question*, 4; see also Martin Heidegger, *What is Called Thinking?* trans. Fred D. Wieck and J. Glenn Gray (New York: Harper and Row, 1968), 22. "The essence of technology is not anything human. The essence of technology is above all not anything technological."

28 *Question*, 13.

29 *Question*, 167.

30 *Question*, 17.

31 Cited in Karsten Harries' "Introduction" to *Martin Heidegger and National Socialism: Questions and Answers*, ed. Günther Neske and Emil Ketterling, trans. Lisa Harries (New York: Paragon House, 1990), xxx. Henceforth cited as Neske and Ketterling, *Heidegger.*

32 Martin Heidegger, "Sketches for a History of Being as Metaphysics," in *The End of Philosophy*, trans. Joan Stambaugh (New York: Harper and Row, 1973), 66. These outlines provide fascinating evidence of Heidegger's usually submerged chronologies. Henceforth cited as *End*.

33 *Question*, 21.

34 *Question*, 20–21. See *VuA*, 28.

35 *Question*, 27.

36 See Hubert L. Dreyfus, "Between Technē and Technology." Dreyfus wants to demonstrate how the conception of Dasein found in *Being and Time* in fact furthers (rather than resists) the ordering drive of technology by making Being itself available to technological understanding.

37   See Heidegger's *Nietzsche, Volume II: The Eternal Recurrence of the Same,* trans. David Farrell Krell (San Francisco: Harper and Row, 1984), 233: "What else is the essence of the modern power-driven machine than one offshoot of the eternal recurrence of the same?" Also *VuA,* 126.

38   *Question,* 33.

39   *Question,* 35.

40   Here I am citing the analysis of Jacques Derrida in *Of Spirit,* trans. Geoff Bennington and Rachel Bowlby (Chicago: University of Chicago Press, 1989), 10–11; and "On Reading Heidegger: An Outline of Remarks to the Essex Colloquium," in *Research in Phenomenology* 17 (1987), 171–74. The latter sketch is particularly clear on the structure of contamination in Heidegger's notion of technics, about which I say more below.

41   See especially Gianni Vattimo, *The End of Modernity: Nihilism and Hermeneutics in Postmodern Culture,* trans. Jon R. Snyder (Baltimore: Johns Hopkins University Press, 1988), esp. chapters 2 and 10. Vattimo's primary contribution to the debates seems to have been his claim that, for Heidegger, Being has become exchange value. Such a superimposition of distinct theoretical languages hardly serves either one.

42   Cited in Harries, "Introduction," in Neske and Ketterling, *Heidegger,* xxix. Remember Nietzsche's Zarathustra: "Die at the right time!"

43   *Question,* 38.

44   *Question,* 41.

45   *Question,* 48.

46   In "Building Dwelling Thinking," Heidegger writes about the overflow of speech permitted by technology. "It is language which tells us about the nature of a thing . . . In the meantime, to be sure, there rages round the earth an unbridled yet clever talking, writing, and broadcasting of spoken words. Man acts as though *he* were the shaper and master of language, while in fact *language* remains the master of man" (*Poetry, Language, Thought,* 146).

47   See also *Discourse on Thinking,* trans. John M. Anderson and E. Hans Freund (New York: Harper and Row, 1966), 54: "I would call this comportment toward technology which expresses 'yes' and at the same time 'no,' by an old word, releasement toward things [*Gelassenheit zu den Dingen*]." The translators note that "Gelassenheit" (the German title of the book) has a mystical sense, as the openness of man toward God. *Gelassenleit* might also point toward a nonviolent disposition toward the world, cool like Zen. Henceforth cited as *Discourse.*

48   *Question,* 49.

49   In "The Principle of Ground" (1956), Heidegger has this to say about "information," a word which "[we] must hear in its American-English accent . . . [Information] means the reporting that instructs modern man, as quickly and as comprehensively as possible, as clearly and completely as possible, about the securing of his needs, their requirement and provision. Consequently, the representation of man's language as an instrument of information gains the upper hand in increasing measure." See "The Principle of Ground," trans. Keith Hoeller, *Man and World* 7 (August 1974), 216.

50   *Question,* 116.

51   *Question,* 126.

52   *Question,* 134.

53   *Question,* 141.

54   *Question*, 135.

55   Martin Heidegger, "Dialogue on Language," in *On the Way to Language*, trans. Peter D. Hertz (New York: Harper and Row, 1971), 17.

56   See *Cahiers du Cinéma* 186 (January 1967), 45–46.

57   *Discourse*, 52.

58   *Discourse*, 51.

59   In Neske and Ketterling, *Heidegger*, 55.

60   Jean Baudrillard, "The Precession of Simulacra," in *Simulations*, trans. Paul Foss, Paul Patton and Philip Beitchman (New York: Semiotext(e), 1983), and Freidrich Kittler, "Gramophone, Film, Typewriter" *October* 41 (Summer 1987) and "Media Wars: Trenches Lightning Stars," *1–800* 1 (Fall 1989). It would be possible to analyze both of these writers in terms of Heideggerian inheritances.

61   On this point, see Michel Foucault, "Nietzsche, Genealogy and History," in *The Foucault Reader*, ed. Paul Rabinow (New York: Pantheon, 1984), 83–4. He specifically cites the "eye," noting that it "was not always intended for comtemplation." Foucault's relation to Heidegger seems particularly close and testy in this essay.

   I should also add that Heidegger explicitly states that this conception is designed to pre-empt any discussion of "historiographically demonstrable changes in nations and continents" ("Overcoming Metaphysics," *End*, 93).

62   See "Parergon" in Jacques Derrida, *The Truth in Painting*, trans. Geoff Bennington and Ian McLeod (Chicago: University of Chicago Press, 1987).

63   *End*, 85.

64   Martin Heidegger, *The Question of Being*, trans. Jean T. Wilde and William Kluback (New Haven: College and University Press, 1958), 43. This is the famous essay in which Heidegger crosses out Being. Interestingly, it is presented as a letter to Ernst Jünger.

65   In a message sent to a Beirut symposium in 1974, Heidegger concludes with this warning: "The questioning thinking of Being is in itself an action that abandons what is most characteristic of it, if it, understood as mere theory, *delivers itself all too quickly* to an unthought practice and the groundless machinations of organization and institution" (Neske and Ketterling, *Heidegger*, 254; my emphasis).

66   See Pierre Bourdieu, *L'ontologie politique de Martin Heidegger* (Paris: Minuit, 1988; originally pub. in 1975), chapter 2. "The philosophical field and space of possibles." In this fascinating dissection, Bourdieu maps Heidegger as a triangulated response to a number of figures, including "post-Mallarmean poetics," neo-Kantians like Cassirer and theoreticians of the "conservative revolution" like Jünger (64). He makes a particularly relevant remark about the "appearance" of philosophy: "The historians of philosophy too often forget that the grand philosophical options which mark out the space of possibilities . . . are presented in the sensible form of persons, apprehended in their manners of being, of behaving, of speaking" (63). No doubt the *nouveaux philosophes* took such lessons to heart.

67   Avital Ronell, *The Telephone Book: Technology—Schizophrenia—Electric Speech* (Lincoln: University of Nebraska Press). Ronell's nuanced, elusive discussion of Heidegger and technology takes place through the "telephone," a concept-metaphor that allows Ronell to connect the "calls" of Being and Others through a Heideggerian textual "switchboard." I have already indicated that the Elsewhere of technics extends

toward that of Being; but instead of seizing on television as the guiding figure for a rereading of Heidegger, Ronell chooses the telephone. At one point, she wonders aloud how she could have chosen the telephone for this extended interpretive gambit, when Heidegger in fact never mentions it (199). A good question. In fact, although she quotes the passage from "The Thing" that mentions television, she suggests that the telephone's very absence there proves that it is somehow even more everywhere than television, both as technology and as the extension of the sacred, inward privilege of calling and listening. But are the private, schizophrenic intensities buzzing across these lines always the poetic evasions Heidegger would have wanted them to be, or, on the contrary, is the telephonic trope just a limited economy conceded to a residual subjectivity that shares the apparatus with new and more successful varieties?

68   Ronell, *The Telephone Book,* 199. She repeats the claim in "The Differends of Man," *Diacritics* 19, nos. 3–4 (Fall–Winter 1989): 73.

69   "Martin Heidegger in Conversation with Richard Wisser," in Neske and Ketterling. Originally published as *Martin Heidegger im Gespräch* (Freiburg/Munich: Verlag Karl Alber, 1970). This edition contains several video stills from the program.

70   Peter Sloterdijk, in *Critique of Cynical Reason,* trans. Michael Elred (Minneapolis: University of Minnesota Press, 1987), 205–6, argues that Heidegger's political perspective remained forever locked in place as a "provincial" response to the radicalism of Weimar Germany.

71   Neske and Ketterling, *Heidegger,* 82.

72   Ibid., 87.

73   Ibid., 120.

Seven. From Post Cards to Smart Bombs

1   Eric Barnouw, *A Tower in Babel: A History of Broadcasting in the United States, Volume 1: to 1933* (New York: Oxford University Press, 1966), 231. The book also contains a photograph (Plate 10) of the broadcast of "The Queen's Messenger." One can make out a man brandishing a pistol in front of a woman's face, and her hand raised to ward it off.

2   See Jacques Derrida, "Philosophie des États Généraux," in *États Generaux de la Philosophie* (Paris: Flammarion, 1979), 32: "[There] are, in the techno-politics of telecommunications, unavoidable (incontournable) stakes, stakes which are also philosophical, very new in some of their forms, their operations, and their evaluation, their route, their market (marché) and their technology."

3   Jean-Luc Godard, "Faire les Films possible là où on est," in *Jean-Luc Godard par Jean-Luc Godard,* ed. Alain Bergala (Paris: Cahiers du Cinéma/Éditions de l'Étoile, 1985) 385. The interview originally appeared in *Le Monde* on 25 September 1975.

4   Jacques Derrida, *La Carte Postale: de Socrate à Freud et au-delà* (Paris: Flammarion, 1980). English translation: *The Post Card: From Socrates to Freud and Beyond,* trans. Alan Bass (Chicago: University of Chicago Press, 1987). Henceforth cited as *The Post Card.* For the record, when Derrida was asked whether the work of Godard had had any influence on his work or his "imaginary," Derrida responded "Not the least influence, to my knowledge." See Carole Desbarats and Jean-Paul Gorce, eds., *L'effet Godard* (Toulouse: Editions Milan, 1989), 110. The question of "influence," of course, is only one way to stage a confrontation.

5   Derrida, *The Post Card*, 100–101.
6   Jacques Derrida, *Marges de la philosophie* (Paris: Minuit, 1972). English translation: *Margins of Philosophy*, trans. Alan Bass (Chicago: University of Chicago Press, 1982). Henceforth cited as *Margins*.
7   Jacques Derrida, *De la Grammatologie* (Paris: Minuit, 1967). English translation: *Of Grammatology*, trans. Gayatri Chakravorty Spivak (Baltimore: Johns Hopkins University Press, 1976). Henceforth cited as *Grammatology*.
8   Jacques Derrida, "Signature Event Context," in *Limited Inc.*, trans. Samuel Weber and Jeffrey Mehlman (Evanston: Northwestern University Press, 1988), 8. See also Derrida, "The Pit and the Pyramid: Introduction to Hegel's Semiology," in *Margins*, 106–8. I owe the latter reference to Fredric Jameson.
9   Derrida, *Grammatology*, 91.
10 Ibid., 45.
11 See, for example, Jacques Derrida, *Dissemination*, trans. Barbara Johnson (Chicago: University of Chicago Press, 1981), 167, on the "system of presence."
12 Jacques Derrida, "Afterword: Toward An Ethic of Discussion" in *Limited Inc.*, 148. The entire essay greatly clarifies Derrida's position on this point. For contrast and continuity, see Derrida, "'Genesis and Structure' and Phenomenology," in *Writing and Différence*, trans. Alan Bass (Chicago: University of Chicago Press, 1978), esp. 166 (on "logos"). This essay was originally published in 1959.
13 Derrida, *Writing and Différence*, 260. This essay, "From Restricted to General Economy: A Hegelianism Without Reserve," is a key text for understanding the antidialectical thrust that animates Derrida's theorizing of limits, values and systems.
14 See Fredric Jameson, *The Prison House of Language* (Princeton: Princeton University Press, 1972), 175–76; here Jameson suggests that Derrida and McLuhan present two sides of the same "cultural reality." Since this book was published in the same year as "Signature Event Context," Jameson could not have taken account of Derrida's powerful critiques of the postulates of communications and media theory since 1972. For Jameson's more recent strategic avoidance of Derridean positions, see his *Late Marxism: Adorno, or the Persistence of the Dialectic* (London: Verso, 1990), esp. 234–35 and 242–45.
15 Derrida, *Limited Inc.*, 20.
16 Marshall McLuhan, *Understanding Media* (New York: Signet, 1964), 67.
17 This comparison merits further investigation. See Chapter 1 for a discussion of Sartre on seriality and broadcasting. See also Derrida, *Limited Inc.*, 136–37, where he speaks of a constantly shifting textual "experience" of history, reality, etc. To this picture we could also add Herbert Schiller's work, for example, *Information and the Crisis Economy* (Oxford: Oxford University Press, 1986), for a sense of the legal-economic regime that attempts to regulate all transmissions.
18 See also Derrida, *Grammatology*, 40–41, 69.
19 Gregory Ulmer, *Teletheory: Grammatology in the Age of Video* (New York: Routledge, 1989) and Avital Ronell, *The Telephone Book: Technology–Schizophrenia–Electric Speech* (Lincoln: University of Nebraska Press, 1989).
20 Jean-Luc Godard, "Godard parle," interview with Christian Perrot and Leon Mercadet, *Actuel* 103 (January 1988): 76. He distinguishes loosely between "producing for diffusion" (television) and "shooting an image" (cinema).

21 Jacques Derrida, "Envoi," in Psyché: Inventions de l'autre (Paris: Galilée, 1987), 109–43. An English translation, "Sending: On Representation," exists but is unreliable: Social Research, 49, no. 2 (Summer 1982) trans. Mary Ann and Peter Caws. This paper, delivered in 1980, is essential to any reading of The Post Card, as is "Telepathy," a "misplaced" addition to The Post Card (also in Psyché) translated by Nicholas Royle, Oxford Literary Review 10, 1985.

22 Jacques Derrida, "My Chances/Mes Chances," trans. Irene Harvey and Avital Ronell, in Taking Chances: Derrida, Psychoanalysis, and Literature, ed. Joseph H. Smith and William Kerrigan (Baltimore: Johns Hopkins University Press, 1984), 27. See also Limited Inc., 151, 159.

23 Derrida, "Envoi," 133. For some reason, the translators of the English version completely deleted the last sentence of this quotation, although its importance to the argument—mine as well as Derrida's—is central.

24 Derrida, The Post Card, 100.

25 For more on this economic trope and its psychoanalytic resonance, see Samuel Weber, "The Debts of Deconstruction and Other, Related Assumptions," in Institution and Interpretation (Minneapolis: University of Minnesota Press, 1987).

26 Ibid., 109–10.

27 Derrida, The Post Card, 12.

28 Ibid., 29.

29 Ibid., 65, 121, 123.

30 Derrida, "Envoi," 127.

31 Ibid.

32 Louis Althusser, "Ideology and Ideological State Apparatuses," in Lenin and Philosophy, trans. Ben Brewster (New York: Monthly Review Press, 1971), 127–86.

33 Ibid., 174, translation modified. See the original version in Althusser's Positions (Paris: Éditions Sociale, 1976), 126.

34 For a development of Althusser's position in linguistics, see Michel Pêcheux, Language, Semantics and Ideology: Stating the Obvious, trans. Harbans Nagpal (London: Macmillan, 1979), esp. 103–9.

35 Derrida, The Post Card, 21–22.

36 Ibid., 104.

37 Ibid., 106.

38 Ibid., 20.

39 Ibid., 138–39. Also see the reflections on multinational corporations and the politics of "telematics" in "The Principle of Reason: The University in the Eyes of its Pupils," trans. Catherine Porter and Edward P. Morris, Diacritics 13, no. 2 (1983).

Eight. Ineluctable Modalities of the Televisual

1 Gilles Deleuze, Cinema 1: The Movement-Image, trans. Hugh Tomlinson and Barbara Habberjam (Minneapolis: University of Minnesota Press, 1986). Originally published as Cinéma 1: L'Image-Mouvement (Paris: Minuit, 1983).

2 Gilles Deleuze, Cinema 2: The Time-Image, trans. Hugh Tomlinson and Robert Galeta (Minneapolis: University of Minnesota Press, 1989). Originally published as Cinéma 2: L'Image-Temps (Paris: Minuit, 1985).

3   Deleuze, *Cinema 1*, xiv. See also "Sur L'Image-Temps," *Pourparlers* (Paris: Minuit, 1990), 83–84.

4   Deleuze, *Cinema 2*, xii–xiii.

5   I take my cue here from Fredric Jameson's suggestion in the introduction of *Signatures of the Visible* (New York: Routledge, 1990), 6.

6   Deleuze gives as concise as possible a definition of "assemblage" in Gilles Deleuze and Claire Parnet, *Dialogues*, trans. Hugh Tomlinson and Barbara Habberjam (New York: Columbia University Press, 1987), 69: "What is an assemblage? It is a multiplicity which is made up of many heterogenous terms and which establishes liaisons, relations between them, across ages, sexes and reigns—different natures. Thus, the assemblage's only unity is that of co-functioning: it is a symbiosis, a 'sympathy'."

7   Henri Bergson, *Matter and Memory*, trans. Nancy Margaret Paul and W. Scott Palmer (London: George Allen & Unwin Ltd, 1911).

8   This is a highly condensed summary. See Deleuze, "Sur La Philosophie," *Pourparlers*, 187. For a discussion of Bergson's understanding of the relationship between images and concepts, see Jean-Joseph Goux, "Monetary Economy and Idealist Philosophy, in *Symbolic Economies: After Marx and Freud*, trans. Jennifer Curtiss Gage (Ithaca: Cornell University Press, 1990) 100–106.

9   Deleuze, *Cinema 1*, ix.

10   Ibid., 57–58.

11   Ibid., xiv.

12   For more precise definitions and extensive elaboration of various Deleuzian terms, see Brian Massumi, *A User's Guide to Capitalism and Schizophrenia* (Cambridge, MA: MIT Press, 1992). On desire, see esp. 161.

13   Ibid., 58–60; Bergson, *Matter and Memory*, 64.

14   Deleuze, *Cinema 1*, 63.

15   This was the problem that occupied Maurice Merleau-Ponty toward the end of his life: how to introduce the body's "thickness" into the phenomenological language of perception? See his unfinished work *The Visible and the Invisible*, trans. Alphonso Lingis (Evanston, IL: Northwestern University Press, 1968), chapter 4, esp. 140ff.

16   For one example, see Gilles Deleuze and Félix Guattari, *A Thousand Plateaus*, trans. Brian Massumi (Minneapolis: University of Minnesota Press, 1987), 146–47. On these pages, "pragmatics" is diagrammed, having four components: "generative, transformational, diagrammatic and machinic." In this book, "pragmatics" replaces the word "schizoanalysis" from the authors' *Anti-Oedipus*, trans. Robert Hurley, Mark Seem, Helen R. Lane (Minneapolis: University of Minnesota Press, 1983). Of the four components, the Deleuze of the cinema books seems most interested in the first and last; that is, in "concrete mixed semiotics" and the physical/expressive "assemblages" that rise from them (i.e., the sensory-motor link, as we will discuss below).

17   Deleuze, *Cinema I*, 64.

18   Deleuze and Guattari, *A Thousand Plateaus*, 76.

19   Gilles Deleuze, "La Photographie est déjà tirée dans les choses," interview by Pascal Bonitzer and Jean Narboni, *Cahiers du Cinéma* 352 (October 1983): 37; reprinted in *Pourparlers*, 71.

20   The great exception cases of the second volume—Eisenstein and Hitchcock—appear out of nowhere, and appear remarkable in part because they seem to avoid all the existential/phenomenological categories that defined prewar thinking about cinema.

21   Deleuze, *Cinema 1*, 70. Deleuze also concludes here that the three basic kinds of movement-image in cinema correspond to three basic kinds of shot: the long shot (perception-image), the medium shot (action-image) and close-up (affection image). This typology makes sense only if it is regarded as a standard that will be repeatedly violated.

22   In an article about Godard and Gorin, Serge Daney proposed an equivalence between the Lacanian subject-supposed-to-know and the cinematic spectator, in order to condemn the power of film to usurp all powers of reference from the viewers. A more contemporary way to pursue the formula would be a reading of Lacanian film theory as a series of displacements and transferences of a critic's will to mastery. See "Le 'groupe Dziga-Vertov,' (2)" *Cahiers du Cinéma* 240 (July/August 1972): 4–9.

23   Deleuze, *Cinema 1*, 204.

24   Ibid., 155–59, 205, 215.

25   For an indispensable account of Deleuze and Guattari's historical toolbox, see Fredric Jameson, "Beyond the Cave: Demystifying the Ideology of Modernism," in *The Ideologies of Theory, Volume Two: The Syntax of History* (Minneapolis: University of Minnesota Press, 1988), 123–28.

26   For example, the cases of experimenters hoping to time, in milliseconds, the process of recognizing a written word or letter by flashing an illuminated square to a subject bound to a chair. As Nietzsche said: aesthetics is just applied physiology. Cited by Friedrich Kittler, *Discourse Networks, 1800/1900*, trans. Michael Metteer with Chris Cullens (Palo Alto: Stanford University Press, 1990), 222, 224.

27   For a discussion of the Taylorism of manufacturing and cinema, see Peter Wollen, "Cinema/Americanism/The Robot," *New Formations* 8 (Summer 1989), 7–34. Wollen, interestingly, also mentions Chanel, whose name I include for different reasons: not that she standardized fashion (Wollen's point) as much as she introduced a durable economy of differentiation: a set of elements that could be varied and inflected from year to year.

28   Deleuze, *Cinema 1*, 206.

29   Ibid.

30   Deleuze, *Cinema 2*, 3; *Cinéma 2*, 10. (The French edition will be cited wherever I have modified the translation.)

31   Deleuze, *Cinema 2*, 7.

32   Ibid., 22–23.

33   Ibid., 81.

34   Ibid., 41. ("Montrer" is the French verb "to show.")

35   Ibid., 68.

36   Ibid., 82–83; *Cinéma 2*, 110–11.

37   Ibid., chapter 5.

38   Deleuze, *Cinema 2*, 207. Deleuze offers a remarkable comment on the work of Resnais: "For memory is clearly no longer the faculty of having recollections: it is the membrane which, in the most varied ways (continuity, but also discontinuity, envelopment, etc.), makes sheets of past and layers of reality correspond, the first emanating from an inside which is always already there, the second arriving from an outside always to come, the two gnawing at the present which is now only their encounter."

39   Ibid., 161.

40   Ibid., 157.

41   Ibid., 179–80.

42   Ibid., 243; *Cinéma 2*, 316.

43   Deleuze and Guattari, *Anti-Oedipus*, 36.

44   Deleuze, *Cinema 2*, 265. Godard mentions that montage has become mixing, which is to say, blending and superimposing, as on tape.

45   See the note on Nam June Paik in Deleuze, *Cinema 2*, 331.

46   Ibid., 27–28.

47   Deleuze and Guattari, *A Thousand Plateaus*, 457–58. During a discussion of the difference between subjection and enslavement, they turn to television. Subjection refers to the ways TV is used and consumed by subjects, while enslavement describes the total incorporation of the viewer to the apparatus. Capitalism, the force behind TV, is defined as an "axiomatic of decoded fluxes." It is also associated specifically with images, as opposed to fetishes and symbols. (See also chapter 3 of *Anti-Oedipus*.) Although this account of TV functions well as an example within the larger terms of that book, such conclusions run on a different historical scheme from Deleuze's *Cinema* books. For one thing, the Guattarian emphasis on the psychic status of the subject/individual has disappeared in these later works.

48   Nam June Paik, "Entretien avec Nam June Paik," interview by Jean-Paul Fargier, Jean-Paul Cassagnac and Sylvia van der Stegen, *Cahiers du Cinéma* 299 (April 1979): 10.

49   In *Anti-Oedipus*, Deleuze and Guattari use the French word "enregistrement" to compress a range of terms, including "circulation" and "diffusion." Throughout this text I have used these closely related terms variably, according to contexts. See translators' note, *Anti-Oedipus*, 4.

50   For a typology of computer-generated video geometries, see Robert Allezaud, "Images primaires, images fractales," *Revue d'esthetique*, 10 n.s. (1986), 69–71. He distinguishes generally between Euclidean spaces and fractal spaces, the former arranged around simple objects and the latter which renders complex objects according to mathematical approximations.

51   Hal Foster, "TV in Two Parts," *TV Guides*, ed. Barbara Kruger (New York: Kuklapolitan Press, 1985), 3.

52   Mary Ann Doane, "Information, Crisis, Catastrophe," in *Logics of Television*, ed. Patricia Mellencamp (Bloomington: Indiana University Press, 1990) 222–39.

53   See Deleuze, *Cinema 2*, 179–82, for a discussion of how different uses of cutting and mixing change the relationship between Wholes which emerge through the unfolding of images and virtual Wholes which remain "outside."

54   Jean Baudrillard, "The Ecstasy of Communication" in *The Anti-Aesthetic*, ed. Hal Foster (Port Townsend, WA: Bay Press, 1983), 129.

55   Jean-Luc Godard, "Godard parle," interview by Christian Perrot and Leon Mercadet, *Actuel* 103 (January 1988): 77.

56   For a suggestive discussion of time, information and money, see Jean-François Lyotard, "Time Today," in *The Inhuman: Reflections on Time*, trans. Geoff Bennington and Rachel Bowlby (Stanford: Stanford University Press, 1991) 66–7.

57   See Deleuze, *Cinema 2*, 265.

58   See, for example, Lauren Rabinowitz, "Animation, Postmodernism, and MTV," *The Velvet Light Trap* 24 (Fall 1989): 99–112. I thank Professor Ken Surin for bringing this interesting piece to my attention.

59 See "Editors' Introduction: Contesting the New World Order," *Polygraph* 5 (1992), 6–8.

60 For a rich discussion of the face as matrix of inward depths and inscriptive surfaces, see Deleuze and Guattari, chapter 7, "Year Zero: Faciality," *A Thousand Plateaus*, 167–91.

61 Fredric Jameson, *Postmodernism: or, the Cultural Logic of Late Capitalism* (Durham, NC: Duke University Press, 1990), 75. What I call "automatic time" is a revision and expansion of what Jameson here calls "machine time." A full discussion of this essay would necessarily address the currents of Kantian aesthetic terms in Jameson's formulations.

62 For Jameson's own account of the evacuation of the scene of representation, see his marvelous little *grand récit* that closes the video essay in *Postmodernism*, 95–96.

63 For more detailed discussion of video art, see David James, "inTerVention: the contexts of negation for video and its criticism," and Beverle Houston, "Television and Video Text: A Crisis in Desire," both in Patti Podesta, ed., *resolution: A Critique of Video Art* (Los Angeles: LACE, 1986). The most comprehensive collection of writing on the subject is Doug Hall and Sally Jo Fifer, eds., *Illuminating Video: An Essential Guide to Video Art* (New York/San Francisco: Aperture and Bay Area Video Coalition, 1990). The growing body of video art criticism, often emerging alongside the artworks themselves, demands an exploration that is beyond the scope of this text.

64 Deleuze, "Postscriptum sur les sociétés de contrôle," *Pourparlers*, 240–47.

BIBLIOGRAPHY

Adorno, Theodor. *The Jargon of Authenticity*. Translated by Knut Tarnowski and Fredric Will. Evanston, IL: Northwestern University Press, 1973.

Allen, Robert C., ed. *Channels of Discourse: Television and Contemporary Criticism*. Chapel Hill: University of North Carolina Press, 1987.

Allezaud, Robert. "Images primaires, images fractales." *Revue d'esthetique* n.s., 10 (1986): 69–71.

Alliez, Eric, and Michel Feher. "The Luster of Capital." *Zone* no. 1/2 (1987): 315–59.

Altman, Rick. "Television/Sound." In *Studies in Entertainment*, edited by Tania Modleski, 39–54. Bloomington: Indiana University Press, 1986.

Althusser, Louis. *For Marx*. Translated by Ben Brewster. New York: Vintage Books, 1970.

———. *Lenin and Philosophy*. Translated by Ben Brewster. New York: Monthly Review Press, 1971.

———. *Philosophy and the Spontaneous Philosophy of the Scientists*. Edited by Gregory Elliott. London: Verso Books, 1990.

———. *Positions*. Paris: Éditions Sociale, 1976.

Althusser, Louis, and Étienne Balibar. *Reading Capital*. Translated by Ben Brewster. London: Verso Books, 1979.

Althusser, Louis, Étienne Balibar, Pierre Macherey, Roger Establet, and Jacques Rancière. *Lire le Capital*. Paris: François Maspero, 1968.

Alvarado, Manuel, ed. *Video World-Wide*. Paris: UNESCO, 1988.

Ang, Ien. *Desperately Seeking the Audience*. New York: Routledge, 1991.

Armes, Roy. *On Video*. New York: Routledge, 1988.

Arnheim, Rudolf. *Radio*. Translated by Margaret Ludwig and Herbert Read. London: Faber and Faber, 1936; reprint, New York: Arno Press, 1971.

Baehr, Helen, and Gillian Dyer, eds. *Boxed In: Women and Television*. London: Pandora Press, 1987.

Barnouw, Eric. *A Tower in Babel: A History of Broadcasting in the United States, Volume 1: 1933.* New York: Oxford University Press, 1966.

——. *Tube of Plenty.* Revised ed. New York: Oxford University Press, 1982.

Barthes, Roland. *Camera Lucida.* Translated by Richard Howard. New York: Hill and Wang, 1981.

——. *Image—Music—Text.* Translated by Stephen Heath. New York: Hill and Wang, 1977.

Baudrillard, Jean. *Amérique.* Paris: Grasset, 1986.

——. *For A Critique of the Political Economy of the Sign.* Translated by Charles Levin. St. Louis: Telos Press, 1981.

——. "The Ecstasy of Communication." In *The Anti-Aesthetic,* edited by Hal Foster. Port Townsend, WA: Bay Press, 1983.

——. *The Mirror of Production.* Translated by Mark Poster. St. Louis: Telos Press, 1975.

——. *Simulations.* Translated by Paul Foss, Paul Patton, and Philip Beitchman. New York: Semiotext(e), 1983.

Benjamin, Walter. *Illuminations.* Translated by Harry Zohn. New York: Schocken, 1969.

Bergson, Henri. *Matter and Memory.* Translated by Nancy Margaret Paul and W. Scott Palmer. London: George Allen & Unwin, 1911.

Bijeker, Wiebe E., Thomas P. Hughes, and Trevor J. Pinch, eds. *The Social Construction of Technological Systems.* Cambridge, MA: MIT Press, 1987.

Bourdieu, Pierre. *L'ontologie politique de Martin Heidegger,* 2d ed. Paris: Minuit, 1988.

Brecht, Bertolt. *Brecht on Theatre.* Translated by John Willett. New York: Hill and Wang, 1964.

——. "Radio as a Means of Communication." Translated by Stuart Hood. *Screen* 20:3/4 (Winter 1979/80): 24–28.

Browne, Nick. "The Political Economy of the TV (Super) Text." In *Television: The Critical View,* edited by Horace Newcomb, 585–99. New York: Oxford University Press, 1987.

Buckingham, David. "Television Literacy: A Critique." *Radical Philosophy* 51 (Spring 1989): 12–25.

Chateau, Dominique. "L'effet zapping." *Communications* 51 (1990): 45–55.

Comolli, Jean-Louis. "Machines of the Visible." In *The Cinematic Apparatus,* edited by Teresa de Lauretis and Stephen Heath, 121–42. New York: St. Martin's Press, 1980.

Couchot, Edmond. "La Synthèse Numérique de l'image: vers un nouvel ordre visuel." *Traverses* 26 (1982): 56–63.

Cubitt, Sean. "Time Shift: Reflections on Video Viewing." *Screen* 29:2 (Spring 1988): 74–81.

——. *Timeshift: on video culture.* New York: Routledge, 1991.

Daney, Serge. "Le 'groupe Dziga-Vertov' (2)." *Cahiers du Cinéma* 240 (July/August 1972): 4–9.

——. *Le salaire du zappeur.* Paris: Éditions Ramsay, 1988.

Debord, Guy. *The Society of the Spectacle.* Detroit: Black and Red, 1983.

Deleuze, Gilles. "Le cerveau, c'est l'écran." Interview by A. Bergala, P. Bonitzer, M. Chevrie, J. Narboni, C. Tesson, and S. Toubiana. *Cahiers du Cinéma* 380 (February 1986): 24–32.

——. *Cinema 1: The Movement-Image.* Translated by Hugh Tomlinson and Barbara Habberjam. Minneapolis: University of Minnesota Press, 1986.

——. *Cinema 2: The Time-Image.* Translated by Hugh Tomlinson and Robert Galeta. Minneapolis: University of Minnesota Press, 1989.

——. "La Photographie est déjà tirée dans les choses." Interview by Pascal Bonitzer and Jean Narboni. *Cahiers du Cinéma* 352 (October 1983): 35–40.

——. *Pourparlers*. Paris: Éditions de Minuit, 1990.

——. "Trois questions sur Six Fois Deux." *Cahiers du Cinéma* 271 (November 1976): 5–12.

Deleuze, Gilles, and Félix Guattari. *Anti-Oedipus*. Translated by Robert Hurley, Mark Seem, and Helen R. Lane. Minneapolis: University of Minnesota Press, 1983.

——. *A Thousand Plateaus*. Translated by Brian Massumi. Minneapolis: University of Minnesota Press, 1987.

Deleuze, Gilles, and Claire Parnet. *Dialogues*. Translated by Hugh Tomlinson and Barbara Habberjam. New York: Columbia University Press, 1987.

Delphy, Christine. *Close to Home: A Materialist Analysis of Women's Oppression*. Translated and edited by Diana Leonard. Amherst: University of Massachusetts Press, 1984.

Derrida, Jacques. "Of An Apocalyptic Tone Recently Adopted in Philosophy." Translated by John P. Leavey, Jr. *Oxford Literary Review* 6 (1984): 3–37.

——. "Comment Donner Raison? How to Concede, with Reasons?" *Diacritics* 19:3–4 (Fall–Winter 1989): 4–9.

——. *Dissemination*. Translated by Barbara Johnson. Chicago: University of Chicago Press, 1981.

——. "Economimesis." Translated by R. Klein. *Diacritics* 11:2 (June 1981): 3–25.

——. *Of Grammatology*. Translated by Gayatri Chakravorty Spivak. Baltimore: Johns Hopkins University Press, 1976.

——. *Limited Inc*. Translated by Samuel Weber and Jeffrey Mehlman. Evanston, IL: Northwestern University Press, 1988.

——. *Margins of Philosophy*. Translated by Alan Bass. Chicago: University of Chicago Press, 1982.

——. "My Chances/Mes Chances." Translated by Irene Harvey and Avital Ronell. In *Taking Chances: Derrida Psychoanalysis, and Literature*, edited by Joseph H. Smith and William Kerrigan, 1–32. Baltimore: Johns Hopkins University Press, 1984.

——. "No Apocalypse, Not Now (full speed ahead, seven missiles, seven missives)." Translated by Catherine Porter and Philip Lewis. *Diacritics* 14:2 (1984): 20–31.

——. "Philosophie des États Généraux." In *États Généraux de la Philosophie*. Paris: Flammarion, 1979.

——. *Positions*. Translated by Alan Bass. Chicago: University of Chicago Press, 1981.

——. *The Post Card: From Socrates to Freud and Beyond*. Translated by Alan Bass. Chicago: University of Chicago Press, 1987.

——. "The Principle of Reason: The University in the Eyes of its Pupils." *Diacritics* 13:3 (Fall 1983): 3–20.

——. *Psyché: Inventions de l'autre*. Paris: Galilée, 1987.

——. "On Reading Heidegger: An Outline of Remarks to the Essex Colloquium." *Research in Phenomenology* 17 (1987): 171–74.

——. "Some questions and responses." In *The Linguistics of Writing*, edited by Nigel Fabb, Derek Attridge, Alan Durant and Colin MacCabe, 252–64. New York: Methuen, 1987.

——. *Of Spirit: Heidegger and the Question*. Translated by Geoff Bennington and Rachel Bowlby. Chicago: University of Chicago Press, 1989.

——. "Telepathy." Translated by Nicholas Royle. *Oxford Literary Review* 10 (1985).

——. *The Truth in Painting*. Translated by Geoff Bennington and Ian McLeod. Chicago: University of Chicago Press, 1987.

——. *Writing and Différence*. Translated by Alan Bass. Chicago: University of Chicago Press, 1978.

Dienst, Richard. "The End of History (Times Three): On *Crime Story.*" *Polygraph* 2/3 (1988): 178–185.

Doane, Mary Ann. "Information, Crisis, Catastrophe." In *Logics of Television*, edited by Patricia Mellencamp, 222–39.

Dreyfus, Hubert. "Between Techne and Technology: The Ambiguous Place of Equipment in *Being and Time.*" *Tulane Studies in Philosophy* 32 (1984): 23–35.

Drummond, Phillip, and Richard Patterson, eds. *Television in Transition.* London: British Film Institute, 1986.

Ellis, John. *Visible Fictions: Cinema Television Video.* London: Routledge, 1982.

Feuer, Jane. "The Concept of Live Television: Ontology as Ideology." In *Regarding Television,* edited by E. Ann Kaplan, 12–21. Frederick, MD: University Publications of America, 1983.

Fiske, John. *Television Culture.* New York: Methuen, 1987.

Fiske, John, and John Hartley. *Reading Television.* London: Methuen, 1978.

Foster, Hal. "TV in Two Parts." In *TV Guides,* edited by Barbara Kruger. New York: Kuklapolitan Press, 1985.

Foster, Hal, ed. *Vision and Visuality.* Dia Art Foundation Discussions in Contemporary Culture no. 2. Seattle: Bay Press, 1988.

Foucault, Michel. *The Foucault Reader.* Edited by Paul Rabinow. New York: Pantheon, 1984.

Freccaro, Carla. "Our Lady of MTV: Madonna's 'Like a Prayer.'" *boundary 2* 19:2 (Summer 1992): 163–183.

Gaines, Jane. *Contested Cultures: Image Properties in the Industrial Age.* Chapel Hill: University of North Carolina Press, 1991.

Geddes, Keith and Gordon Bussey. *Television: The First Fifty Years.* London: National Museum of Photography, Film, and Television, 1986.

Godard, Jean-Luc. "Godard parle." Interview by Christian Perrot and Leon Mercadet. *Actuel* 103 (January 1988): 72.

——. (Introduction à une véritable histoire du cinéma.) Paris: Albatros, 1980.

——. *Jean-Luc Godard par Jean-Luc Godard.* Edited by Alain Bergala. Paris: Cahiers du Cinéma/Éditions de l'Étoile, 1985.

——. "Le Dernier Rêve d'un Producteur—Nord contre Sud ou Naissance (de l'image) d'une Nation." *Cahiers du Cinéma* 300 (May 1979).

Goodwin, Andrew. *Dancing in the Distraction Factory: Music Television and Popular Culture.* Minneapolis: University of Minnesota Press, 1992.

Goux, Jean-Joseph. *Symbolic Economies: After Marx and Freud.* Translated by Jennifer Curtiss Gage. Ithaca: Cornell University Press, 1990.

Guattari, Félix. "La machine à images." *Cahiers du Cinéma* 437 (November 1990): 70–72.

——. *Molecular Revolutions: Psychiatry and Politics.* Translated by Rosemary Sheed. Harmondsworth: Penguin Books, 1984.

Guillaume, Marc. "Téléspectres." *Traverses* 26 (1982): 18–28.

Hall, Doug, and Sally Jo Fifer, eds. *Illuminating Video: An Essential Guide to Video Art.* New York/San Francisco: Aperture/Bay Area Video Coalition, 1990.

Hall, Peter, and Paschal Preston. *The Carrier Wave: New Information Technology and the Geography of Innovation 1846–2003.* London: Unwin Hyman, 1988.

Hanhardt, John, ed. *Video Culture: A Critical Investigation.* Rochester, NY: Visual Studies Workshop, 1986.

Haraway, Donna. "Manifesto for Cyborgs: Science, Technology and Socialist-Feminism in the 1980s." *Socialist Review* 80 (1985).

Harvey, David. *The Condition of Postmodernity.* Oxford: Basil Blackwell, 1989.

———. *The Limits to Capital.* Chicago: University of Chicago Press, 1982.

Heath, Stephen. "Representing Television." In *Logics of Television,* edited by Patricia Mellencamp, 267–302. Bloomington: Indiana University Press, 1990.

Heath, Stephen, and Gillian Skirrow. "Television: A World in Action." *Screen* 18 (Summer 1977): 7–59.

———. "An Interview with Raymond Williams." In *Studies in Entertainment,* edited by Tania Modleski, 3–17. Bloomington: Indiana University Press, 1986.

Heidegger, Martin. *Basic Writings.* Edited by David Farrell Krell. New York: Harper and Row, 1977.

———. *Being and Time.* Translated by John Macquarrie and Edward Robinson. New York: Harper and Row, 1962.

———. *Discourse on Thinking.* Translated by John M. Anderson and E. Hans Freund. New York: Harper and Row, 1966.

———. *The End of Philosophy.* Translated by Joan Stambaugh. New York: Harper and Row, 1973.

———. *An Introduction to Metaphysics.* Translated by Ralph Mannheim. New Haven: Yale University Press, 1959.

———. *Martin Heidegger im Gespräch.* Freiburg/Munich: Verlag Karl Alber, 1970.

———. *Nietzsche, Volume II: The Eternal Recurrence of the Same.* Translated by David Farrell Krell. San Francisco: Harper and Row, 1984.

———. *On the Way to Language.* Translated by Peter D. Hertz. New York: Harper and Row, 1971.

———. *Poetry, Language, Thought.* Translated by Albert Hofstadter. New York: Harper and Row, 1971.

———. "The Principle of Ground." *Man and World* 7 (August 1974): 207–22.

———. *The Question Concerning Technology and other Essays.* Translated by William Lovitt. New York: Harper and Row, 1977.

———. *The Question of Being.* Translated by Jean T. Wilde and William Kluback. New Haven: College and University Press, 1958.

———. *Vorträge und Aufsätze.* Pfullingen: Neske, 1954.

———. *What Is Called Thinking?* Translated by Fred D. Wieck and J. Glenn Gray. New York: Harper and Row, 1968.

Horkheimer, Max, and Theodor W. Adorno. *The Dialectic of Enlightenment.* Translated by John Cumming. New York: Continuum, 1988.

Houston, Beverle. "Viewing Television: The Metapsychology of Endless Consumption." *Quarterly Review of Film Studies* 9:3 (Summer 1984): 183–195.

Jameson, Fredric. *The Ideologies of Theory.* 2 vols. Minneapolis: University of Minnesota Press, 1988.

———. *The Political Unconscious: Narrative as a Socially Symbolic Act.* Ithaca: Cornell University Press, 1981.

———. *Postmodernism, or, The Cultural Logic of Late Capitalism.* Durham: Duke University Press, 1990.

———. *The Prison-House of Language.* Princeton: Princeton University Press, 1972.

——. *Signatures of the Visible*. New York: Routledge, 1990.

Jhally, Sut. *The Codes of Advertising: Fetishism and the Political Economy of Meaning in Consumer Society*. New York: Routledge, 1987.

Kant, Immanuel. *Critique of Judgement*. Translated by J. H. Bernard. New York: Hafner Press, 1951.

Kaplan, E. Ann. *Rocking Around the Clock: Music Television, Postmodernism, and Consumer Culture*. New York: Methuen, 1987.

Kaplan, E. Ann, ed. *Regarding Television*. Frederick, MD: University Publications of America, 1983.

Kaplan, E. Ann, and Michael Sprinker, eds. *The Althusserian Legacy*. London: Verso Books, 1993.

Kittler, Friedrich. *Discourse Networks, 1800/1900*. Translated by Michael Metteer with Chris Cullens. Palo Alto: Stanford University Press, 1990.

——. "Gramophone, Film, Typewriter." Translated by Dorothea von Mücke with Philippe L. Similon. *October* 41, 101–48.

——. "Media Wars: Trenches, Lightning, Stars." *1–800* 1 (Fall 1989): 5–9.

Kluge, Alexander. "On Film and the Public Sphere." Translated by Thomas Y. Levin and Miriam B. Hansen. *New German Critique* 24/25 (Fall/Winter 1981–82): 206–20.

Lacan, Jacques. *Télévision*. Paris: Éditions du Seuil, 1974.

Lacoue-Labarthe, Philippe, and Jean-Luc Nancy, eds. *Les fins des hommes: à partir du travail de Jacques Derrida*. Paris: Galilée, 1981.

Lardner, James. *Fast Forward: Hollywood, the Japanese, and the VCR Wars*. New York: New American Library, 1987.

Lentricchia, Frank. *After the New Criticism*. Chicago: University of Chicago Press, 1980.

Lévy, Patrick. "Introduction à Heidegger." *Cahiers du Cinéma* 186 (January 1967): 45–6.

Lipietz, Alain. *The Enchanted World*. Translated by Ian Patterson. London: Verso Books, 1985.

Lukács, Georg. *History and Class Consciousness*. Translated by Rodney Livingstone. Cambridge, MA: MIT Press, 1971.

Lyotard, Jean-François. *The Inhuman: Reflections on Time*. Translated by Geoffrey Bennington and Rachel Bowlby. Palo Alto: Stanford University Press, 1991.

——. *The Lyotard Reader*. Edited by Andrew Benjamin. Oxford: Basil Blackwell, 1989.

——. "Time Today." Translated by Geoff Bennington and Rachel Bowlby. *Oxford Literary Review* 11 (1989): 3–20.

McArthur, Colin. *Television and History*. London: British Film Institute, 1978.

MacCabe, Colin. *Godard: Images, Sounds, Politics*. Bloomington: Indiana University Press, 1980.

MacCabe, Colin, ed. *High Theory, Low Culture: Analyzing popular television and film*. New York: St. Martin's Press, 1986.

McLuhan, Marshall. *Understanding Media*. New York: Signet, 1964.

Mandel, Ernest. *Late Capitalism*. Translated by Joris de Bres. London: Verso Books, 1975.

Marx, Karl. *Capital, Volume I*. Translated by Ben Fowkes. New York: Vintage Books, 1977.

——. *Capital, Volume II*. Translated by David Fernbach. Introduction by Ernest Mandel. Harmondsworth: Penguin Books, 1978.

——. *Capital, Volume III*. Translated by David Fernbach. Harmondsworth: Penguin Books, 1983.

——. *Grundrisse.* Translated by Martin Nicolaus. New York: Vintage Books, 1973.

Masterman, Len, ed. *Television Mythologies: Stars, Shows, and Signs.* London: Comedia Publishing, 1984.

Mattelart, Armand, Xavier Delcourt, and Michele Mattelart. *International Image Markets: In Search of an Alternative Perspective.* Translated by David Buxton. London: Comedia Publishing Group, 1984.

Mattelart, Michele, and Armand Mattelart. *Les Carnaval des Images: La Fiction Bresilienne.* Paris: La Documentation Française, 1987.

Mellencamp, Patricia, ed. *Logics of Television: essays in cultural criticism.* Bloomington: Indiana University Press, 1990.

Merleau-Ponty, Maurice. *The Invisible and the Visible.* Translated by Alphonso Lingis. Evanston, IL: Northwestern University Press, 1968.

——. *The Phenomenology of Perception.* Translated by Colin Smith. London: Routledge and Kegan Paul, 1962.

Metz, Christian. *Film Language: A Semiotics of the Cinema.* Translated by Michael Taylor. Oxford: Oxford University Press, 1974; reprint, Chicago: University of Chicago Press, 1991.

Modleski, Tania. *Loving With a Vengeance.* New York: Methuen, 1982.

——. "The Rhythms of Reception: Daytime Television and Women's Work." In *Regarding Television,* edited by E. Ann Kaplan, 67–74.

Morley, David. *Family Television: Cultural Power and Domestic Leisure.* London: Comedia Publishing, 1986.

Morris, Meaghan. "The Banality of Cultural Studies." In *Logics of Television,* edited by Patricia Mellencamp, 14–43.

Morse, Margaret. "An Ontology of Everyday Distraction: The Freeway, The Mall, and Television." In *Logics of Television,* edited by Patricia Mellencamp, 193–221.

——. "Talk Talk Talk: the Space of Discourse in Television News, Sportcasts, Talk Shows, and Advertising." *Screen* 26:2 (March/April 1985): 2–15.

Nelson, Joyce. *The Perfect Machine: TV in the Nuclear Age.* Toronto: Between the Lines, 1987.

Neske, Günther, and Emil Ketterling, eds. *Martin Heidegger and National Socialism: Questions and Answers.* Translated by Lisa Harries. New York: Paragon House, 1990.

Nichols, Bill. "The Work of Culture in the Age of Cybernetic Systems." *Screen* 29: 1 (Winter 1988): 22–46.

Paik, Nam June. "Entretien avec Nam June Paik." Interview by Jean-Paul Fargier, Jean-Paul Cassagnac, and Sylvia van der Stegen. *Cahiers du Cinéma* 299 (April 1979): 10–15.

Panzieri, Raniero. "The Capitalist Use of Machinery: Marx versus the 'Objectivists.'" In *Outlines of a Critique of Technology,* edited by Phil Slater. London: Ink Links, 1980.

Pêcheux, Michel. *Language, Semantics and Ideology: Stating the Obvious.* Translated by Harbans Nagpal. London: Macmillan, 1979.

Penley, Constance, and Andrew Ross, eds. *Technoculture.* Minneapolis: University of Minnesota Press, 1991.

Petro, Patrice. "Mass Culture and the Feminine: The 'Place' of Television in Film Studies." *Cinema Journal* 25:3 (Spring 1986): 5–21.

Podesta, Patti, ed. *resolution: a critique of video art.* Los Angeles: LACE, 1986.

Pribham, E. Deidre, ed. *Female Spectators: Looking at Film and Television*. London: Verso Books, 1988.

Rabinowitz, Lauren. "Animation, Postmodernism, and MTV." *The Velvet Light Trap* 24 (Fall 1989): 88–112.

Rodman, Howard. "The Series That Will Change TV." *Connoisseur* (September 1989): 139–44.

Ronell, Avital. "The Differends of Man." *Diacritics* 19: 3–4 (Fall–Winter 1989) 63–75.

——. *The Telephone Book: Technology—Schizophrenia—Electric Speech*. Lincoln: University of Nebraska Press, 1989.

Rose, Jacqueline. *Sexuality in the Field of Vision*. London: Verso, 1986.

Rosen, Philip, ed. *Narrative, Apparatus, Ideology: A Film Theory Reader*. New York: Columbia University Press, 1986.

Rosen, Philip T., ed. *International Handbook of Broadcasting Systems*. Westport: Greenwood Press, 1988.

Ryan, Michael. *Marxism and Deconstruction: A Critical Articulation*. Baltimore: Johns Hopkins University Press, 1982.

Sartre, Jean-Paul. *Being and Nothingness*. Translated by Hazel Barnes. New York: Washington Square Press, 1966.

——. *Critique of Dialectical Reason, Volume 1*. Translated by Alan Sheridan-Smith. London: Verso Books, 1976.

——. *Critique of Dialectical Reason, Volume 2*. Translated by Quintin Hoare. London: Verso Books, 1991.

Schiller, Herbert. *Information and the Crisis Economy*. New York: Oxford University Press, 1986.

Schneider, Cynthia and Brian Wallis, eds. *Global Television*. Cambridge, MA: MIT Press, 1989.

Schwichtenberg, Cathy, ed. *The Madonna Connection: Representational Politics, Subcultural Identities, and Cultural Theory*. Boulder, CO: Westview Press, 1993.

Sexton, Adam, ed. *Desperately Seeking Madonna*. New York: Delta, 1993.

Sloterdijk, Peter. *The Critique of Cynical Reason*. Translated by Michael Elred. Minneapolis: University of Minnesota Press, 1987.

Smith, Anthony. *The Geopolitics of Information*. New York: Oxford University Press, 1980.

Smith, Barbara Herrnstein. *Contingencies of Value: Alternative Perspectives for Critical Theory*. Cambridge, MA: Harvard University Press, 1988.

Spivak, Gayatri Chakravorty. *In Other Worlds: Essays in Cultural Politics*. New York: Methuen, 1987.

Sprinker, Michael. *Imaginary Relations: Aesthetics and Ideology in the Theory of Historical Materialism*. London: Verso Books, 1987.

Steiner, George. *Martin Heidegger*. New York: Viking Press, 1978.

Udelson, Joseph H. *The Great Television Race: A History of the American Television Industry 1925–1941*. Tuscaloosa: University of Alabama Press, 1982.

Ulmer, Gregory. *Teletheory: Grammatology in the Age of Video*. New York: Routledge, 1989.

Varis, Tapio. *International Flow of Television Programs*. Paris: UNESCO, 1985.

Vattimo, Gianni. *The End of Modernity: Nihilism and Hermeneutics in Postmodern Culture*. Translated by Jon R. Snyder. Baltimore: Johns Hopkins University Press.

Vernet, Marc. "Incertain zapping." *Communications* 51 (1990): 33–44.

Vernier, Jean-Marc. "L'image pulsation." *Revue d'esthetique* n.s., 10 (1986): 129–34.

Vertov, Dziga. *KINO-EYE: The Writings of Dziga Vertov.* Edited by Annette Michelson, translated by Kevin O'Brien. Berkeley: University of California Press, 1984.

Virilio, Paul. *War and Cinema: The Logistics of Perception.* Translated by Patrick Camiller. London: Verso Books, 1989.

Weber, Samuel. *Institution and Interpretation.* Minneapolis: University of Minnesota Press, 1987.

——. "Upsetting the Set Up: Remarks on Heidegger's Questing After Technics." *Modern Language Notes* 105:5 (December 1989): 977–91.

White, Mimi. "Crossing Wavelengths: The Diegetic and Referential Imaginary of American Commercial Television." *Cinema Journal* 25:2 (Winter 1986): 51–64.

Williams, Alan. "Is Sound Recording Like a Language?" *Yale French Studies* 60 (1980): 51–66.

Williams, Raymond. *Keywords.* New York: Oxford University Press, 1983.

——. *Politics and Letters.* London: Verso Books, 1979.

——. *Problems in Materialism and Culture.* London: Verso Books, 1980.

——. *Raymond Williams on Television: Selected Writings.* Edited by Alan O'Connor. London: Routledge, 1989.

——. *Television: Technology and Cultural Form.* New York: Schocken, 1974.

——. *Towards 2000.* London: Chatto and Windus, 1983.

Winston, Brian. *Misunderstanding Media.* Cambridge, MA: Harvard University Press, 1986.

Wollen, Peter. "Cinema/Americanism/The Robot." *New Formations* 8 (Summer 1989): 7–34.

——. *Readings and Writings: Semiotic Counter-Strategies.* London: Verso Books, 1982.

——. *Signs and Meaning in the Cinema.* Bloomington: Indiana University Press, 1972.

Wolton, Dominique. *Eloge du grand public: une théorie critique de la télévision.* Paris: Flammarion, 1990.

World Radio and Television Handbook. Copenhagen: Billboard, 1991.

Zimmerman, Michael E. *Heidegger's Confrontation with Modernity: Technology, Politics, Art.* Bloomington: Indiana University Press, 1990.

Žižek, Slavoj. *Looking Awry: An Introduction to Jacques Lacan through Popular Culture.* Cambridge: MIT Press, 1991.

——. *The Sublime Object of Ideology.* London: Verso Books, 1989.

Index

Richard Dienst is Assistant Professor in the Department of English and Director of the English and Philosophy Program at Purdue University. He was a founding editor of *Polygraph* and has published articles on cultural studies and contemporary theory.

Library of Congress Cataloging-in-Publication Data
Dienst, Richard, 1962–
Still life in real time : theory after television /
Richard Dienst.
— (Post-contemporary interventions)
Includes bibliographical references and index.
ISBN 0-8223-1451-7 (alk. paper). —
ISBN 0-8223-1466-5 (alk. paper : pbk.)
1. Television—Philosophy.   I. Title.
PN1992.55.D54   1994
302.23'45—dc 20   93-37942 CIP